PARTY AT THE BALLOT BOX

Party at the Ballot Box

Mobilizing Black Women Voters

Melissa R. Michelson, Stephanie L. DeMora, and Sarah V. Hayes

NEW YORK UNIVERSITY PRESS

New York

NEW YORK UNIVERSITY PRESS
New York
www.nyupress.org

© 2025 by New York University
All rights reserved

Please contact the Library of Congress for Cataloging-in-Publication data.
ISBN: 9781479835751 (hardback)
ISBN: 9781479835768 (paperback)
ISBN: 9781479835805 (library ebook)
ISBN: 9781479835799 (consumer ebook)

This book is printed on acid-free paper, and its binding materials are chosen for strength
and durability. We strive to use environmentally responsible suppliers and materials to the
greatest extent possible in publishing our books.

The manufacturer's authorized representative in the EU for product safety is Mare
Nostrum Group B.V., Mauritskade 21D, 1091 GC Amsterdam, The Netherlands.
Email: gpsr@mare-nostrum.co.uk.

Manufactured in the United States of America

10 9 8 7 6 5 4 3 2 1

Also available as an ebook

CONTENTS

FIGURES AND TABLES

TABLES

FOREWORD

NYKI ROBINSON

Growing up in Baltimore, Maryland, I had no desire to work in politics. If you had told me twenty years ago that I'd go on to start an organization centered on voting, I would have said bull crap. It wasn't until I got my first "real" job in the mayor's office in the city of Baltimore in 2007 that I really began to realize the importance of government, politics, and relationships.

After working in the mayor's office, I went to the governor's office and then to a government agency. And after losing my good government job following a gubernatorial transition, I decided to move on to an idea I had months prior. On November 30, 2015, the birthday of Shirley Chisholm, we launched Black Girls Vote—an organization committed to engaging, educating, and empowering Black women. I rallied a group of volunteers and we hit the ground running by registering voters and hosting events, debates, educational sessions, and more. Our ongoing mission has been to amplify Black women, the power of our vote, and how our votes and voices should be respected.

Like many others in 2020, we had no idea the pandemic was upon us. Black Girls Vote had so many voter engagement ideas, activities, and other things planned. However, with the pandemic hitting us in March and a primary election upon us, we knew we had to pivot fast.

My colleague Sam Novey and I were on a Zoom call discussing ideas, and I said, "Because voters can no longer party at the polls this election cycle, how about they party at the mailbox?" Not only would we bring the party to their homes, but we also wanted them to have a sense of pride in their community, in being a Baltimorean. So everything in the box— the treats, the signage, the shirt, the button—would be pro-voting and pro-Baltimore. It would feel like Baltimore. And that's when Party at the Mailbox (PATM) was born.

In addition to pitching our idea to potential funders, Sam thought conducting a randomized controlled trial (RCT) could be groundbreaking for a campaign like this. Having less knowledge of RCTs, I trusted his expertise, and soon after, Sam set up an initial Zoom call. On May 13, 2020, I had the pleasure of meeting Donald P. Green, Michael Hanmer, Melissa Michelson, Tyson King Meadows, and Lester Spence. I wasn't sure how the call would go, nor did I have much experience discussing political science research with highly accomplished academics who live, eat, and breathe this stuff. So my goal was to show up as myself and sell the vision.

I remember quite a few things from that call, but what stood out the most was when Dr. Michelson shared with me that she had heard of Black Girls Vote. Here she was, a white woman in Northern California who had heard about Black Girls Vote. That was an aha moment. I was not only excited and thrilled but also proud of our small yet mighty team.

Baltimore's primary election was on June 2, 2020, and our pilot would include over two thousand voter education and engagement boxes—something the city had never seen before. So we would create a movement and my first RCT; cool, right?

It was cool, but the pressure was on. Not only was I pitching a Baltimore activation, but I told potential investors that we could scale and replicate this in battleground cities across the US. On Election Day, the early reports said Baltimore had its highest voter turnout in over thirty years, and from my lens, PATM had a lot to do with that. We not only had thousands of social media impressions, but we also had over ten thousand people join our virtual election night party. The energy around PATM was like nothing we'd ever seen before. And our RCT proved that this was true. Voters who received the boxes voted at a 2.5 percent higher rate than those who hadn't received a box; low-propensity voters in the household voted at a 12.7 percent higher rate. Those data from our inaugural RCT gave us quantitative and qualitative research in our favor. They also gave us the confidence to seek additional funding for expansion for the 2020 general election.

To be honest, the money didn't fall as quickly as we anticipated. I just knew this groundbreaking experiment would spread like wildfire, and folks in every city would want a PATM activation. We were pretty much down to the wire, and if we didn't secure funding ASAP, we would have to nix our vision of expansion in this unprecedented election. Designing the elements, ordering materials, and building a team for a massive campaign like this takes a lot of time and preparation, so we needed donors, and we needed them soon. And after at least twenty pitches, I met with the Cohens, Carolyn and Joe. In mid- to late August 2020, the tide began to turn. We had met with Carolyn previously, but this time she wanted to include her brother Joe. And after our Zoom call, within an hour, Sam and I received an email that said they were going to invest $120,000 in PATM. They pledged to give us our first major investment for expansion. I remember screaming so loudly in my apartment building, I'm surprised no one called the cops. I immediately called Sam and said, "Oh my God, we did it." And we're still doing it. We have been building and learning not only from our community partners but also from each other. We created and replicated something exciting for voters, particularly Black women voters. And if I could broadcast any message, that message would be "Invest in Black women."

Very seldom do you see academia and community partners unite in this capacity. Especially for something fun and celebratory—in this case, we are celebrating democracy. A lot of Black people don't like the term *research*. We sometimes need more clarification about the goals, objectives, and research process. That way, we can manage expectations but also build trust. This partnership allowed me to grow as a nonprofit organization leader. In my work with Dr. Michelson and her team, we both grew, learned, and challenged each other when necessary.

We've received awards, published papers, facilitated workshops, won grants, and so much more. That's why I say, and will continue to say, invest in Black women. Invest in their ideas, their tenacity, and their grit. Because people invested in the concept of PATM, the idea for this book was conceived. And there are so many other beautiful, brilliant, Black women who have ideas and are looking for someone to invest in them. Many Black women are willing and open to experiments and experiences, which could lead to more trailblazing unions between academia and community partners. There are some more Dr. Michelsons and Nykis out there (well, not exactly as cool as us, but you get the point) who are innovative and capable of creating programs like PATM.

I am thrilled about this book and humbled to share some of the journey that began in 2020. And to date, we're still creating and changing the outcomes of elections by getting folks enthusiastic about voting and celebrating them. I hope you enjoy this book as much as I did. Thank you to Dr. Michelson for sticking with my team and me. We created something magical and unique. Now let's read about it.

With love,
Nyki

A special thank you to my mommy, Sherri Ronee' Fraling, may she continue to rest in peace; my amazing son, Nyle; family, friends, supporters, and team Black Girls Vote; our internal PATM team members, Sam Novey, Tasmin Swanson, Tenne Thrower, Akil Trice, Patricia Watson, Savannah Frazier, Cortney Robertson, Dea Thomas, Allison Fisher, Ashley Daniels, Stephanie DeMora, and Sarah Hayes; and our external partners and donors, especially the Cohens: Carolyn, Joe, and Larry.

1

A History of Partying to the Polls

On Saturday, May 30, 2020, a caravan of forty cars slowly made its way through the streets of West Baltimore, the cars transformed into a moving billboard of homemade get-out-the-vote signs. Leading the caravan was a voter education sound truck amplifying the voice of Black Girls Vote founder Nykidra "Nyki" Robinson, whose organization was one of those invited by the No Boundaries Coalition of Central West Baltimore to join the event. To the accompaniment of honks from other vehicles and cheers from passersby, Robinson urged members of the community to remember to fill out and return their vote-by-mail ballots for the June 2, 2020, primary election. Most Baltimore voters, especially those in the majority-Black community of West Baltimore, traditionally participate in elections by showing up to their local polling place, but health considerations stemming from the COVID-19 pandemic led the city to move to an all-mail election.[1] As part of their effort to increase participation and get those mail-in ballots returned, these community organizations were using a car caravan to turn absentee voting into a community event. The caravan route ended at a ballot drop-off box where organizers cheered on citizens as they cast their votes.

Three days later, Black Girls Vote and Baltimore Votes hosted a virtual voting party on Facebook, bringing together local DJs, local and national elected officials, and over eleven thousand viewers over the course of the two-hour election-night event. Well-known local DJs—DJ AirMax, DJ Pretty Girl Tiara LaNiece, and DJ Quick Silva—played a steady stream of danceable music interspersed with announcements of raffle prizes and opportunities to chat with elected officials who dropped in, including President of the Maryland State Senate Bill Ferguson, Speaker of the Maryland House of Delegates Adrienne Jones, and the Reverend Jesse Jackson Jr. Many virtual dance party guests were decked out in Party at the Mailbox (PATM) T-shirts, which had been distributed to Baltimore voters as part of a voter education effort by the two organizations in the weeks before the election along with local snacks, balloons and noise-makers, and colorful posters. Those face-to-face deliveries of boxes filled with information about voting and items with ties to the local community, such as Baltimore's Berger cookies (an institution since the 1830s), spread voting awareness across Baltimore via social media and decorated car windows, mailboxes, and front doors. Baltimore voters were voting safely from home as individuals, but the PATM project brought them together in a spirit of community celebration.

These and other celebrations of democracy around the country illustrate the community engagement and joy that can accompany election events. Especially in Black neighborhoods, showing up to vote on Election Day—or for early voting or even to drop off completed mail-in ballots—is a declaration not just of one's decision to vote but of one's commitment to show up for one another, to celebrate the power of every individual and also the power of the larger group, and to give a hat tip to the ancestors who made those votes possible. It is an honoring of the Black civil rights movement and the successful fight for the Black franchise, and also a commitment to show up for one's community by demanding accountability from elected officials and attention to the public policy needs of Black Americans. Whether marked with a virtual dance party, a Souls to the Polls walk from a house of worship, a polling place festival, or simply the act of returning a vote-by-mail ballot via the US Postal Service, voting is a celebration of community.

In this book, we posit that this power of voting as a celebration of community can be used to increase voter turnout, particularly in Black communities. We call this theory the Voter Community Celebration Model. We define this model as a get-out-the-vote (GOTV) engagement method where (1) the individual is acknowledged and intentionally celebrated as an active participant in American democracy as a voter (regardless of party affiliation), (2) voting is viewed as a fun and educational family activity, and (3) voting is openly celebrated as an act of public service in the voter's entire local residential community. Our focal example is the PATM campaign that emerged during the COVID-19 pandemic, first piloted in Baltimore, for the June 2020 primary under the direction of Black Girls Vote founder Robinson and Baltimore Votes cofounder Sam Novey. The PATM project helped cultivate that celebratory spirit at a time when many Baltimoreans, like many other Americans, were sheltering in place to mitigate the spread of the virus. We describe the various iterations of the PATM project through multiple election cycles in 2020, 2021, 2022, and 2024, as well as other community celebrations of turnout such as Souls to the Polls and Precinct Parties, to support our theory that these celebrations of community can be a powerful driver of high voter turnout in Black communities and other cohesive communities. Despite the increasingly fraught environment of modern elections in our hyperpolarized politics, generating a celebratory atmosphere evokes positive emotions and encourages the prosocial behavior of voting.

It's an Experience

As Robinson noted repeatedly throughout the PATM campaign, "It's not just a box, it's an experience." And the community experienced it together. Around the country, household members took to walking around their neighborhoods during the early months of the COVID-19 pandemic to break up the monotony of social distancing and sheltering at home. Residents in many communities posted teddy bears in car and home windows to make those walks more like a treasure hunt for younger neighbors. In the summer of 2020 in Baltimore, those car and home windows also featured PATM posters and balloons. Social media exploded with unboxing videos and testaments from residents who found the project a welcome respite from the isolation they were feeling, as well as a positive reminder of their pride in being Baltimoreans. As Denise, a Baltimore mother of two,[2] told us in a focus group conducted after the June 2020 election, seeing the signs as she walked around Baltimore with her children left her with a sense of community:

> The signs were great. I loved the signs. We put them all over. We put them on the door, and we put them on the fence, and we put them all over. Given that it is during a pandemic and we are doing walks all the time, my kids have such a great time spotting the signs as they walked and seeing those and having that kind of connection. It was this added connection that I thought was really special in a time when people felt particularly

isolated. . . . I loved having another way to do that and to engage my whole family in doing that, and to connect with our neighbors who do not know necessarily how to do that.

That the signs were visible to passersby out for a walk also meant that folks who didn't personally get a box could feel like they were part of the project. Demand for the boxes far outstripped supply and, as we describe in chapter 3, not delivering boxes to everyone who asked for one was a crucial aspect of our plan to robustly evaluate the impact of the PATM project. That said, media coverage of the project and the visibility of the boxes and their contents on social media and on neighborhood streets meant that many nonrecipients felt included in the celebration. Phyllis, a Black woman who works as a social worker, told us after the election,

> I didn't get a box. I applied for one, but I wasn't able to get one. But with that being said, I'm sure that they . . . because they had put it on the news, and I'm sure they got more responses than they anticipated. Yeah, but I think that was an amazing idea. And I felt like it's a really good initiative. . . . I think that that's the type of work that we need to be doing, to really go into the home and kind of make, make voting fun. Make it something that like, "Yo, I want to share this with my friends."

Because Phyllis had seen PATM covered by local news, she didn't feel left out when she didn't get a box. Instead, she felt like it was helping make voting fun—making voting a shared celebration with friends. Juliette, a Baltimore middle school teacher, also told us she enjoyed the PATM project despite not receiving a box, in part because she observed the social media celebration it generated:

> I didn't personally receive a box. . . . I had such a fun time following along with people on social media who did and I thought, this year in particular, the idea of really celebrating what it feels like to vote from home and, you know, to be encouraged and to see people have a reason to publicly post on social media to talk about their voting experience is not something that I had ever seen in the city, in such a way. Like there's a handful of people will go, go vote, they'll post the . . . post a picture like with their "I voted" sticker. But this, I think, encouraged a lot more people to talk

about their voting experience and to share publicly that they were voting. And that, to me, is so important, the idea of normalizing voting. Like it's not just a certain kind of person who votes—everyone can vote. And I think that's what this campaign showed in a way that I haven't seen in other years on social media.

Juliette felt part of the celebration of voting by mail, even without receiving a box, because she knew it was something happening across the city of Baltimore and being shared on social media by people she followed. It wasn't the box that was creating the celebratory feeling, it was "the experience"—the idea that the city was doing this together.

It wasn't just social media. Local radio and television stations featured stories about the project, and local community partners spread the word about how to request a box, while also distributing food aid and other services. The signs and balloons on local doors and in car windows, social media posts, and coverage in the media helped make PATM an event that touched the whole community. Crucial to our understanding of how the project affected turnout as a community event is that it made an impression even on those who didn't receive a box but who wanted one. It wasn't the box that was nudging them to vote, it was the broader idea of coming together as a community to celebrate voting. It was bringing people together—virtually—and making voting fun.

In the midst of a pandemic and needing to socially distance, the community was celebrating their neighbors, as well as their democracy. This was reflected in the election results: Baltimore City turnout in the election was historic, far exceeding participation in other parts of the state, as shown in figures 1.1 and 1.2. This included forty-six thousand voters who had never before participated in a primary election, seventeen thousand of whom had never before cast a vote in any election.

That an effort like PATM was able to generate increased voter turnout by turning the election into a virtual party is not without precedent. History and political science scholars have demonstrated that turnout is enhanced by cultivating community celebrations around elections, although those previous efforts all entailed face-to-face events. For the first half century of the new United States, voting was done by voice and in public, and with a festive atmosphere. "Elections were a chance to weigh in on important business, but they were also an opportunity to let

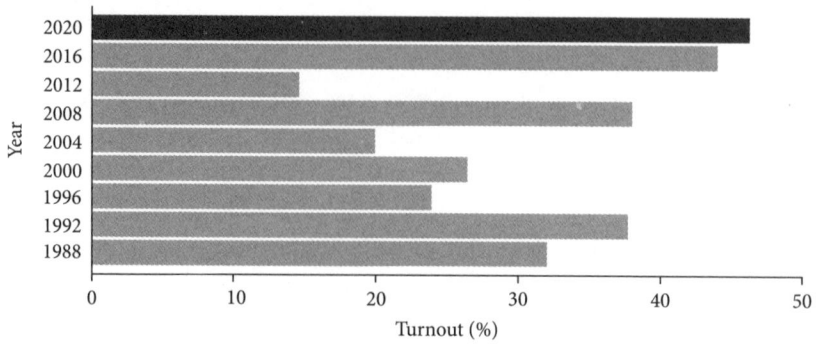

Figure 1.1: Voter Turnout in Baltimore Presidential Primary Elections, 1988–2020

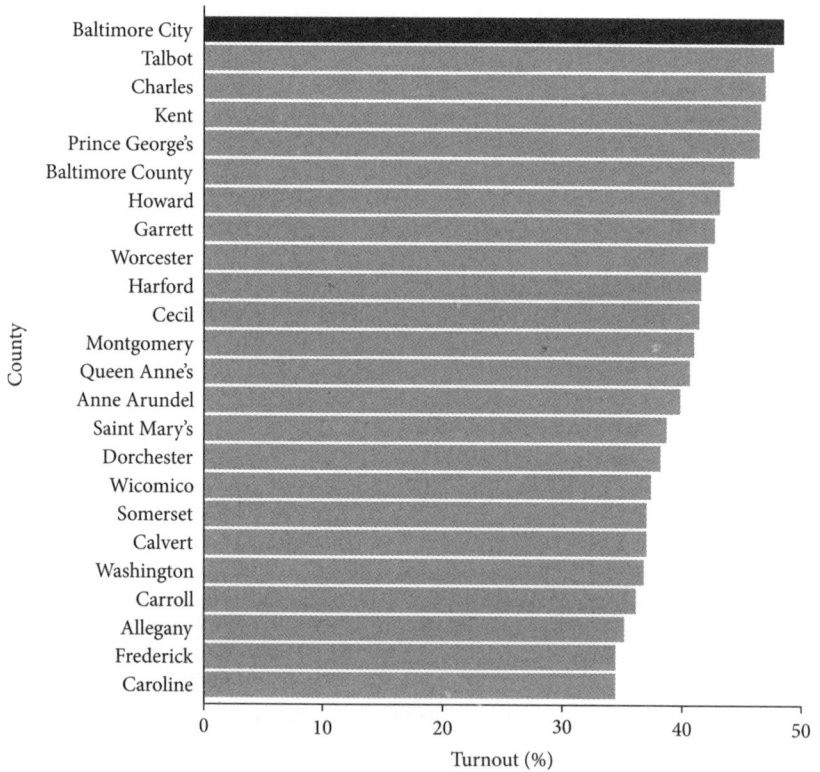

Figure 1.2: Voter Turnout in June 2020 Baltimore Presidential Primary Election, by County and in Baltimore City

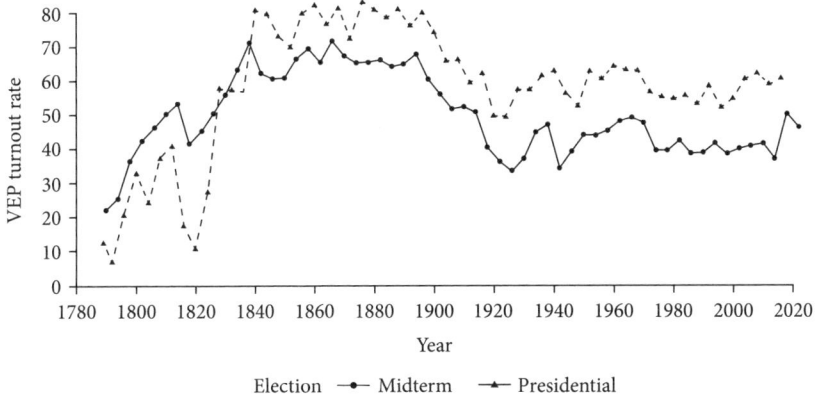

Figure 1.3: Voter Turnout in the US, 1789–2020

loose and party" (Blakemore 2019). Turnout was also extremely high, sometimes exceeding 80 percent of eligible voters, as shown in figure 1.3 (M. McDonald, n.d.). In contrast, most voting today is done privately and sedately, and turnout is far lower. Many election campaigns host election-night parties, but these celebrations are held after the polls are closed and focus not so much on getting out the vote but on (hopefully) celebrating victories. Voters also celebrate voting by wearing "I voted" stickers or using "I voted" tags and frames on social media, but these celebrations are more akin to virtue signaling and do not necessarily convey a spirit of community celebration. Many Americans vote primarily out of a sense of civic duty or due to what political scientists call minimax regret—minimizing the regret they might feel if their preferred candidates don't win (Ferejohn and Fiorina 1974; Blais and Achen 2019).

The PATM effort in Baltimore City in June 2020 was also a celebration of voting, but not with quite the same flavor as those eighteenth- and nineteenth-century festivals. In the early days of the US, these boozy, rowdy parties were used by candidates and their supporters to create a clientelist relationship between candidates and voters. The food and beverages that candidates provided to voters, literally called treating, encouraged eligible citizens to go to the polls and vote for those candidates. In contrast, PATM urged a celebration of voting for the local community, and as noted earlier, the project encouraged that perspective even among individuals who did not receive a box. The June 2020 pilot project urged turnout not in favor of any of the candidates on the primary ballot but in favor of Baltimore. The phrase on the PATM posters, "I love Baltimore so I vote"—still visible on the doors and windows of local residences long after Election Day had passed—embodied this community spirit (figure 1.4). White voters in early America were invited to party as a treat from candidates that was meant to cultivate election victories. Voters in the Black communities of Baltimore partied in June 2020 for their neighbors and their city. In chapter 4, we review extension projects conducted in 2021 and 2022 that focused on sending packages to eligible voters without the same focus on community. To preview those results, we find negligible evidence that it was the boxes doing all of the work. In the absence of a community-wide celebration of voting such as that generated in the June 2020 pilot in Baltimore, increases in turnout among voters who received the packages of information and local goodies were much smaller. Voters don't just want a box. They want a party.

Eighteenth-Century Black Election Day Festivals

The idea of celebrating elections within Black communities was not an original one in 2020. In the late 1700s and early 1800s, free Black people in the North celebrated Election Day, despite their ineligibility to vote. Historians disagree on the degree to which these festivals were a precursor to Black politics, but they agree that they were episodes of community joy and celebration. Shane White (1994, 16) notes enslaved people in the North created "distinctively African American festivals" in the middle third of the eighteenth century, gradually transforming events initially organized by white slave owners. By the end of the 1800s, Election Day was a "richly textured and important" African American cultural event (S. White 1994, 15)—"a rare and valued opportunity for African Americans, who were few and sparsely settled, to socialize among themselves" (16). "In Boston on Negro Election Day blacks congregated on the common, drinking, gambling, dancing, and generally enjoying themselves without interference from whites" (17). A similar description from historian Ira Berlin, describing events in New England cities in the late 1700s and early 1800s, notes, "The celebration of Negro election day took a variety of forms, but everywhere it was a day of great merrymaking that drew blacks from all over the countryside" (1980, 53). Berlin continues,

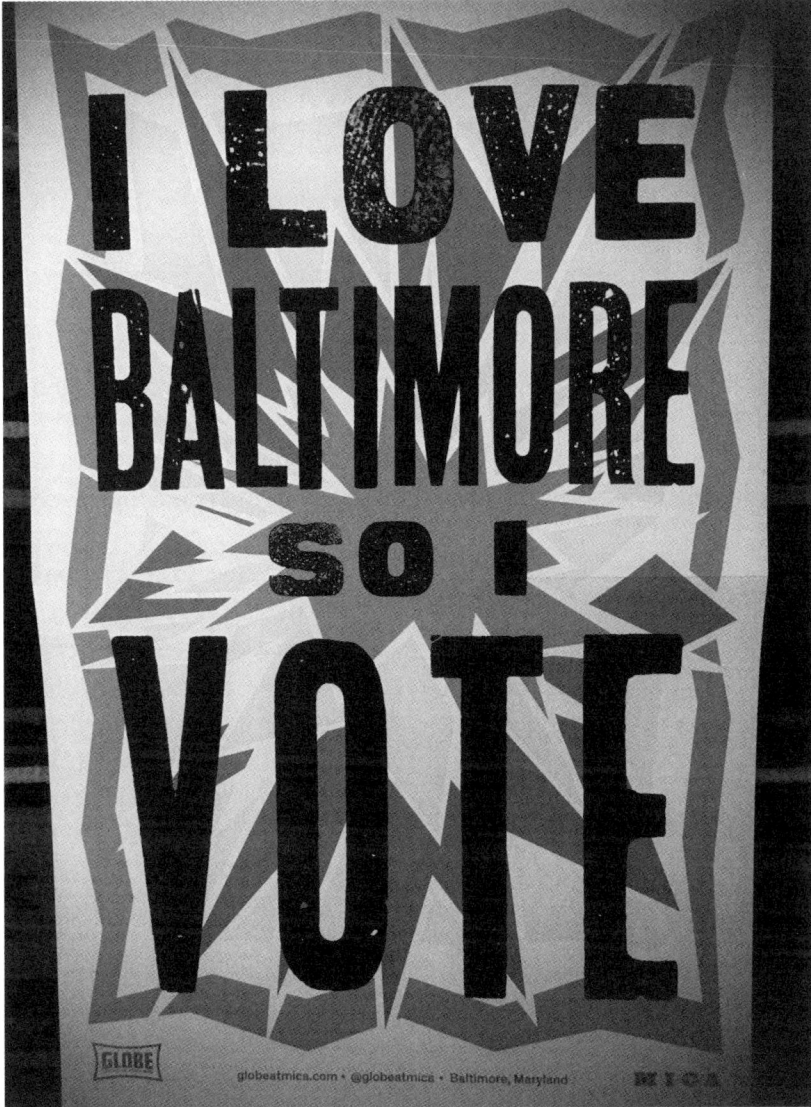

Figure 1.4: "I Love Baltimore So I Vote" Poster

Negro election day culminated with the selection of black kings, governors, and judges. These officials sometimes held symbolic power over
the whole community and real power over the black community. While
the black governors held court, adjudicating minor disputes, the blacks
paraded and partied. . . .

Negro election day permitted a seeming release from bondage, and it
also provided a mechanism for blacks to recognize and honor their own
notables. Most important, it established a framework for the development
of black politics. (1980, 53–54)

According to Berlin, these Election Day festivals were a celebration of
local Black communities. The elected governors and other leaders had
some limited power (e.g., to settle disputes), but that wasn't the focus of
the celebratory festivals. Instead, they were a day to come together as a
community.

That spirit of bringing the Black community together in celebration has
carried over into modern Black politics. During the post–Civil War Jim
Crow era, voting in groups was a means of ensuring the safety of Black
voters. In the modern era, bringing voters from places of worship to
early-voting locations was also a means of fighting disenfranchisement by
providing transportation to the polls. Now a national movement, Souls
to the Polls events organized by Black churches bring Black Americans
together in private cars, on buses, or on foot to go to the polls. In rural
areas, these bus rides are also open to noncongregants, providing crucial
transportation for those who otherwise would have more trouble casting
a vote (Martin 2016; D. Daniels 2020). Souls to the Polls is about more
than a ride—it is about coming together as a community to participate in
electoral politics.

Black Voter Turnout Projects

Souls to the Polls is just one of many modern projects aimed at increasing Black voter participation. Other ongoing efforts include Stroll to
the Polls, Stacey Abrams's organizations Fair Fight Action and the New
Georgia Project, Black Voters Matter, and the National Coalition on Black
Civic Participation, to name just a few. Black communities and community organizations regularly organize registration and voter turnout

efforts. But there is little robust research published about those efforts in political science journals and books because of the ongoing focus on randomized controlled trials (RCTs).

Voter mobilization RCTs are similar in design to a medical experiment where a treatment group is given a new drug or treatment while a control group is given a placebo or traditional treatment. The difference in outcomes between patients randomly assigned to either get the new drug or treatment or not is thus a measure of its effects. In a GOTV RCT, eligible voters are randomly assigned to either get the treatment (an encouragement to participate in an upcoming election) or be in the control group; any observed difference in turnout in the treatment group compared with the control group can then be attributed to that random event (the encouragement to vote). Political scientists have been using RCTs to study the effects of various GOTV tactics and messages for decades, generating insights into how voters in a variety of communities behave in response to those mobilization efforts (García Bedolla and Michelson 2012; Green and Gerber 2024). As detailed later in this chapter, however, only a handful of those RCTs have examined how to increase Black turnout. RCTs were also used to evaluate the effect of the PATM project; details on these are provided in chapters 3, 4, and 5.

Evaluations of Souls to the Polls and similar community efforts have not been the subject of RCTs. Thus, while many observers (including community organizers) believe that these efforts are effective, the lack of robust analytical proof in the form of RCT data has created a disconnect between what communities know about getting out the Black vote and what Black politics scholars know about getting out the Black vote. This lack of RCT data notwithstanding, these community-based programs are widely understood to be important and effective, bringing Black voters to the polls and raising the national visibility of Black electoral power (Doubek and Inskeep 2021; Hazelton 2022; Moody-Ramirez et al. 2023).

Even casual observers of Black electoral politics and civic engagement projects are likely familiar with the various efforts led by Stacey Abrams. In 2013, while serving in the Georgia House of Representatives, she launched the New Georgia Project, with the aim of increasing outreach and participation by those historically marginalized in the state, including people of color and young voters. The New Georgia Project to this day continues to help Georgians register to vote, defend voting rights, push for expanded voting access, and turn out for elections, with a focus on increasing participation among Black Georgians. In 2018, Abrams received the Democratic nomination to be the governor of Georgia but lost by a razor-thin margin to then–Secretary of State Brian Kemp. Abrams attributed her loss to what she claimed was "deliberate and intentional" voter suppression actions by Kemp, particularly his removal from the voter rolls of voters of color and young voters (Taylor 2018). Kemp's office purged 1.4 million inactive voters from the voter rolls and put 53,000 voter registrations on hold (70 percent of which were for Black voters) due to minor discrepancies between registration forms and government records (e.g., dropped hyphens or using nicknames instead of full names, such as Tom for Thomas). This "exact match" system was challenged in court and was dropped in April 2019. Abrams went on to create a new organization, Fair Fight Action, which works to promote fair elections and mitigate voter suppression.

Abrams continued to work to increase Black voter turnout and reduce suppression of Black voters between 2018 and her second bid for the governor's seat in 2022. While she lost her races for governor, her successful efforts to increase Black turnout were widely seen as having provided the margin of victory for other Black candidates, including US Senator Raphael Warnock in 2020 and again in 2022, and for Democratic candidates in the state, including President Joe Biden in 2020. Without RCT data, we cannot determine with certainty the degree to which Abrams's efforts had these purported effects, but many political observers, community organizers, and politicians nevertheless see her efforts to expand voter turnout as having changed the game (Wootson 2022).

Another prominent effort to increase Black voter participation in recent years is Black Voters Matter, founded by LaTosha Brown and Cliff Albright in 2016. They originally focused on increasing Black turnout for the 2017 special election in Alabama, where Black turnout helped Doug Jones defeat Roy Moore and win a seat in the US Senate. In 2018, they launched a series of bus tours focused on rural areas in the South, riding a black bus covered with affirming messages about Black political power. Their message is about power, "not just about participation" (Asmelash 2020). Subsequent efforts included bus tours in Southern and swing states in 2019, as well as a 2020 We Got Power bus tour that visited Alabama, California, Mississippi, North Carolina, and Tennessee and contacted an estimated ten million Black voters (Epstein 2020). In response to the COVID-19 pandemic, Black Voters Matter shifted to a series of virtual town halls for the latter part of the 2020 campaign cycle, but in 2022 they returned to their original model of bus tours, this time visiting Florida, Georgia, Michigan, Missouri, North Carolina, Ohio, Pennsylvania, Texas, and Wisconsin. Black Voters Matter also supported hundreds of local organizations in a dozen states. The organization is credited, alongside Fair Fight and the New Georgia Project, with helping turn Georgia blue in 2020.

Many other organizations, at the local, state, and national levels, have worked for years, if not decades, to increase Black voter turnout and fight suppression of Black voters. The fight for the franchise that was "won" with ratification of the Fifteenth Amendment to the US Constitution in 1870 and again with the 1965 Voting Rights Act continues to the modern day. These efforts have generated best practices for how to build on local community knowledge, to empower communities through grassroots organizing, and to use legal challenges and courts to push back against laws and policies that disenfranchise Black voters and other historically marginalized communities. Black Girls Vote and PATM build on this rich history. In addition, the PATM project adds the component of RCTs, allowing for robust empirical evaluation of the effect of their efforts and comparisons to RCTs conducted by other groups and with other communities of voters. These efforts also build on the Election Day festivals piloted in 2005.

Twenty-First-Century Election Day Festivals

In 2005, a group of political scientists led by Donald Green who were seeking to find ways to effectively increase voter turnout piloted the idea of an election festival in the small town of Hooksett, New Hampshire. A week of publicity preceded the event, including flyers in the local newspaper, lawn signs, and prerecorded phone calls made to three thousand Hooksett households. On Election Day, the festival was held on the front lawn of the local middle school, just outside the local polling place, drawing a large crowd. A large tent offered free snacks and drinks, including sandwiches and cotton candy. A professional DJ played family-friendly music. Green's team reported that the festival successfully created a festive atmosphere: "People of all ages milled about the party tent. Young children snacked and played catch. Elderly couples took advantage of the chairs around the tent to sit, listen to the music, and eat the free sandwiches we provided. The free food relieved some harried parents of dinner preparation that evening, and they mingled with their friends and neighbors" (Addonizio et al. 2007, 723). That November, the same team of scholars organized a similar voting-day festival in front of an elementary school polling place in New Haven, Connecticut, for the city's low-salience municipal election. The festival was advertised with flyers, posters, and lawn signs, and the principal of the school sent flyers to parents, students, and teachers. A round of prerecorded phone calls was also conducted. Again, a large crowd of local residents attended the festival. Describing the festival, the scholars noted, "As in Hooksett, people of all ages milled around the party tent. An impromptu dance contest broke out among the children, the prize being 14 one-dollar bills collected from the audience. Mothers and fathers mingled with their friends and neighbors. The party-goers devoured an enormous quantity of hot dogs and hamburgers" (2007, 723). As with the election celebrations in Black communities in the late 1700s and early 1800s, and the celebrations of Black voters surrounding Souls to the Polls events, these polling place festivals celebrated community while celebrating voting. The major takeaway from the two festivals was not "the enormous quantity of hot dogs and hamburgers" consumed, or even the impromptu dance contest. Instead, it was the positive effect on voter turnout.

Green's team repeated the festivals twelve more times in 2006. The racial makeup of the fourteen test sites varies, but none are majority Black, and most are majority Anglo (non-Latino white).[3] All fourteen elections were low to medium salience, ranging from a municipal race where no candidates faced challengers to contested midterm federal elections. The scholars estimate that on average the festivals increased the odds of turnout by 2.5 percentage points (SE = 1.2), at a cost of twenty-eight dollars per vote. These estimates were generated using the science of RCTs. To put this in perspective, nonpartisan mailed encouragements to vote generally increase turnout by less than 0.5 percentage points, on average. Phone calls made by volunteers increase turnout by an average of 2.8 percentage points, while door-to-door canvassing increases turnout by an average of 4.0 percentage points (Green and Gerber 2024).

Green and Oliver McClellan have since organized several rounds of additional election festival RCTs, with mixed results. These included eight election festival RCTs conducted for the 2016 general election. In this high-salience context, they find an average estimated effect of 3.8 percentage points (SE = 1.6). Estimated effects of further follow-up RCTs with a much larger set of festivals are weaker: Over one hundred festivals were conducted across multiple sites in 2017 and 2018, with no measurable effect on turnout. Green and McClellan posit that this may be due to the widespread rain on both election days, which likely influenced festival attendance (it rained at 87 percent of election festival sites in 2017 and 75 percent in 2018). Looking at a smaller number of early-vote festivals conducted in 2018 ($N = 7$)—on days when Mother Nature did not interfere with the festivals—they find an effect of 3.5 percentage points (SE = 1.2). Overall, they conclude that election festivals are an effective and cost-effective means for increasing voter turnout, with a pooled estimate including all studies from 2005 through 2018 of 1.6 percentage points (SE = 0.81) (Green and McClellan 2017, 2020).

The small effects for the large number of festivals conducted in 2017 and 2018 sit in stark contrast to the consistently strong effects found in the earlier RCTs and in the 2016 general election. Overall, we interpret these results as suggesting that the tactic of making voting a celebratory community event is effective across low-, medium-, and high-salience elections but that the focus on single-day events leaves the tactic vulnerable to weather events or other disruptions. Another factor is that these events "lacked the community-level barrage of publicity typical of the most successful early parties" (Donald P. Green, personal communication, March 9, 2023). This contrasts with Black community celebrations of the vote that take place over several days or weeks, such as with Souls to the Polls, which brings voters out during early-voting periods on multiple Sundays. PATM is more akin to historical Black community celebrations that were spread out over time; this avoids potential unanticipated disruptions and allows for word about the celebration to spread and for excitement about the election to build over time, and thus to generate a larger impact on turnout.

These smaller later and overall effects notwithstanding, Party at the Polls festivals are the model on which PATM was based. There is a rich literature on the most effective ways to get out the vote, both generally and when specifically targeting low-propensity communities of color. These range from traditional methods including door-to-door canvassing, phone banking, and mail, to newer tactics including text messages and relational organizing. For Robinson, generating a celebratory atmosphere was crucial; Black voters in 2020 needed to party (at the mailbox).

Generating Reciprocity

Other scholars have studied the power of increasing turnout using political favors or tangible incentives. As noted earlier, PATM provided items to voters, but the impact of the project was felt far beyond those who directly received them. Still, there are parallels to these previous, incentive-based efforts. The use of cash or other incentives to motivate voter turnout and vote choice is widespread in the developing world, where the exchange of clientelist goods is not illegal; multiple studies document its pervasiveness and effectiveness at increasing turnout (Vicente 2014; Murugesan 2020). Specific material advantages, including access to public services, jobs, cash, and gifts, are used in democracies in countries in the Americas, Africa, Asia, and the Middle East to deliver material advantages to political supporters (Murugesan 2020). While in some instances this takes the form of vote buying, in other instances where individual votes cannot be monitored (where there is a secret ballot), politicians and political parties reward supporters for showing up at the polls, which Simeon Nichter (2008) differentiates as "turnout buying."

In the United States, where compensating individuals for voting is a violation of federal law, there have nevertheless been strong traditions in some communities of building relationships with voters using incentives, a strategy likely to induce feelings of reciprocity among potential voters (Cialdini 2021). According to *Street Fight*, the 2005 movie chronicling the 2002 Newark, New Jersey, mayoral race between incumbent Sharpe James and Cory Booker, both candidates plied voters with gifts and food, including flowers, perfume, potholders, chartered buses to Atlantic City, and tickets to concerts and the circus. The degree to which this tradition persists is uncertain; no recent news stories or academic publications have explored the practice.

Academic efforts to test the effect of financial incentives on turnout have met with mixed results. Costas Panagopoulos conducted two GOTV RCTs offering cash payments for participation in local California elections in 2007 and 2010 (thus eluding federal bans on paying citizens to vote); his results suggest that nonnominal payments are more effective than simple reminders at increasing turnout (Panagopoulos 2013a). Victoria Shineman conducted a "super-treatment" GOTV RCT in a local California election in 2011, combining cash payments with information about how to register and vote, as well as multiple emailed reminders about the election, which generated a large increase in turnout as well as statistically significant increases in political knowledge (Shineman 2018).

In summary, we thought that, in addition to motivating turnout as a celebration of community, PATM might also increase turnout by creating a clientelist relationship with some voters, nudging them to participate in order to reciprocate the box that they received. Note that this was never conveyed to the voters, and PATM staff were careful to never imply that they were requiring a promise of turnout in return for participation in the program or acceptance of a box delivery. But the psychological effect of the boxes could nevertheless have induced feelings of reciprocity (Cialdini 2021). The rule of reciprocation is why we try to repay favors and to give birthday presents to those who have remembered our own birthdays. The rule is so strong, Cialdini notes, that in English and in many other languages the phrase "much obliged" often is used as a substitute for "thank you" (2021, 24). The rule of reciprocity is why marketing plans often include free samples, and why fundraising mailers often include free return address labels or greeting cards; these create feelings of obligation in the recipients that lead them to reciprocate with a purchase or donation. The PATM materials, if they generated feelings of reciprocity among recipients, could theoretically have increased turnout as a consequence of recipients thinking that they owed it to the PATM program to comply with their request.

Celebrating Democracy During a Pandemic

The success of the election festivals explored by Donald Green and his collaborators notwithstanding, in-person festivals are not always feasible or appropriate, such as when voting is spread out over a long period of time (e.g., early-voting periods) or is conducted mostly or completely using mail-in ballots. In 2020 in particular, precautions taken to keep voters safe during the pandemic included reduced in-person voting options and an increased emphasis on vote-by-mail.

The need to do so was illustrated by the March 2020 primary in Wisconsin. On April 3, Wisconsin's Democratic Governor Tony Evers called a special session of the state legislature to delay the election and shift to a mail-in election; the Republican-controlled legislature refused, so Evers issued an emergency order making the change on April 6. That order was appealed to the Wisconsin Supreme Court, which blocked it, paving the way for voting to begin the next day. Local election officials in the state's major cities, including Milwaukee and Green Bay, had already decided to operate fewer polling places (down from 180 to 5 in Milwaukee, and from 31 to 2 in Green Bay), and many poll workers declined to show up to work, citing public health concerns. The combination of fewer polling places and fewer poll workers meant long lines to vote, especially in Black neighborhoods. Postelection analyses found a spike in COVID-19 cases, likely linked to the lack of social distancing experienced when voters chose to wait in those lines and cast their ballots (Cotti et al. 2020).

Press coverage of the Wisconsin primary election framed it as forcing voters to choose between democracy and their health; most other states did not present voters with the need to make this choice, instead quickly revising their voting laws and procedures either to allow for expanded use of mail-in balloting or in some cases to shift to entirely all-mail elections and either mailing every voter a vote-by-mail application or mailing ballots to all registered voters. As a result of these changes, the share of voting conducted via mail-in ballots increased dramatically (DeSilver 2020). This shift in voting procedures meant that parties, candidates, and organizations had to shift their GOTV tactics to encourage voters to vote by mail rather than to encourage them to show up at their local polling place. PATM was specifically designed by Robinson to replace the election festivals that had proved so promising in earlier elections to be effective in this new electoral context, and with a focus on Black voters.

Party at the Mailbox

The power of a celebratory, community-based effort to raise turnout among low-propensity voters also builds on scholarship about the power of group consciousness, linked fate, and emotions to motivate political behavior. *Group consciousness*, first identified by W. O. Brown in 1931, is a politicized in-group identification wherein individuals believe that their group's status and interests are best achieved through collective action (see McClain et al. 2009). Black group consciousness predicts higher voter turnout than would be expected given individuals' socioeconomic status, as well as other forms of political participation. Black Americans with strong feelings of group consciousness see collective action as a way to benefit their group as a whole as well as themselves as individuals (Austin 2018). Celebrations of community prime group consciousness to encourage these behaviors. The belief in voting as a means of advancing Black people as a community is akin to the belief in voting as civic duty. We delve further into this idea of voting as a civic duty and a sense of group consciousness in chapter 6.

Relatedly, *linked fate* measures the degree to which an individual member of a broader group feels that their interests are inextricably linked to the interests of the identity group (Dawson 1994; McClain et al. 2009). Individuals with strong feelings of linked fate feel bound by that membership; it's not just that they feel close to other members of the group, but that they are incentivized to cooperate with other members and give priority to group objectives. Michael Dawson, who coined the term, describes linked fate as a *"black utility heuristic"*: the perception that individual life chances depend heavily on those of Black Americans as a whole, leading to the rational substitution of group utility for individual utility in political decision-making and a strong moral and emotional commitment to the group (Dawson 1994, 10). Reviewing the linked fate literature, Claudine Gay and colleagues (2016) find that Black Americans consistently report strong feelings of racial linked fate, which in turn leads to support for group solidarity. PATM engaged with registered voters in their communities as members of strongly felt in-groups—for example, as Black Baltimoreans and as Black women. In chapter 2, we delve more deeply into how theories of linked fate, and especially the linked fate felt by Black women, are related to our concept of voting as a celebration of community.

Finally, there is the emotional component of voting as a celebration of community—specifically joy. Much of the voting literature focuses on voting as a duty, and notions of group consciousness and linked fate also take a serious tone, emphasizing the need to stick together to fight discrimination and uplift communities. They reference the Black civil rights movement, the ongoing fight for equality at the voting booth, and the need to demand inclusion in the polity. These explanations for why Black Americans turn out to vote at such high rates are powerful, but cheerless; they do not reflect the palpable joy expressed by participants in Souls to the Polls activities or the festive mood reported at the 1963 March on Washington (Kenworthy 1963). Tracey Michae'l Lewis-Giggetts (2020, xx) describes Black joy as "a salve we need in the midst of a reality that on its worst day can be insidiously paralyzing." It is "a radical demonstration of our humanity" that cultivates personal and collective healing" (xxi), "rooted in a deep love for who we collectively are as Black people" (xxii).

We hypothesized that efforts to mobilize voters by cultivating a celebratory community environment would be particularly successful in majority-Black communities given the strong tradition among many Black Americans of voting as a celebration of community. Since the Reconstruction era, Black American organizations and institutions have maintained a rich history of mobilizing their communities to vote. Black Americans have a unique political socialization where most of their political cues are generated at the grassroots level in familial and community spaces (Walton 1985; T. Lee 2002; Harris-Lacewell 2004; Walton and Smith 2012). As a result, Black Americans view voting as an important activity or value to uphold in community. In chapter 6, we share evidence of these attitudes from our interviews and focus group conversations.

The communal, celebratory nature of Black civic engagement has a rich history. Groups such as churches, social fellowships, fraternities and sororities, and suffrage clubs have taken an active part in not only advocating for Black Americans' right to vote but encouraging their communities to exercise that right with community events and meetings including voter registration efforts and town halls (Giddings 1984, 1988;

Higginbotham 1993; Smooth 2018; D. Daniels 2020; A. Daniels 2021). Building on this practice, these types of organizations have developed new and innovative ways to engage potential voters. Black churches have worked for sixty years to increase voter turnout, more recently under slogans such as Souls to the Polls (D. Daniels 2020). The effectiveness of these church-based programs can be seen in research showing that Black early-voting turnout in Florida spikes on Sundays (Herron and Smith 2012).

In 2020, this celebratory community spirit was particularly evident among members of Alpha Kappa Alpha, a Black sorority that Democratic vice-presidential nominee Kamala Harris joined as a student at Howard University, as well as members of the other Black fraternities and sororities that make up the Divine Nine. As the election approached, *The Washington Post* reported that sorority members were celebrating Harris's nomination and working to increase turnout among members (Janes 2020). The organization that branched out to create PATM, Black Girls Vote, shares the same historical lineage as these organizations, particularly Black women-led organizations, which create unique programs and initiatives to engage Black voters (Vroman 1965; Giddings 1984; Higginbotham 1993; Collins 2000; Dowe 2016; Smooth 2018); the founder and president of both organizations, Robinson, is herself a member of Delta Sigma Theta, one of the Divine Nine.

RCTs Mobilizing Black Voters

Voter mobilization research has been the focus of extensive scholarship since 2000, but not with equal attention to all types of voters. Summarizing the GOTV literature in 2020, David Searle and Marisa Abrajano write, "The paucity of research on how candidates, political parties and outside groups target African Americans and whether or not they are persuaded or mobilized by these efforts cannot be emphasized enough" (2020, 259). We turn now to explanations for this notable gap in the scholarly literature and a review of what we do know about how best to increase Black turnout, particularly using the robust methodology of RCTs.

This gap in existing scholarship is attributable to two major factors. First, Black voters have traditionally been strong supporters of the Democratic Party, and they have also been located in noncompetitive geographic areas, thus reducing interest in how best to increase their levels of participation. In close presidential elections in battleground states, Black voters can attract significant attention and investment from candidates and campaigns, but in most elections efforts to encourage Black turnout are limited to relatively small, local efforts led by grassroots organizations and churches, and most Black voters do not receive invitations to participate. This reflects strategic decisions made by candidates and campaigns, which know that Black voters can be relied on as loyal Democratic voters (Frymer 1999; I. White and Laird 2020). Even in battleground states, people of color are less likely to be mobilized compared with white voters (Ramírez et al. 2018).

Excluding the presidential races that included Barack Obama, Black turnout is generally lower than white turnout (Fraga 2018; M. McDonald, n.d.). Rashawn Ray and Mark Whitlock (2019) argue that Black Americans are not less likely to want to vote, but that their lower voter turnout rates are due to their being systematically denied the ability to do so, particularly in the wake of the *Shelby v. Alabama* (2013) Supreme Court decision that rolled back Voting Rights Act protections. In many geographic areas, Black voting rights are restricted through the use of voter ID requirements and limits on early voting. A 2024 report from the Brennan Center for Justice found that the gap between Black and white turnout has consistently grown since the *Shelby* decision, particularly in areas of the country previously covered by the Voting Rights Act (Morris and Grange 2024).

The dearth of published work on how best to mobilize Black voters is significant because of the increasingly visible role played by Black voters in US politics, as evidenced by the results of the 2020 presidential election, and also because we should not assume the relevance of best practices generated from GOTV efforts in non-Black communities. As Michael Dawson (1994, 5) notes, "African-American politics, including political behavior, is *different*. It has been shaped by historical forces that produced a different pattern of political behavior from the pattern found among white citizens." Dawson attributes this different pattern of behavior to his theory of linked fate: that the historical experiences of African Americans lead them to use group interests as a proxy for self-interest. Individuals will consider racial group interests when making political choices when they believe their own life chances are linked to those of Black Americans as a group.

The second factor contributing to the gap in scholarship on GOTV efforts aimed at Black voters is the focus in the past quarter century on RCTs for producing robust evidence about the power of GOTV efforts, combined with the reluctance by many Black people to cooperate with external efforts to experiment with their communities. This stems from historical instances of unethical scientific exploitation of Black people, including the prominent examples of Tuskegee and Henrietta Lacks.

In 1931, the US Public Health Service, working with the Tuskegee Institute in Macon, Alabama, enrolled hundreds of Black men in a study to record the effects of untreated syphilis over time. By 1943, penicillin was widely used to treat the disease, but it was not offered to study participants, who were instead offered placebos such as aspirin and mineral supplements, even as they suffered severe health problems, died, or passed the disease on to their spouses and children. The study ended in 1972 after its existence was revealed in a news story by the Associated Press, and in 1974 survivors and heirs received a $10 million settlement. In 1997, then-President Bill Clinton issued a formal apology for the study, noting, "To our African American citizens, I am sorry that your federal government orchestrated a study so clearly racist" (Clinton 1997; Centers for Disease Control and Prevention 2023).

Henrietta Lacks was a young Black woman who in 1951 went to the Johns Hopkins Hospital for medical treatment for what was later determined to be cervical cancer. A sample of her cells was collected and, surprisingly, did not die; instead, they doubled every twenty to twenty-four hours. These unique "HeLa" cells (from her first and last name) continue to be used in medical research. However, consent for the use of her cells was never obtained from Lacks or her family, nor was the family compensated. Decades later, Lacks's descendants sued, noting in their legal complaint that "the exploitation of Henrietta Lacks represents the unfortunately common struggle experienced by Black people throughout history. . . . Too often, the history of medical experimentation in the United States has been the history of medical racism." The suit was settled in August 2023, although the terms of the settlement were not publicly disclosed (Skene and Brumfield 2023).

This rational reluctance to cooperate with scientific inquiries not-withstanding, there are a handful of published GOTV RCTs that include significant numbers of Black participants. After the modern GOTV experimental subfield was launched in 2000 (Gerber and Green 2000), scholars around the country sought to extend those findings with RCTs in different geographic areas and with different communities. Early efforts focusing on Black voters included mostly indirect tactics: a November 2000 collaboration with the National Association for the Advancement of Colored People using direct mail and commercial phone banks (Green 2004), leafleting campaigns in partisan races (Gillespie 2005), and nonpartisan campaigns targeting predominantly Black precincts (Azari and Washington 2006). These initial efforts, however, generated negligible effects on participation. In November 2009, a social pressure mail experiment successfully increased Black voter turnout in New Jersey's gubernatorial election (Panagopoulos 2013b).

Door-to-door canvassing efforts by local community organizations, in contrast, have consistently increased Black voter turnout. This includes efforts conducted by the now-defunct Association of Community Organizations for Reform Now (ACORN) in November 2001 in Detroit, Michigan, and in November 2003 in Kansas City, Missouri. The target populations in these cities at the time were 94 percent and 64 percent African American, respectively. Contact with an ACORN canvasser increased turnout in these RCTs by 7.8 percentage points in Detroit and by 8.5 percentage points in Kansas City (Green and Michelson 2009). RCTs in South Los Angeles, California (a mixed Black and Latino community), in 2006 and 2008 found that door-to-door canvassing efforts by members of the local organization Strategic Concepts in Organizing and Policy Education (SCOPE) were effective at increasing Black voter turnout. Black South Los Angeles voters were particularly likely to be mobilized when contacted by a Black canvasser and when contacted by a canvasser from their local community (García Bedolla and Michelson 2012; Sinclair et al. 2013; Michelson and García Bedolla 2014). In contrast, a November 2018 door-to-door effort aimed at increasing Black turnout in Washington, DC, that did not use local Black canvassers had negligible effects (Scott, Michelson, and DeMora 2021). More recently, a team of scholars analyzed a randomized GOTV effort conducted by a community organization in Ohio with majority-Black low-income public housing residents. The estimated effect of their canvassing was a 3.1 percentage-point increase in turnout, but due to the small sample size there is a high degree of uncertainty about that estimate, and it is not statistically significant (Grumbach et al. 2024).

The positive effects generated by many previous face-to-face efforts to increase voter participation among Black citizens support Lisa García Bedolla and Melissa Michelson's theory of sociocultural cognition regarding the power of personalized outreach to low-propensity voters, and also theories about the power of shared Black consciousness. Black voters are uniquely influenced to be loyal to the Democratic Party and to participate in elections due to well-understood behavioral norms with roots in Black liberation politics (I. White and Laird 2020). Reinforcing Dawson's theory of Black linked fate, Ismail White and Chryl Laird argue that the roots of Black political unity were established through the adversities of slavery and segregation, when Black Americans forged uniquely strong social bonds for survival and resistance. These tight communities have continued to produce and enforce political norms including Democratic Party identification in the post–civil rights era. The social experience of race for Black Americans is thus fundamental to their political choices. Black voters are uniquely influenced by the social expectations of other Black Americans to prioritize the group's ongoing struggle for freedom and equality. When they navigate the choice of supporting a political party, this social expectation translates into affiliation with the Democratic Party.[4]

Black voter turnout does not necessarily follow rules about political participation developed from studies of white Americans (Philpot et al. 2009). Tasha Philpot and her coauthors make this point in their summary of pathbreaking work by Dawson (1994), Fredrick Harris (1999), and Eric McDaniel (2008): "Unlike other groups in society, indigenous institutions that surfaced out of Blacks' unique history play as important a role in determining Blacks' motivation to engage in politics as do individual-level characteristics or other group attachments such as party identification" (Philpot et al. 2009, 999). Harris (1999) documents the example of Black clergy mobilizing their congregation members during the civil rights movement and also observes that Black parishioners overwhelmingly support church-based political activism. McDaniel (2008, 19) notes that Black church-based activism reflects the relative lack of other resources among Black Americans, including few Black elected officials at the federal level, few and less well-funded interest organizations that represent the Black community, even fewer Black political action committees, and ongoing registration and voting restrictions that systematically disenfranchise eligible Black voters. Conducting RCTs with Black voters is crucial for determining how best to increase Black turnout. Studies in other communities (e.g., the election festivals conducted by Green and his colleagues) do not necessarily predict how well similar events would influence participation in majority-Black neighborhoods.

The very limited number of published RCTs examining Black GOTV efforts does not reflect the high level of mobilization activity regularly delivered by Black-serving organizations, including churches. White and Laird note that Black voters in Alabama delivered the margin of victory for Doug Jones in his bid for the US Senate in a special election in December 2017. Although 60 percent of Black voters were unaware of the scheduled election just a few weeks earlier, high Black turnout (and near-unanimous support for Jones) gave Democrats a victory. This turnout was fueled "by relentless on-the-ground mobilization efforts of black organizations and black social networks" (I. White and Laird 2020, 2). Black voters are also credited with the success of the two Democratic candidates for the US Senate who were chosen in a special election in Georgia on January 5, 2021 (M. Lee et al. 2021). The lack of RCT evidence for these conclusions does not mean that they are not based on facts. PATM builds on the collective wisdom that guides modern efforts to mobilize Black voters. The success of PATM as documented in our RCTs speaks to the strength of that inherited wisdom.

The 2020 Pandemic and Vote-by-Mail

Among the many ways that the COVID-19 pandemic upended life in the United States in 2020 was a disruption of usual methods of mobilizing voters to participate in elections. Just as millions of voters were being asked to cast their ballots in primaries and caucuses, and later for the November elections, they were also asked to shelter indoors and practice social distancing. Community organizations with plans to engage in door-to-door canvassing and other best practices for increasing voter turnout had to innovate with new, pandemic-safe methods of registering and mobilizing eligible voters. One notable innovation came from Black Girls Vote, a nonpartisan community organization based in Baltimore. Their pilot project, PATM, sought to increase vote-by-mail participation in the June 2, 2020, primary. Reflecting the decrease in Black American turnout in 2016 compared with the previous two presidential elections, the project also sought specifically to shift attitudes and identities—to create a greater sense of identity as voters and to generate feelings of shared community.

We conducted a multimethod evaluation of the PATM pilot, using an RCT, an internet survey, one-on-one interviews with registered voters and community leaders, and focus groups. We documented significant shifts in attitudes and behavior, including a double-digit increase in voter turnout among low-propensity voters who shared a household with someone who participated in the pilot project. Building on those results, we expanded to three cities for the November 3, 2020, elections, adding Detroit and Philadelphia. In late 2021, we launched a fifth effort in the Atlanta metropolitan area, for the US Senate runoff elections on January 5, 2021; while we lack RCT data for that iteration of the project, we do have survey, interview, and focus group data. Shifting gears, we moved to implement what we call the *skinny sleeve* alternative in PATM efforts for the off-year gubernatorial election in Richmond, Virginia, on November 2, 2021. The skinny sleeve was a large, padded envelope containing fewer items than the *classic box* we used in earlier iterations, which was a cardboard box with a larger number of items. The skinny sleeve version was used again in Detroit and Atlanta in November 2022, and in Philadelphia in November 2024. For these iterations, we shifted several aspects of the project, including randomly sending out packages to selected multivoter households in majority-Black ZIP codes, as we describe in chapter 5.

As fear of COVID-19 lessened, even as the pandemic continued, most elections shifted back to in-person and hybrid models, with many voters (especially Republicans) choosing to vote at their local polling place due to increased skepticism about the security of returning a ballot through the US Postal Service (M. Parks 2022). PATM thus became a party that was not focused on returning one's ballot through the mail but rather one that came to voters in the mail. As the implementation of the project shifted over time, however, the core philosophy remained the same: that individuals in majority-Black communities would be more likely to vote if they were encouraged to think about voting as something done as a celebration of their community. This emphasis on celebration merged with existing attitudes toward voting as a duty—a duty to the Black ancestors who fought successfully for the right to vote—and celebration of Black community and Black voices by showing up for that community on Election Day.

Hypotheses

For our initial set of PATM efforts, we hypothesized that individuals who opted to ask to receive a box of informational materials and other goodies from the PATM campaign would be more likely to vote. We also expected this effect to spill over onto other members of their households and to their communities. In other words, because individuals receiving boxes were encouraged to share the contents with their households and neighbors, we expected those household members and neighbors to also be more likely to vote even if they did not opt into the program. In fact, we have considerable evidence that they did so, including anecdotal accounts from our postelection qualitative data as well as visual data collected from the target neighborhoods. Long after the elections, PATM materials were still visible from sidewalks in Baltimore. We expected the effect to be particularly notable in Black communities due to the nature of those communities, the feelings of linked fate shared by many Black Americans, and the spirit of voting as a celebration of community that PATM primed with its educational materials. Our hypotheses are summarized as follows:

> H1: Members of households randomly assigned to receive a PATM box will be more likely to vote compared with members of households randomly assigned to not receive a box.
>
> H2: As a result of the spirit of community duty primed by the PATM box, recipients will also report stronger feelings of political efficacy (which will make them more likely to vote).
>
> H3: As a result of the community identities and duty to community primed by the PATM box, recipients will also be more likely to report political identities as voters and as members of their cities.

The common thread of these hypotheses, and of the project overall, is that we expect voters in Black communities to respond to the PATM materials in a way that reflects their identities as Black Americans and the histories of voting and civic duty in Black America. Because Black Americans have historically celebrated their linked fate at the ballot box and voted in part due to feelings of civic duty linked to their identities as members of Black communities, and because the PATM boxes primed that linked fate and community civic duty, the boxes increased turnout in Black neighborhoods. Turnout is also likely to increase among non-Black Americans, but we expect the strongest results among Black voters.

Through repeated RCTs and surveys, interviews, and focus group discussions with hundreds of community members, we were able to explore voter responses to PATM, and we find significant support for our Voter Community Celebration Model. Priming members of Black communities with educational materials that encourage voting as an expression of membership in a local Black community, and as a celebration of that local Black community, significantly increases voter turnout among members of that community.

At the same time, not all PATM projects were equally successful. In some cities, especially in November 2020, the measurable effect of our efforts was negligible; we explore possible explanations for this variation in effect in subsequent chapters and summarize those findings in the conclusion. Not all PATM efforts were the same in their implementation and effectiveness. In Baltimore, the project benefited from the strong base of trust built up by Black Girls Vote and Baltimore Votes in earlier elections, and the strong network of local community organizations that served as project partners. In other cities, PATM worked to find trusted local partners, but the PATM initiatives were newcomers to those cities and did not have the same name recognition. When we spoke to voters after each election, few of them (other than those in Baltimore) were familiar with Black Girls Vote or PATM outside of the limited information they had from signing up for or receiving a box. The 2020 and 2021 rounds were also generally in high-salience elections, and in more widely dispersed geographic areas. We tested the importance of these factors in our final set of PATM efforts, in 2022 and 2024.

Remainder of the Book

The next chapter reviews the literature underlying our Voter Community Celebration Model and how it is linked to Black identity, the history of Black struggles for the franchise, linked fate, and other racialized understandings of voting and citizenship. It provides historical data about rates of participation in the Black community, compared with other ethnic and racial communities in the United States, both overall and among men and women. It also reviews the specific relationship that many Black communities have had with voting, including Souls to the Polls and Stroll to the Polls, and other scholarship and community organizational efforts focused on Black voter registration and mobilization.

In chapter 3, we move on to a detailed account of the pilot PATM effort in Baltimore for the June 2020 primary election, and the challenges faced by Black Girls Vote and Baltimore Votes to get the project funded and into the field. Those challenges notwithstanding, we demonstrate with an RCT that the pilot increased turnout among low-propensity household members of PATM box recipients by 12.7 percentage points. We also share results from the successful extension in November 2020 that included not just the city of Baltimore but also Baltimore County, a separate geographic entity. Going beyond those quantitative data, we use our survey, interview, and focus group discussion data with Baltimoreans to illustrate the many ways in which PATM made voting a celebration of community that changed attitudes and behaviors.

Moving beyond our original community of Baltimore, in chapter 4 we review the roadshow: various extensions of PATM that took place in Detroit and Philadelphia in November 2020 and the Atlanta metropolitan area in January 2021 (for the US Senate runoff elections). Using mixed-methods data including RCTs, surveys, interviews, and focus groups, we explore results from these replication efforts and the hows and whys of outcomes that differed. These rich data allow us to further explore our Voter Community Celebration Model.

In chapter 5, we explore the implementation of the skinny sleeve: an innovation first tested in the Virginia gubernatorial election with a PATM effort in Richmond in November 2021. For this round, we implemented several changes, including randomly sending recipients either a classic box (resembling boxes from earlier PATM cities) or a skinny sleeve (a large, padded envelope with fewer items included). Both were delivered via the US Postal Service and distributed randomly to households in majority-Black neighborhoods. With those results in hand, we conducted a final set of PATM efforts, using just the skinny sleeve, in two cities in November 2022 (Detroit and Atlanta) and one city in November 2024 (Philadelphia). These changes were made specifically to test how to deliver the program at a lower cost per vote, and also how it might be scaled up to reach more voters in more communities. Results here speak to the challenges faced by a local community organization hoping to go national, and the pressures imposed by funders. They also help clarify the Voter Community Celebration Model by narrowing the variables at play and exploring the effect of returning to cities from earlier efforts to test how that helps build trust and local buy-in.

In chapter 6, we dig deeper into our qualitative data, exploring the multifaceted understanding of voting as a duty (the "D" factor) that participants voiced during our many conversations with them, including dozens of focus groups. Participants talked about voting as a duty to their ancestors who fought for the franchise, as a duty to their communities who need a political voice, and as a duty to speak up for their preferred public policies. Their definition of duty differs from traditional understandings of the word. These data enrich our understanding of why Black people vote and how efforts to encourage voting can channel duty to community in ways that make those efforts more effective. This duty to community, then, is part of the mechanism of why PATM was so effective, even among individuals not directly engaging with PATM materials.

In our concluding chapter, we circle back to the Voter Community Celebration Model to review lessons learned from our multiple rounds of PATM and the various types of data used to evaluate its effect on local communities. We offer details for how local cities and community organizations can replicate the PATM experience in their own communities and increase voter turnout among low-propensity voters, not only to the benefit of democracy and a strong participatory culture but also for the spillover effects PATM has on feelings of community and political efficacy. To preview those conclusions, we find that efforts that mobilize voters as members of a community, and not just as individual voters, are more effective, and that PATM can move voters to the polls in low-, medium-, and high-salience elections. We offer takeaways about how to partner with academics to the benefit of both local community organizations and the scholarly understanding of real-world politics, and we encourage others to have their own community parties.

2

Black Identities and Black Turnout

This chapter delves more deeply into the rich tapestry of literature surrounding Black political engagement and elaborates on the underlying goals and guiding principles of the Party at the Mailbox (PATM) initiative. We expand on the thought behind PATM and our strategies for increasing Black voter turnout. Specifically, we detail how our innovative Voter Community Celebration Model is intricately connected to the historical struggles for the franchise, linked fate, and other racialized understandings of voting and citizenship. Using historical data, we juxtapose rates of participation within the Black community to those of other ethnic and racial communities in the United States. We also examine the unique relationships that have developed between many Black communities and voting, and institutions like Black churches and Black Greek letter organizations. Compared with other chapters in this book, this chapter takes a more academic look at the mechanisms of Black political behavior, particularly of Black women. Practitioners and casual readers should feel free to skip ahead to chapter 3, where we return to the narrative of our project.

Black Girls Vote and the PATM project both center the voices and power of Black women. Casual observers of modern partisan politics might assume that Black women are an empowered community within the Democratic Party, given the many Black elected and appointed female officials on the national stage (including former Vice President and 2024 Democratic nominee for President Kamala Harris and Supreme Court Justice Ketanji Brown Jackson). High rates of voter turnout and Democratic Party loyalty among Black women have been crucial to recent Democratic election victories. In 2008 and 2012, 96 percent of Black women voted for the Democratic presidential nominee (Barack Obama), as did 94 percent of Black women in 2016 (Hillary Clinton), 90 percent of Black women in 2020 (Joe Biden), and 92 percent of Black women in 2024 (Kamala Harris). The power of this level of support was enhanced by strong turnout: 75 percent of eligible Black women cast a ballot in 2008, as did 74 percent in 2012, 66 percent in 2016 and 2020, and 63 percent in 2024. These high rates of partisan loyalty and turnout belie the long-standing and enduring barriers to political power faced by Black women (and other members of historically marginalized communities).

In this chapter, we dive into political theories that explain Black political mobilization, with particular emphasis on Black women. We detail how Black women's political identity and civic engagement are shaped by their intersectional identities both as Black and as women, two groups that have historically been disenfranchised and marginalized in US politics. By prioritizing and centering the voices and power of Black women, Black Girls Vote programming aligns with the rich political history of Black suffrage and maintains the long-standing tradition of political participation that is central within Black communities. We provide a theoretical account of why centering Black identity is so important to facilitate effective mobilization of the Black community.

Black Political Identity

Scholarly examinations of Black politics often examine the role of institutions and collective behavior in shaping Black identity. These studies chronicle the diverse ways in which Black communities have participated in politics throughout American history, even in the face of institutional constraints and exclusion. At the heart of this research is an effort to understand how civic participation persists amid adversity. Black political identity in America is fundamentally intertwined with an ethos of community connection. From battles for citizenship and the franchise to more contemporary policy issues, racial visibility has remained a cornerstone of Black political identity in large part because of historical and ongoing marginalization.

Black voter turnout has been consistently high compared with other historically marginalized racial and ethnic groups (Fraga 2018). This was particularly the case in 2008 and 2012 when the Black vote also outpaced the white vote, reflecting the historic candidacies of the first Black US president, Barack Obama. More recently, high turnout among Black voters has been credited with securing the 2020 nomination of Joe

Biden as the Democratic Party presidential nominee thanks to a Black-powered primary victory in South Carolina, and the 2023 reelection of Democratic Governor of Kentucky Andy Beshear.

Black political scientists and sociologists have extensively researched why Black political behavior remains distinct from that of other racial and marginalized groups. Recognizing that Black Americans tended to have lower levels of occupational status, education, and income, some early scholars hypothesized that Black turnout would equal white turnout were those differences to disappear (Olsen 1970, 682). Others argued that, even then, there would be racial differences. Anthony Orum (1966, 33) posits, "Various forms of the prevalent social segregation of Negroes are viewed as conducive to their isolation from civic affairs; this isolation, in turn, accounts for both a low level of participation in associations and a low voting turnout." Nicholas Danigelis (1977, 32) summarizes this perspective, known as isolation theory, as the idea that racism creates a "double barrier to participation" among Black people: "First, threats of violence and disenfranchisement techniques are immediate impediments; in addition, the framework of prejudice produces apathy among blacks and prevents them from acquiring the necessary political sophistication." Notwithstanding legal barriers and white prejudice, Black Americans often exhibited high rates of participation, including voting. In the 1950s and 1960s this generated two competing theories: compensatory theory and ethnic community theory.

Proponents of compensatory theory held that Black Americans, aware of barriers to their socioeconomic success, compensate with high rates of political participation to generate positive self-evaluations and higher levels of self-esteem (Myrdal et al. 1944; Orum 1966). Proponents of ethnic community theory, in contrast, claimed that high rates of Black participation are attributable to racial consciousness among Black Americans, the result of shared experiences of discrimination and the effectiveness of organized political activity to improve their collective conditions (Lane 1959; Olsen 1970). Scholars later tried to operationalize these competing theories using various measures of political trust and efficacy, but different operationalizations led to inconsistent findings and contradictory conclusions (see London and Giles 1987 for a review).

Christopher Ellison and David Gay (1989) tested these competing models using American National Election Studies surveys from 1968 and

1980. They conclude that "while the compensatory approach may have offered a useful explanation of black political participation when it was developed in the 1940s and 1950s, it finds no support in this analysis" (Ellison and Gay 1989, 113). They find mixed support for ethnic community theory and call for further research on participatory norms within the Black community and the role of voter mobilization efforts by local community organizations.

In the seminal book *Behind the Mule* (1994), Michael Dawson posits that Black Americans with a strong sense of racial identity and who see their individual fates to be linked to the fates of Black Americans generally—in other words, who have a strong sense of *linked fate*—will be more likely to make their political decisions based on what is best for Black Americans generally rather than their personal preferences. This concept of linked fate is defined as related to but separate from the concept of group consciousness, which is a politicized in-group identification that engenders collective action (Miller et al. 1981). The two concepts are closely related, and both stem from feelings of racial discrimination (Sanchez and Vargas 2016). Most modern understandings of contemporary Black political attitudes and behavior are rooted in theories of shared group consciousness and the role of historical and contemporary racism (Allen et al. 1989; Chong and Rogers 2005; Dawson 1994; McClain et al. 2009).

Dawson (1994) posits that linked fate explains why Black political participation remains high, stable, and consistently Democratic. This observation holds true even when standard predictors of turnout, including time, resources, and civic skills (Verba et al. 1995), might predict lower levels of participation, or when differences in economic status might predict a larger degree of partisan variation. Nadia Brown and Danielle Casarez Lemi (2021, 97) note that rates of political participation among Black women "defy" traditional political participation models. That Black women are more likely to vote, even compared with other women of color, controlling for those standard predictors of turnout, has been demonstrated in multiple studies over time (Alex-Assensoh and Stanford 1997; Burns et al. 2001; Farris and Holman 2014).

Black turnout is consistently nearly as high as white turnout despite documented evidence that the barriers to participation for Black Americans are higher. Using data from hundreds of thousands of smartphone users, M. Keith Chen et al. (2022) found that residents of entirely

Black neighborhoods waited 29 percent longer to vote at polling places and were 74 percent more likely to spend more than thirty minutes at their polling place, compared with entirely white neighborhoods, during the 2016 presidential election. Justin Grimmer and Jesse Yoder (2022) found that photo identification laws in North Carolina in place during the 2016 general election deterred only 0.06 percent of white voters, but 0.13 percent of Black voters, because Black voters are less likely to have the appropriate ID. There are also disparities in access to early-voting locations. Using county-level data from 2008 and 2012, Elliott Fullmer (2015) found that the percentage of county residents who identify as Black is negatively associated with early-voting site density. In other words, Black neighborhoods have fewer early-voting locations, making it more difficult for Black residents to access that convenience measure.

Recent work has examined under what conditions Black individuals will exhibit behaviors driven by feelings of linked fate, including the role of feelings of attachment to one's group (Lopez Bunyasi and Smith 2019) or just whether individuals identify as Black (Smith et al. 2019). Expanding on this, work by Ismail White and Chryl Laird (2020) offers further insight into the enduring unity of Black voters in their political engagement and support for the Democratic Party. In their book *Steadfast Democrats*, they argue that Black socialization and social pressure are key to understanding Black political behavior. More specifically, these powerful social bonds, and the expectation to prioritize group needs, influence many Black Americans to support the Democratic Party even as more individuals consider themselves ideologically conservative (I. White and Laird 2020). A Pew Research Center study of two decades of public opinion data found that while the percentage of white Democrats who called themselves liberal had grown from 30 percent in 2000 to 55 percent in 2019, the percentage of Black Democrats who called themselves liberal remained relatively stable, increasing from 25 percent in 2000 to 29 percent in 2019. In the same study, 43 percent of Black Democrats called themselves moderate in 2019 and 25 percent called themselves conservative (Gilberstadt and Daniller 2020).

At the same time, Black voters consistently support Democratic candidates—91 percent in 2016 for Hillary Clinton and 90 percent in 2020 for Joe Biden—and have done so since the 1984 and 1988 presidential campaigns of Jesse Jackson Jr. "Taken together, his two campaigns cemented the bond between African Americans and the Democratic Party and significantly increased the size, visibility and clout of black voters within the party's coalition" (Kornacki 2019). This has manifested in an increased role of the Black vote in choosing the party's presidential nominees. In 2016, 24 percent of votes cast in the Democratic primary were cast by Black Americans. Since 1992, every successful Democratic nominee for president has won a majority of Black primary votes (Kornacki 2019).

Current research on Black electoral behavior has generally focused on expanding linked fate theory to see how it applies to various Black subgroups. Black Americans face marginalization due to their racial identity but can also have other marginalized identities, such as gender identity and sexuality. While an individual may be marginalized because of their racial identity, secondary marginalization means that further marginalization can occur within an already marginalized group (Cohen 1999). Secondary marginalization, sometimes also called intersectional discrimination (Strolovitch 2007), affects political attitudes and behaviors. Multiple scholars have noted that Black women, in particular, possess an intersectional linked fate that reflects how their racial and gender identities intersect with one another and their patterns of civic engagement (Simien 2005; N. Brown 2014; Scott, Brown, et al. 2021).

Black Women and Political Identity

Black women not only possess a distinct racial identity but also occupy a unique intersectional position, encompassing their identities as both Black individuals and women, that influences their political participation (Simien 2005; N. Brown 2014). The concept of intersectionality, a term coined by Kimberlé Crenshaw (1991), refers to the way in which individual identities overlap, and how individuals with multiple historically marginalized identities are affected by those identities. For example, while women are often marginalized and disadvantaged compared with men (sexism), and Black people are often marginalized and disadvantaged compared with white people (racism), Black women are affected by both sexism and racism simultaneously—their gender and race identities intersect. Crenshaw notes, "Because of their intersectional identity as both women and of color within discourses that are shaped to respond to one or the other, women of color are marginalized within both. . . . The intersection of racism and sexism factors into Black women's lives in ways that cannot be captured wholly by looking at the race or gender dimensions of those experiences separately" (1991, 1244).

Intersectionality can also generate positive effects. Clyde Wilcox (1990) found that Black racial consciousness inspires gender consciousness among Black women. The two types of consciousness operate in tandem to influence the political behavior and shape the attitudes of Black women (Gay and Tate 1998; Simien and Clawson 2004).

Patricia Hill Collins notes that "the political dimension of oppression has denied African-American women the rights and privileges routinely extended to White male citizens" (2000, 4). She continues, "The supposedly seamless web of economy, polity, and ideology function as a highly effective system of social control designed to keep African-American women in an assigned, subordinate place" (5). Reflecting their positionality as a historically oppressed group on multiple dimensions, Black women work to oppose oppression, to resist institutionalized racism and prevailing social and economic injustice (Collins 2000, 9). They are committed to justice "both for U.S. Black women as a collectivity and for that of other similarly oppressed groups" (9). Being a Black feminist, for Collins, means recognizing the "everyday, taken-for-granted knowledge" of Black women and giving Black women a path toward affirming and expressing that consciousness in a way that empowers Black women (32). This is precisely the mission of Black Girls Vote and the collaboration between PATM and the various community partners in each city where PATM conducted an activation. The project celebrates Black women in their communities, recognizing their political power as regular voters, and thus encourages residents of those communities not only to vote but to continue to work to mobilize individuals in their households and neighborhoods.

Black American civil society and commitment to community, its "distinctive ethos," are rooted in the history of slavery and the forced segregation of Black Americans into all-Black geographic areas (E. Brown 1994). This humanist vision of Black feminist thought means that Black women are often engaging in political action as a means of empowering their communities or, as Alice Walker defines *womanism*, of empowering Black men and women. They are engaging in political action in their communities to support those communities and all human communities (Walker 1983; Steady 1981, 1987). This humanist perspective was also endorsed by former congresswoman Shirley Chisholm, the inspiration for Black Girls Vote (see foreword; Chisholm 1970).

Black women work to change discriminatory policies and procedures, in order to bring about institutional transformation, through their challenges to the subordination of Black women (Collins 2000). They see the social injustice faced by Black women as linked to broader, coalitional struggles for social justice. Until recently, public-sphere actions on behalf of the Black community were seen as the realm of Black men, while Black women have also been socialized to believe that they should be working on behalf of their race, albeit in the private sphere (Davis 1981; Terborg-Penn 1985; Collins 2000).

Nikki Giovanni writes that "the purpose of any leadership is to build more leadership. The purpose of being a spokesperson is to speak until the people gain a voice" (1988, 135). This theme of Black women's activism "reflects a belief that teaching people how to be self-reliant fosters more empowerment than teaching them how to follow" (Collins 2000, 219). The community spirit of PATM reflects this longtime style of Black women's political activism. Black Girls Vote founder Nyki Robinson worked with long-standing community organizations, raised up and partnered with local groups and especially with Black women-led local groups, and fostered the political involvement and voices of women who received PATM boxes. This exemplifies the model of leadership embodied by Black civil rights activists such as Septima Clark and Ella Baker, and endorsed by Angela Davis, who urged activists, "We must strive to 'lift as we climb'" (Davis 1989, 5).

Black women have always had a commitment to uplifting their communities, fighting for social justice, and bringing up others along the way. Black women have led the charge and have turned out to vote at higher rates than Black men since at least 1978 (Center for American Women and Politics, n.d.). By promoting voter turnout as a means of achieving the ultimate goal of improving their communities, PATM aligns with the tradition of Black women leveraging their voices to uplift those of others and to fight institutionalized racism and sexism in a horizontal model of inclusion and uplift (Jones 2020). Individual Black women who received a PATM package were asked to vote, but also to use the materials inside the packages to educate and mobilize other individuals in their households and neighborhoods. This is consistent with how Black women working in their communities have seen connections between activism and mothering, family and community. As Collins observes, "African-American women have long engaged in motherwork designed to build strong Black identities capable of withstanding the assaults of White supremacist rhetoric and practice" (2000, 223). Politicized motherwork by Black women is the activist base of Black women's community work. "Such work does not explicitly advocate for Black women but instead sees Black women's advancement occurring in the context of community" (224).

Black women's participation has always been a cornerstone to the continuation of the Black political union (Tate 1991). Within Black communities, women play a vital role in various aspects of Black socialization. Because of their intersecting identities, Black women have remained committed to engaging in the political process through diverse channels such as churches, student organizations, and social networks. Although their political participation may occur through nontraditional avenues, it has fostered social connection that serves as a catalyst for civic participation in the Black community. While Black women play an integral role in all facets of civic participation through community, research has shown that they have utilized sites of cultural significance to advance their work. Most notably, the Black political theoretical framework created by Melissa Harris-Lacewell (2004) explains that everyday Black spaces have long served as sites to discuss Black political ideology. In her analysis, she finds that Black Americans form and maintain rich, culturally diverse connections with one another in spaces such as barbershops and beauty salons, through television and social media programming such as the BET (Black Entertainment Television) network, and through Christian churches. These spaces have traditionally been intercultural and intergenerational, and, generally speaking, they span across socioeconomic statuses. Each space, the leaders within them, and how they have contributed to civic engagement are distinct yet connected as branches of a broader Black community.

Black women's leadership within church communities is part of this tradition of encouraging civic engagement. Often described as the "invisible institution" (Barnes 2006), churches have traditionally been sites of civic engagement and political participation. They hold significant cultural and religious significance for Black Americans. Belonging to a church is highly important to Black Christians, and belonging to a church with a majority-Black congregation is even more important (Mohamed et al. 2021). Churches have historically been some of the few establishments that were owned and operated by people within the Black community. While churches are primarily used for religious worship services, they have always operated as multifunctioning centers for all things pertaining to those Black communities. A large portion of this work has included engaging church members in other forms of civic and political participation (McClerking et al. 2005). Traditionally, this involves church members gathering together to organize voter engagement drives and participating in political protests.

For instance, Souls to the Polls is a nationwide initiative designed by Black churches to increase voter turnout from their congregations. This tradition has lasted over sixty years and reaches across denominations (Daniels 2020). The long history of these events, also known as COGIC (Church of God in Christ International) Counts and AME (African Methodist Episcopal Church) Voter Alert, is testament to how stable and important civic participation is to the Black community. Some observers have noted that "Super Sunday" comes every week during election season in many Black churches, with politically active ministers devoting part of their sermons to reminders about the importance of turning out to vote. These events often include external speakers such as elected officials and other prominent public figures. Black voters who regularly attend a politically active church are more likely to vote than Black voters who attend a nonpolitical church (R. Brown and Brown 2003). Within churches, women have played an integral role in ensuring that these events occur (Barnes 2006; Ngunjiri et al. 2012).

Black Greek letter organizations (BGLOs) have also played a role in the promotion of Black political participation and community engagement and continue to hold an important role in Black communities as a cultural site of celebration of Black identity and leadership. N. Brown and Lemi (2021, 100) note that while BGLOs were founded to help Black students succeed academically, they are also "politically grounded and civically engaged," and they seek to serve Black communities, in part, by cultivating social norms and providing civic skills. One of the norms promoted by BGLOs is political participation.

Black sororities are a particularly powerful path to political leadership for Black women, and many notable Black women elected officials trace their political origins to their participation in a Black sorority (Dowe 2016). Examples include Shirley Chisholm, the first African American woman to run for Congress, who was a member of the Delta Sigma Theta sorority, and former Vice President Kamala Harris, the first Black, Asian, and woman vice president, who was a member of Alpha Kappa Alpha. These are just two of the traditional BGLOs known as the Divine Nine.[1] Members of the Divine Nine are a powerful political force in modern US politics, credited with pushing forward the confirmation of Attorney General Loretta Lynch in 2015, the first Black woman to ever hold the position, and working to elect Vice President Harris in 2020 (T. Johnson 2015; G. Parks and Hughey 2020).

Efforts in 2020 included Stroll to the Polls, an effort to encourage turnout launched by Atlanta Alpha Kappa Alpha member Maisha Land. This creative effort resulted in a viral video featuring members of the Black sororities of the Divine Nine (Alpha Kappa Alpha, Delta Sigma Theta, Zeta Phi Beta, and Sigma Gamma Rho) donning their sorority colors while walking and dancing to encourage voter turnout (K. Bates 2020, 11Alive 2020). The joy exhibited by sorority members in the Stroll to the Polls video is an example of the broader phenomenon of Black joy, a critical component of Black identity, unity, and culture.

Celebration, in its most general sense, refers to expressing joy for an event, person, or situation. The notion of Black joy as resistance has been defined as a celebration of survival in the face of oppressive institutions. Black joy represents the celebration and affirmation of the positive aspects of Black life, community, and culture. By fostering joy and organizing celebratory events, the Black community counters the dominant Eurocentric narratives regarding Black people and reinforces a strong sense of group identity (Lu and Steele 2019). The Stroll to the Polls campaign highlighted the power of Black joy as a catalyst for political engagement and demonstrated the crucial role Black sororities play in promoting civic participation. Through their vibrant displays of unity, sisterhood, and the celebration of their shared history, these sororities exemplify the potential of Black joy to inspire action and bring about change in the face of adversity.

Black Voter Turnout

Black linked fate, Black institutions such as churches and BGLOs, and Black joy, among other factors, all play a role in generating increased voter participation. However, since Black Americans won the right to vote with the Fifteenth Amendment, they have faced barriers to exercising the franchise. Black voter turnout and political participation, including running for (and winning) elected office, surged in the initial period after the Civil War, while federal troops and oversight ensured that those constitutional rights were respected. But after the end of Reconstruction in 1877 and the rise of Jim Crow, Black Americans faced increasing and often violent voter suppression (Feagin and Hahn 1970). The struggle for Black suffrage continued with the civil rights movement, as well as through organizational efforts led by churches and secular community organizations, including legacy organizations such as the National Association for the Advancement of Colored People and the National Urban League and newer groups such as Black Girls Vote, Black Voters Matter, and Fair Fight Action, among others.

Because of the aggressive legal attacks on Black voters' rights, political organizations became an important element of Black communities. Fears of recourse prompted organizations to play an even more central role in Black political participation. Already sites of cultural significance and meeting locations for Black people, churches, hair shops, and community centers became informal institutions to discuss politics and the new fight for suffrage. These locations were instrumental for the civil rights movement and continue to hold great significance for organizations that work alongside them. Throughout the years, Black political organizations, coupled with important Black cultural locations that foster social connections, have been a primary driver for Black get-out-the-vote campaigns.

Black Get-Out-the-Vote Efforts

Get-out-the-vote (GOTV) initiatives for Black communities have relied on organizations like Black Girls Vote for a variety of reasons. Candidates and political campaigns aren't cheap. They require financial support to have any chance of success. And previous exclusion tends to disproportionately economically disadvantage Black political candidates, campaigns, and others critical to the electoral ecosystem (Scott 2022). Thus, Black voter turnout has always relied on community resources and mutual support. From holding information sessions to providing spaces for town halls, political organizations have used various outreach strategies to continue encouraging Black voter turnout. Additionally, civil rights organizations have partnered with Black political organizations because they realized that they are more successful with them (Whitby 2015).

Black political organizations are important to Black mobilization because they understand the cultural and racial significance of voting for Black Americans. These organizations not only understand the historical struggles and challenges faced by Black communities but also actively work to dismantle systemic barriers to political participation. Their work has been crucial to increasing voter turnout and overall encouragement in politics (Leroux 2007).

Community organizations serve as effective and indispensable tools for fostering widespread political participation among Black communities. Given the long history of disenfranchisement, these civic organizations play a crucial role in mobilizing Black voters in the face of institutional barriers. They fulfill an information and resource need for members of Black communities who may not have all the necessary tools or information to exercise their right to vote. These organizations can offer such support in various ways, from informing voters on updated local voting laws to arranging church-assisted rides to polling places. For example, in 2020 Atlanta organizers provided bottles of water to community members who were waiting in long lines to vote, a common occurrence at precincts with large proportions of Black voters. A few months later, the Republican-controlled Georgia legislature passed an election law that, among other provisions, prohibited providing food and water to voters waiting those long lines, a nod to how vital a role organizations play in combatting voter suppression. That provision of the law was later struck down by a federal court.

Voter Community Celebration Model

Drawing on this history of the role of Black women in politicized motherwork, the unwavering commitment to civic engagement by Black institutions including churches and BGLOs, and the strong roles of

Black linked fate and Black joy in shaping Black political attitudes and behavior, we hypothesized that a community organization centered on Black women that worked to increase turnout by using a celebratory message would be effective at increasing voter turnout. By tapping into these deeply rooted cultural and social factors, an organization like this would be well positioned to motivate and empower Black communities to action.

In 1957, Anthony Downs argued that an individual rational voter should almost never vote because of the very low likelihood that their vote would change the outcome of an election, even if they had a very strong preference for one political party, or candidate, over another. The equation predicting the size of the reward for voting (R) was a function of the benefit (B) of one's preferred candidate winning multiplied by the probability (P) that one's vote would matter and offset by the cost (C) of voting. This generated the equation $R = (B \times P) - C$. Given how many voters participate in elections, Downs estimated that no one would ever rationally vote. In 1968, William Riker and Peter Ordeshook revisited Downs's equation, arguing that there are benefits that accrue to individuals who exercise their right to vote that are independent of their contribution to the outcome of an election. They measured these benefits, summarized in a D term (for citizen duty), using four survey questions about the duty to vote, and found that the D term did in fact change the voting calculus such that voting could be considered rational. This changed the equation to $R = (B \times P) - C + D$.

Riker and Ordeshook specify that in theory this D term might include (1) "satisfaction from compliance with the ethic of voting"; (2) "satisfaction from affirming allegiance to the political system"; (3) "satisfaction from affirming a partisan preference"; (4) "satisfaction of deciding, going to the polls, etc."; and (5) "satisfaction of affirming one's efficacy in the political system" but operationalize it as citizen duty (1968, 28).

Following their work, other scholars have further explored factors used by individuals as they calculate their own decisions about whether to vote. Political psychologists have explored to what extent self-efficacy, a psychological measure for self-motivation to act, fits into the equation. They have found that when elections are perceived to be close elections, individuals with high self-efficacy will be more motivated to vote (Darmofal 2010). However, the leading theory takes into account how a sense of moral obligation may factor into the equation. A moral obligation—a sense of duty to oneself, their community, or their nation more broadly—may be driving voters' will to participate in voting even if it doesn't make rational sense to do so. Political theorists have found that having a sense of civic duty influences the original *calculus of voting* model. Political theory has an extensive literature on why citizens believe that voting, and larger participation in the political sphere, is an ethical norm (Verba and Nie 1972). The findings of empirical work have also been consistent with this idea. Robert Goldfarb and Lee Sigelman (2010) detail how incorporating duty into the calculus of voting model changes our understanding of voter turnout and model measurement. In their theoretical review of the turnout puzzle, they suggest that further research should examine what adding a duty constraint does to the performance of voting models. In a two-panel survey design, André Blais and Christopher Achen (2019) found that modeling duty into their statistical model predicted and outperformed turnout performance more than traditional specifications. Additionally, they found that duty can be the determining factor even when preferences for specific candidates are low. This suggests that turnout models that exclude or don't consider civic duty are missing a fundamental explanatory element.

When the subfield of GOTV randomized controlled trials (RCTs) was launched by Alan Gerber and Donald Green in 2000, they included a test of the power of a civic duty message. Their project randomly assigned targeted voters to receive a message about civic duty, the closeness of the election, or neighborhood solidarity. They note, "The civic duty script appeals to a sense of obligation. It states a norm that citizens are expected to vote and contends that democracy depends on political participation. This appeal parallels a central explanation of large-scale collective action, the notion that citizens derive intrinsic satisfaction from participation" (Gerber and Green 2000, 656). The RCT found no measurable difference between responses to the three messages, suggesting that civic duty was no more powerful at motivating voters than other GOTV messages. Subsequent GOTV RCTs found similar null results for competing messages.

In 2006, Gerber, Green, and Christopher Larimer conducted an RCT in Michigan that aimed to distinguish "between the intrinsic rewards that voters obtain from performing this duty and the extrinsic rewards that voters receive when others observe them doing so" (2008, 33). One treatment group received a traditional message about voting as a civic duty, while others were told that their behavior was being monitored, sometimes just by the researchers, but sometimes also indicating that their behavior would be shared with their household members or even with their neighbors. They found the messages that triggered concern about extrinsic rewards (and the social norm of voting) far more powerful than messages that only cued the intrinsic reward of voting. Including social monitoring messages that remind voters that voting behavior is public—thus cueing the external voting norm—is now a standard best practice in voter mobilization scripts, as are other messages that remind voters of the social norm of a duty to vote. Subsequent studies have explored the best ways to incorporate duty in both theoretical and empirical models of voter turnout. For example, models of voter turnout have found that when political trust in government is low, it could result in a decline in voter turnout because voters no longer feel a sense of duty to uphold democracy (Wang 2016).

Less well understood is how members of historically marginalized communities develop a sense of civic duty to a polity from which they are often excluded. As noted in chapter 1, this gap in knowledge reflects a lack of interest in learning how best to motivate Black voters (given their already high rates of turnout, their tendency to vote for Democratic Party candidates, and their tendency to not be seen as providing the margin of victory for close races), as well as the rational reluctance of Black communities to participate in RCTs. Because of high voter turnout, Black voters have not often been targeted by GOTV efforts. In the aggregate of Black voters, the literature has perceived them to be already activated, so it would be difficult to measure an effect. However, there's still much to be gained by constructing a better understanding of where sources of duty fit into a larger discussion of the consistently high levels of Black political engagement. More specifically, we believe our model helps to further explain how duty may operate differently in the voting calculus for Black voters.

Recent research has sought to disentangle the factors that influence the sense of connection among Black voters and to what extent this perception varies. I. White and Laird (2020) found that while sharing a history of racial oppression rooted in slavery and segregation is one explanation for Black linked fate, social connections and networks matter more for Black communities compared with other factors. We take this conversation and place it within the GOTV literature. While Black political behavior is consistent and we can explain why, we seek to understand how celebration of these social connections may activate a sense of duty to vote. We are interested in modeling duty activation through community celebration.

As mentioned earlier, our model builds on the calculus of voting model. This model accounts for civic duty in considering the costs and benefits of voting. We model how both racial and regional identity help make civic duty salient, thus increasing voter turnout. Moreover, we posit that community connection and celebration are vital components in reminding community members why they vote and what it means to be a voter. PATM was run through a nonprofit organization that was rooted in racial identity celebration, Black Girls Vote. This calls back to the theory of linked fate, social connections, and other broad theories of representation. Programs that promote a celebratory atmosphere around race-conscious civic engagement practices help Black voters recognize that community partners not only understand the historical plight of disfranchisement but are currently engaged in the struggle against it. There is a sense of familiarity and comfort that Black voters feel when programs are geared specifically for Black people by Black people.

Regional identity is an important cultural aspect of Black identity. It acts similarly to ethno-racial classification for Black Americans, demarcating specific histories, cultural practices, traditions, and communication styles. Additionally, different regions have unique experiences with voter suppression. Thus, in our model we argue that it is not enough to make racial identity salient; a *regional-racial* identity must be made salient as well. In other words, PATM primed voters' identities as members of specific Black communities in each city: as Baltimoreans (McDougall 1993), Detroiters (One Detroit 2023a), Atlantans (Driskell 2017), and so on. Starting with the Baltimore pilot in June 2020, Nyki Robinson believed that the boxes needed to have a local feel to be effective, and our data support this belief. In city after city, voters told us how much they valued the regional items in their PATM boxes. It aided in reminding them they are active members in their community and encouraged a civic engagement that was based on showing up for one's racial group and also for one's regional-racial group—the local Black community.

These two attributes are vital to creating an atmosphere of community celebration. Such celebration creates space for two important aspects of civic duty to flourish. It is through community celebration that Black voters are reminded of their historic victories and ultimately how political progress is a communal, and not solely individual, act of protest. Community celebration also reinforces communal ties with one another that are important in maintaining higher levels of Black voter turnout.

Our model is designed to explain why and the extent to which voter community celebration is an important part of Black voter turnout and civic engagement. The academic literature has provided explanations for high turnout among Black voters compared with white voters (Danigelis 1977, 1978; Ellison and Gay 1989; Fairdosi and Rogowski 2015), and our model suggests that one reason is that voter community celebration emphasizes racial-regional identity and helps to activate civic duty. This is important for understanding why voters turn out despite the costs. While our model explains Black political behavior, we believe that it has the potential to map onto other groups with a shared history of marginalization and struggle.

In summary, the Voter Community Celebration Model predicts that a community-based effort that primes Black linked fate (especially among Black women), that is seen as a celebration of a local community, and that increases feelings of political efficacy will generate meaningful increases in voter turnout. Through the PATM program, Black Girls Vote partnered with dozens of local community organizations in each city in which PATM was active to prime Black identity with boxes of informational and celebratory items. As detailed in subsequent chapters, we find strong evidence that PATM increased turnout among Black women and their household members. In some instances, effects were centered more on Black women recipients of the boxes, while in others the effects were shown mostly among low-propensity household members. Results varied across cities and elections. In the next few chapters (chapters 3, 4, and 5), we detail the original and subsequent PATM iterations, exploring the nuances of each effort and the results of our RCTs and qualitative data collection. After a detour to delve more deeply into the relationship between Black joy and Black civic duty (chapter 6), we summarize our results across those different iterations and return to the Voter Community Celebration Model in our concluding chapter. As shown in those subsequent chapters, community celebrations of Black identity are an effective means to building political participation.

3

Baltimore Votes

On June 2, 2020, after the polls closed for Baltimore's delayed primary election, Black Girls Vote and Baltimore Votes held a virtual Party at the Mailbox (PATM) dance party hosted by Black Girls Vote founder and CEO Nyki Robinson and project lead Tenne Thrower. As Robinson said repeatedly throughout the PATM pilot project, "It's not just a box, it's an experience." Boxes had been delivered, votes had been cast, and now the experience was culminating in a celebration. More than eleven thousand viewers joined the Zoom party to dance and sing along. For two hours, sets from DJ Pretty Girl Tiara LaNiece, DJ AirMax, and DJ Quick Silva entertained the crowd, which joined enthusiastically from their homes. Robinson and Thrower introduced and chatted with high-profile guests from the city, including the Reverend Jesse Jackson Jr. and the president of the Maryland State Senate, gave shout-outs to Black Girl Magic and the power of civic responsibility, and awarded swag to trivia question winners.

While the pandemic precluded a classic in-person gathering, the community was still coming together—celebrating Baltimore and celebrating democracy. Even before the results were in, it was clear from the large, enthusiastic crowd that PATM had struck a chord. Weeks later, proof of the power of celebration of community displayed at the dance party came in the form of turnout data from the city, showing a huge burst in turnout despite the delayed election date and the shift to vote-by-mail ballots. For Robinson and those who believed in her project, it was a huge vindication. Our postelection survey showed that, compared with participants who did not receive a PATM box, PATM participants were more likely to think of themselves as Baltimoreans and to report voting. A few weeks later, analysis of the randomized controlled trial (RCT) conducted by our academic team provided quantitative proof: PATM increased turnout. By a lot. The spirit of celebration wasn't just talk. It was action.

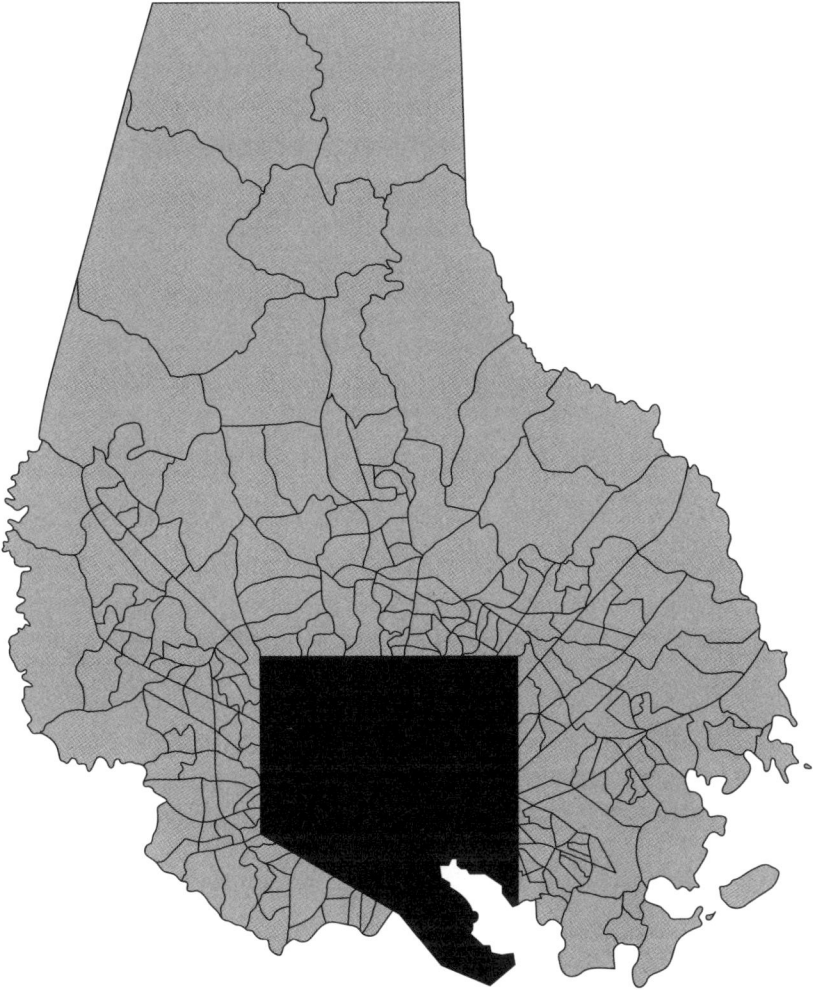

Figure 3.1: Map of Baltimore City and Baltimore County
Note: Baltimore City is shaded black, Baltimore County is shaded grey.

In this chapter, we detail the RCT for the PATM pilot effort conducted for the June 2020 primary in the city of Baltimore and the follow-up RCTs for the general election conducted in both Baltimore City and Baltimore County. Baltimore is an independent city that is surrounded almost entirely by Baltimore County but is a separate political entity; the two do not overlap geographically (figure 3.1). The two groups who came together to pilot PATM, Black Girls Vote and Baltimore Votes, are both local to Baltimore City and had been active in working to increase voter engagement in both the city and the county for several years. In June 2020, they chose to focus the RCT in Baltimore City, where they have a more established network and reputation, to keep the pilot effort a more manageable size. However, they were still active in Baltimore County and some PATM packages were distributed there for the June 2020 election. After the pilot in Baltimore City established the effectiveness of PATM, we extended the evaluation component of the project to include both Baltimore City and Baltimore County in the RCTs conducted in November 2020. Later in this chapter, we detail the geographic differences as well as the differences in racial makeup between these two locations and RCTs.

This chapter includes narrative descriptions of those projects and results from our quantitative analyses (including both RCTs and surveys). Qualitative data from focus groups and interviews with voters and leaders of local organization partners is shared in chapter 6. We find substantial evidence that, in both elections, PATM successfully cultivated celebrations of community that drove voters to the polls, especially low-propensity voters. First, we introduce Baltimore and the history of political activity by its Black residents.

Baltimore

Baltimore has a long history of racial conflict and violence that has plagued the city and pushed Black residents together as a community. The trade of enslaved people was present in the city until the 1860s, as documented by a historical marker in the Jonestown neighborhood at the corner of East Pratt Street and President Street. The marker reads, "Although the United States banned the Transatlantic Slave Trade in 1808, a domestic trade from the Upper South to the emerging cotton-growing regions of the Deep South thrived until the 1860s. Baltimore-based dealers supplied the trade, operating slave pens at the Inner Harbor, on Fell's Point, and across the city, including near this location. Between 1808 and the abolition of slavery in Maryland in 1864, an estimated thirty thousand people were 'sold South' from Baltimore." Frederick Douglass, who once lived on Philpot Street in Fells Point, Baltimore, described the Baltimore slave trade in his 1852 "What to the Slave Is the Fourth of July?" speech

(Douglass 1852): "To me the American slave-trade is a terrible reality. When a child, my soul was often pierced with a sense of its horrors. I lived on Philpot Street, Fell's Point, Baltimore, and have watched from the wharves, the slave ships in the Basin, anchored from the shore, with their cargoes of human flesh, waiting for favorable winds to waft them down the Chesapeake." When Union army troops passing through the city on April 19, 1861, were attacked on Pratt Street by Confederate sympathizers, sparking a deadly riot, Baltimore became the site of the first casualty of the Civil War (Ezratty 2013).

Baltimore was also home to one of the largest populations of free Black Americans in the United States prior to the Civil War (Fields 1985). An urban industrial city, Black laborers came to Baltimore in the early nineteenth century to work in the shipyards, railroads, and steel plants, building the foundation for a growing Black middle class that expanded to work in fields including medicine, education, and law. This led in turn to increased interest and involvement in local politics, including the founding in 1915 of the Progressive Women's Suffrage Club, which sought to educate and register Black Baltimoreans to vote (A. Daniels 2023).

Black activists in Baltimore were part of the civil rights movement as early as 1947, when Black students at Morgan College (today Morgan State University) organized the Baltimore freedom movement to push back against segregation in the city. High-school-aged children in Baltimore organized interracial sporting events to demonstrate their support for integration in this early period. Movements like this gained the support of the National Association for the Advancement of Colored People (NAACP) and lasted several years, eventually winning additional rights for Baltimoreans but also for all Black Americans (Baltimore Heritage, n.d.).

Baltimore is a very segregated city, earning the highest ranking of *hypersegregated* along with just seven other metropolitan areas in a 2015 analysis by Douglass Massey and Jonathan Tannen (Massey and Tannen 2015). One of our roadshow cities (see chapter 4), Detroit, also makes this list. Baltimore's pattern of segregation has generated what Lawrence Brown (2021) has dubbed the *White L* and the *Black Butterfly*. The White L is the area around the Inner Harbor and stretches north into the neighborhoods of Homeland and Guilford. The low-income

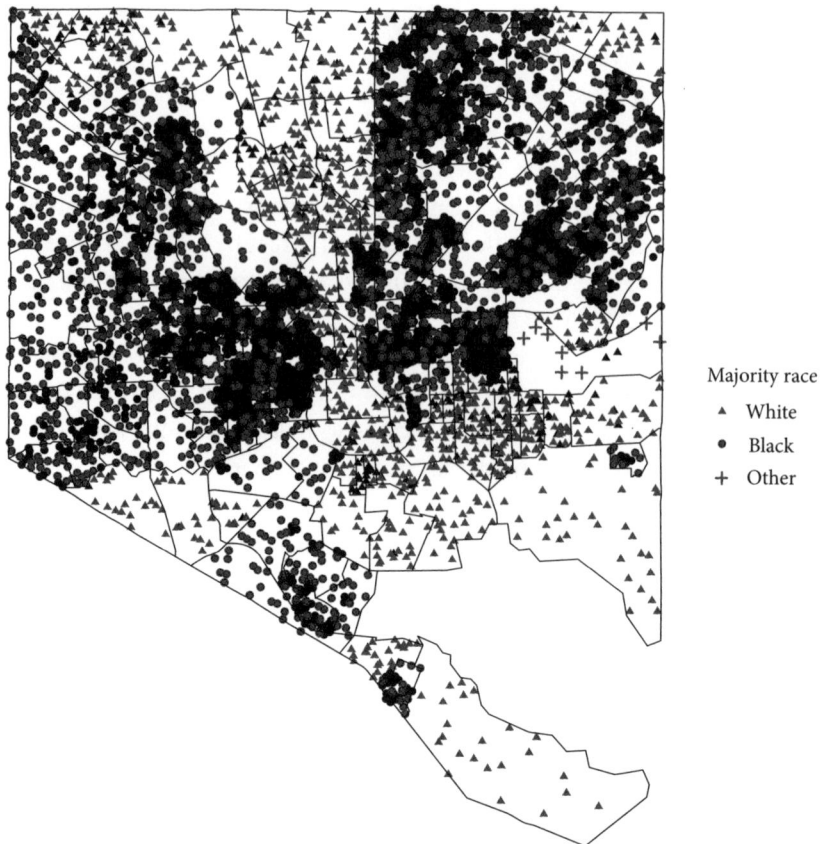

Figure 3.2: Hypersegregated Baltimore: The White L and the Black Butterfly. Each point represents one hundred people in the majority race for that tract. Created with the 2019 five-year American Community Survey data on single races. Baltimore City is low income and overwhelmingly Black, surrounded by wealthy, white suburbs.

majority-Black neighborhoods of East and West Baltimore are visually represented by the butterfly's wings, as shown in figure 3.2. Baltimore City is low income and overwhelmingly Black, surrounded by wealthy, white suburbs. The 2020 U.S Census data show that Baltimore City is 62.3 percent Black and the poverty rate is 20 percent. Baltimore County, in contrast, is majority white and only 31.3 percent Black, with a poverty rate of just 8.9 percent, as shown in table 3.1.

Baltimore has long been a majority-Black city, but it only recently became a city with Black political power. After the Great Depression, the

Table 3.1: 2020 Census Demographic Data for Baltimore City and Baltimore County, Maryland

Race	Baltimore City	Baltimore County
White alone	29.7%	58.8%
Black or African American alone	62.3%	31.3%
American Indian and Alaska Native alone	0.3%	0.5%
Asian alone	2.5%	6.5%
Native Hawaiian and Other Pacific Islander alone	0.0%	0.1%
Two or more races	3.2%	2.8%
Hispanic or Latino	5.4%	6.2%
White alone (not Hispanic or Latino)	27.3%	54.2%
Income		
Median household income (in 2020 dollars), 2016–2020	$52,164	$78,724
Per capita income in past twelve months (in 2020 dollars), 2016–2020	$32,699	$41,089
Persons in poverty	20.0%	8.9%

Source: "QuickFacts: Baltimore County, Maryland; Baltimore City, Maryland," US Census Bureau, accessed January 31, 2025, https://www.census.gov/quickfacts.

city's electoral structure was changed, replacing a bicameral legislature made up of many small districts with a unicameral legislature including just seven multimember districts. This allowed the white Democratic political machine led by Jack Pollack to control city elections and politics through the mid-1950s. In 1954, Black Republican Harry Cole successfully ran for a seat in the state legislature; his victory inspired a voter registration drive conducted by the NAACP, local Black churches, and the *Baltimore Afro-American* newspaper. In 1958, a Black slate of candidates won multiple races, further challenging the Pollack political machine (McDougall 1993, 91–92).

A decade later, Baltimore was one of over a hundred US cities that erupted in protest in reaction to the April 4, 1968, murder of Martin Luther King Jr. In the words of Rev. Marion Bascom (2006), a community leader who was in Baltimore at the time, "There was so much hope in the community, and it was shattered by the untimely death of Martin Luther King, and the town went crazy. Not only Baltimore, but almost every city in the country experienced the same thing, it was almost as if blacks in every community had suddenly been inoculated with [a] hypodermic needle and caught the disease of disturbance. And so, they began to set fires, and it was just horrible. You could smell smoke anywhere in Baltimore City." The riot on April 6, 1968, began slowly on the East Side of the city—a plate-glass window at the Fashion Hat Shop was smashed at around 5:30 p.m., a store (Sun Cleaners) was looted at around 6:00 p.m., and the first business (Ideal Furniture Company) was set on fire at 6:15 p.m. The violence escalated over the course of the evening, as did confrontations with law enforcement. At 10:00 p.m., Governor Spiro Agnew, at the request of the mayor, called in the National Guard and issued a curfew. On April 7, the city was occupied by fifty-five hundred National Guardsmen, four hundred state troopers, and twelve hundred city police officers. That evening, violence erupted on the other side of town, the West Side of Baltimore, leading Agnew to ask the federal government to intervene. President Lyndon Johnson immediately sent three thousand US Army soldiers, a force that later grew to over five thousand (Yockel 2007).

The looting and arson left six dead, seven hundred injured, and millions in property damage. Baltimore wasn't the only city that responded to King's death with rioting, but it was one of the hardest hit. Between the assassination of King on April 4 and Easter Sunday, April 14, there were uprisings in cities in thirty-six states and the District of Columbia, resulting in forty-three deaths, thirty-five hundred people injured, and millions of dollars in property damage—$12 million or more in Baltimore alone, according to various estimates (Yockel 2007; Levy 2011). Historian Peter Levy sums up these various disturbances this way: "During Holy Week 1968, the United States experienced its greatest wave of social unrest since the Civil War" (Levy 2011, 6). The riots also contributed to the rise of Agnew as a law-and-order conservative and "defender of suburbia," and later that year he was chosen as Richard Nixon's vice-presidential running mate (Csicsek 2011; Levy 2011).

The spark of the 1968 protests was King's assassination, but the wave of violence was about more than that single event. It was the result of widespread racial segregation and simmering racial tensions, both of which persisted after the riots. In subsequent years, the rise of shopping malls and chain stores led to the shuttering of small businesses, while white flight to the suburbs increased.

Those same tensions erupted in Baltimore half a century later, on April 19, 2015, when a twenty-five-year-old Black man named Freddie Gray died after suffering a spinal cord injury while in police custody and falling into a weeklong coma. Once again, the city erupted in violence, not just in response to the death of a Black man but in response to another generation's worth of pent-up frustrations about racial inequalities and economic disparities, including ongoing concerns about a lack of accountability for Baltimore police brutality against Black people. Protests and tensions died down when charges were filed against the involved law enforcement officers, but in the end no officers were found criminally responsible, and the Trump administration's Justice Department declined to file federal civil rights charges (Lopez 2016; Booker 2018).

The racial breakdown of the city of Baltimore changed from 24 percent Black in 1950 to 35 percent Black in 1960 and over 46 percent Black by 1970, the combined result of white residents leaving for the suburbs and Black residents moving in as part of the Great Migration. When the incumbent mayor announced in 1971 that he would not seek reelection, the election of the city's first Black mayor seemed possible. White candidate William Donald Schaefer won the Democratic primary with ninety-five thousand votes, while Black candidate George Russell won fifty-eight thousand—a vote share large enough to inspire white politicians to gerrymander the city districts to limit the political power of the city's growing Black population (McDougall 1993, 93). Schaefer was elected governor in 1986; in January 1987, he resigned from his mayoral seat, elevating Baltimore City Council President Clarence H. "Du" Burns to become the first Black mayor of the city. Burns ran for a full term as mayor later that year but was defeated by Kurt Schmoke in the Democratic primary. Baltimoreans then elected Schmoke as their first elected Black mayor in November 1987, and he was reelected in 1991. That same year, the city council reversed the gerrymandering of the past to create five majority-Black districts (out of a total of six districts) despite opposition from Mayor Schmoke, who thought majority-Black districts would discourage racial coalitions with white Baltimoreans (McDougall 1993, 97–98).

The shifting population affected not only city politics but also the housing market and the makeup of Baltimore communities. As the Black population increased, white Baltimoreans left the city for Baltimore

County. According to scholar Harold McDougall, "Block-busting, zoning, and redlining increased racial segregation in the city and encouraged white flight, especially to suburban, prosperous, and predominantly white Baltimore County" (1993, 98). The hypersegregation documented by Massey and Tannen means that Black Baltimoreans have limited access to better schools and jobs and are exposed to extreme environmental toxins, contributing to increased environmental racism.

Baltimore's long-standing and severe segregation created a hostile environment, but one that ultimately resulted in the perseverance of Black Baltimoreans and tight-knit Black communities. This includes various Black churches and interfaith organizations such as Baltimoreans United in Leadership Development (BUILD). Formed by a group of church leaders in 1977, BUILD now represents a coalition of congregations, public schools, and neighborhood associations across the city. Today, BUILD continues its work and is "dedicated to making our city a better place for all Baltimoreans to live and thrive. For more than 40 years, BUILD has worked to improve housing, increase job opportunities, and rebuild schools and neighborhoods, among other issues" (BUILD Baltimore, n.d.). Many such community organizations active in Baltimore today focus on increasing voter registration, turnout, and other forms of engagement to empower local neighborhoods. This includes the two organizations that came together in 2020 to launch PATM, Black Girls Vote and Baltimore Votes (supported by the No Boundaries Coalition of Central West Baltimore).

These historical events—especially of 1968 and 2015—continue to affect the city of Baltimore and were part of the background against which Black Girls Vote conducted the PATM project. Despite visible Black leadership in city government, the city is marked by stark economic inequality, high Black unemployment, and persistent issues of police brutality against Black residents (Serwer 2015). Robinson embedded the project in the community both to build on existing social networks and to ensure that the project was well received by Black Baltimoreans. Subgrants were made to local community organizations that agreed to promote PATM and encourage their members to sign up. Sample boxes were hand-delivered to local influencers. Robinson and her team at Black Girls Vote approached local residents and leaders as native Baltimoreans seeking to cooperate to help boost participation and political voice. Outreach also recognized the hardships imposed by the COVID-19 pandemic, and PATM efforts with community partners often were paired with food giveaways or messages about how to support one another and keep tabs on vulnerable neighbors (e.g., through phone trees). The strength of the pilot in particular, and of the entire PATM project more generally, was boosted by this recognition of the challenges faced by communities that might not always seem immediately connected to electoral politics and the importance of supporting one another through the pandemic.

The June 2020 Primary

For the pilot effort, Black Girls Vote and Baltimore Votes sought to build on their efforts from the 2018 midterm election, when they cooperated to host polling-place parties throughout the city. They hoped PATM would mirror the festive atmosphere of those and other previous election festivals to build community and participation in the June 2, 2020, vote-by-mail primary in Baltimore City (see chapter 1). The intervention was a hand-delivered cardboard box designed to encourage recipients to celebrate vote-by-mail participation in their own homes. Several organizations, including Stand Up Baltimore and Just Our Youth Baltimore, worked in partnership by offering their physical spaces to assemble and store the boxes. The anchor organizational partner was Baltimore Votes, a local voter advocacy organization focused on local voter turnout. Baltimore Votes had cooperated with Black Girls Vote in 2018 to host election festivals in Baltimore, including over seventy festivals in the city, and thus had a strong community presence and a base of trust coming into 2020, as well as a close working relationship with Black Girls Vote leadership. The two organizations worked closely together to organize and execute the PATM pilot (and the subsequent replications). Baltimore Votes provided support for PATM in multiple ways; their cofounder Sam Novey noted, "We shifted our budget from Parties at the Polls to support the Party at the Mailbox pilot, raised emergency funds to support the evaluation, and deployed our communications team and email list to promote the campaign. We also mobilized our past Parties at the Polls partners and board members to promote the campaign in their communities and host community activations like car parades and

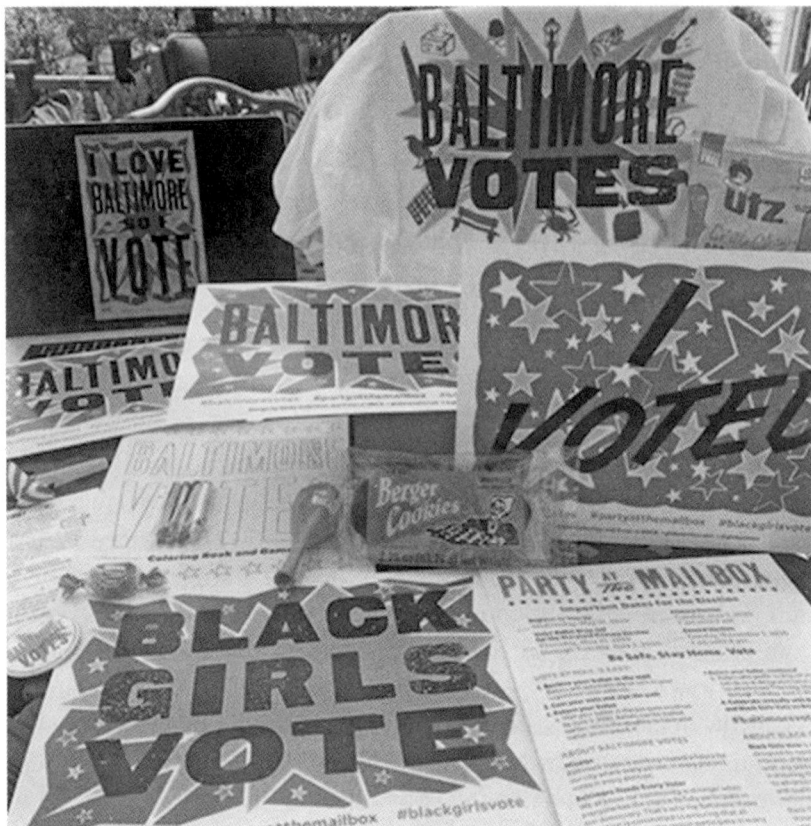

Figure 3.3: The Baltimore Pilot PATM Box

voter education events" (personal communication, September 10, 2021). Support from Baltimore Votes provided key institutional and financial support for the PATM idea pitched by Black Girls Vote. This included contacting academic researchers interested in structuring the effort to allow for a robust test of its effectiveness, which led to formation of the research team that authored this book.

The Baltimore pilot box included informational materials on voting but also festive items such as a T-shirt, balloons, posters, local snacks like Berger Cookies, and a coloring book with crayons, as shown in figure 3.3. The PATM materials intentionally incorporated Black-centered engagement materials that gave a nod to the practice of voting as a community celebration and collective effort. The posters and other printed items were decorated with iconic graphics from the Globe Collection and Press at the Maryland Institute College of Art. Globe's signature style of bold letterpress wood type with a distinctive distressed patina on top of Day-Glo backgrounds is immediately recognizable by Baltimore residents. Globe resonates as a longtime local print shop that has produced graphics supporting local and national Black artists and entertainers since the 1930s as well as modern political movements including Black Lives Matter. The posters deliberately omitted the election date to signal that the community celebration should extend beyond Election Day and that civic engagement is a year-round endeavor.

Participants were recruited via social media and local news media, as well as in partnership with local, trusted community organizations. Local community organizations were given subgrants to promote the program while supporting Baltimore residents (e.g., through food giveaways); overall, PATM partnered with sixty local community organizations for the pilot effort. Social influencers were given boxes and asked to share about them with their networks. Individuals interested in receiving their own box were directed to sign up via a Google form on the program's main website. Overall, 3,390 people registered for a chance to receive a PATM box before the Baltimore primary election, providing their full name, address, and birth year—a minimal amount of personal information meant to allay fears about privacy. From this information, we matched 1,098 individuals from the interest lists to their voting records; 680 were randomly assigned to the treatment group and 418 to the control group.[1] Our analysis examines turnout and behavior of these 1,098 party "hosts" as well as their 2,018 party "guests" (household members who are registered voters), 1,189 of whom were in treatment households and 829 in control households. Each day, Black Girls Vote told the authors how many boxes were on track to be delivered, their delivery capacity, and if there were any undeliverable boxes. This allowed the evaluation team to adjust the treatment and control lists and pull more names when necessary. The deliveries stopped on June 1 (the day before the election).

Individuals who signed up (regardless of their assignment to treatment or control) were also invited to on- and offline activities including a car caravan (described in chapter 1) and the election-night music party on Facebook, which generated visits from eleven thousand viewers. But the star of the show was the boxes. They were hand-delivered (in a pandemic-safe way) by local partner organizations, adding human interaction to the outreach. The boxes and the way they were delivered were both a part of the treatment and designed to promote feelings of celebration: Deliveries were not just boxes left on doorsteps, they were human interactions (coordinated via text messages) between people excited to deliver them and voters excited to receive them. As boxes began to be delivered—and unboxed in Instagram videos—excitement grew. Participants posted celebratory photos on social media. The campaign generated significant local and national media attention. Locally, PATM was featured on the front page of *The Baltimore Sun* and highlighted by WBAL (the local NBC affiliate); nationally, PATM was featured in news outlets including *Forbes* magazine and *USA Today*, as well as on MSNBC's *The ReidOut* with Joy Reid. *Forbes* reporter Jason Moscow interviewed a twenty-year-old college student, Allison Rice, who first heard about PATM "when it was mentioned at the virtual Baltimore Mayoral Stoop Stories, an event at which every mayoral candidate shared a personal tale. At that point, Rice signed her family up to receive a box, and upon its arrival, she said, 'It felt like opening a gift'" (Moscow 2020). Moscow notes, "Because the box shared simple information about 'the importance of spreading awareness to get young people out to vote,' the box's reception felt more 'authentic,' as opposed to the more patronizing mail that comes in from countless campaigns. Allison explained, 'It felt like it was coming from people who care about the city and are excited about the next generation.'" This authenticity—the perception among recipients that the PATM boxes were from people who cared about the city of Baltimore and its residents, as opposed to coming from a campaign as part of a last-minute effort to win an election—underlies the success of the program.

As detailed in chapter 6, respondents who we interviewed or who participated in one of our focus groups shared that they were able to use the box contents before the election, such as by wearing the T-shirt around town or sharing the box with their housemates. The crab-flavored chips and the other local items made them feel like the boxes were about their community (table 3.2). Sharing those items with household members emphasized that community connection and their pride in being from Baltimore.

Table 3.2: Box Contents and Their Links to Baltimore

Item	Significance
T-shirt	A "Baltimore votes" T-shirt branded with the iconic and very locally recognizable Globe Collection and Press artwork.
Pin	A "Baltimore votes" pin for participants to give as a gift to others or to wear on Election Day.
Posters	Locally themed posters (i.e., "Black Girls Vote," "I love Baltimore so I vote," "I voted," "Baltimore votes") were extremely visible signals of the project. They could decorate homes for voting parties or be placed on mailboxes or windows of cars and homes.
Stickers	"Vote 2020" stickers were included to take place of the "I voted" sticker many receive when voting in person. This was intended to allow PATM participants to have that same feeling of pride even when voting by mail.
Crab chips	Crab chips have long been a favorite of Baltimoreans and are flavored with Chesapeake Bay Crab Seasoning or Old Bay Seasoning. Some boxes included Herr's brand Old Bay chips, while other included Utz brand crab chips.
Berger Cookie	This is a local award-winning cookie made by DeBaufre Bakeries. The cookie originated in the 1800s in East Baltimore, and the cookies are well loved by Baltimoreans.
Crayons and coloring book	Children were invited to the party through the inclusion of crayons and a Baltimore Votes coloring book.
Balloons, party horns	PATM-themed balloons, and party horns, added to the festive atmosphere around voting.
Voting information	Information about vote by mail as well as local in-person voting.

Pilot Results

Randomized Controlled Trial

We hypothesized that members of households assigned to receive a PATM box (i.e., the treatment group) would be more likely to vote compared with members of households that did not receive a box (i.e., the control group). We had different expectations for individuals who signed up for a box ("hosts") compared to other members of their households ("guests"). Specifically, we expected that hosts would already be likely to turn out to vote because they were engaged enough to sign up to receive a box, but that the effect would be concentrated among guests, especially household members less likely to turn out.

We robustly measure the effect of PATM on voter turnout by comparing postelection validated voter turnout in the treatment and control groups.

Table 3.3: PATM: Baltimore Primary 2020 Pilot RCT

	N	Control turnout (%)	Treatment turnout (%)	Difference
Everyone	3,116	57.2	59.7	2.5*
Low-propensity voters	277	19.0	31.4	12.4*
High-propensity voters	1,839	85.7	84.1	−1.6
Hosts	1,098	89.0	87.4	−1.6
High-propensity hosts	1,052	91.3	89.5	−1.8
Low-propensity hosts	46	31.3	40.0	8.7
Guests	2,018	41.1	43.8	2.7*
High-propensity guests	787	78.7	76.5	−2.2
Low-propensity guests	231	16.9	29.6	12.7*
Guests with missing propensity data	1,000	17.8	20.9	3.1

Notes: Asterisks indicate differences that are statistically significant ($p < 0.05$, one-tailed). Our analysis includes all household members, not just the individuals who signed up to participate. This increases our sample size from 1,098 (1,869 in treatment + 1,247 in control) to 3,116. Around 1,000 "guests" had missing data on propensity and are, therefore, not included in high or low propensity categories of this table.

RCTs are often nicknamed the "gold standard" in empirical research, as they hold constant all other factors and allow precise measurement of the effect of independent variables. In GOTV research like ours, that independent variable is the encouragements to vote delivered to those randomly assigned to treatment.

Results from the pilot were enormously encouraging, as shown in table 3.3. Turnout increased by 2.5 percentage points among members of treatment group households, compared with the control group. We looked separately for effects among high- and low-propensity voters, defining high-propensity voters as those with a 50 percent or higher likelihood of participating.[2] Individuals who signed up to receive a PATM delivery (our party "hosts") tended to be high-propensity voters and very likely to vote in the June primary regardless of whether they were assigned to treatment. Turnout for party hosts was 89.0 percent in the control group and 87.4 percent in the treatment group. While there is a large difference in turnout for low-propensity hosts (31.3 percent in the control group and 40 percent in the treatment group), the number of participants is too small to generate robust statistical evidence that the boxes increased turnout. Among household members (party "guests"), evidence is stronger that PATM increased turnout. Looking at all guests regardless of vote propensity, turnout was 41.1 percent in the control group and 43.8 percent in the treatment group, a statistically significant difference of 2.7 percentage points. Among lower-propensity party guests, the effect is even larger. Here, turnout increases from 16.9 percent in the control group to 29.6 percent in the treatment group, a statistically significant effect of 12.7 percentage points ($p = 0.00$).[3] As shown in figure 3.4, the effect of attending a PATM party (living in a household with a voter who received a box) increases among guests (household members) as vote propensity decreases.

The effects are largest for low-propensity members of households that received a box but who did not personally go to the PATM website to ask to receive one. This finding is consistent with the evidence collected in our interviews and focus groups: Individuals who signed up to receive a box were already likely to vote, but the boxes were a catalyst for talking about the election with their household members and making those household members feel part of the celebration of voting and community that the PATM project was cultivating. Based on our conversations with voters who participated in PATM, we learned participants were able to use the box contents to talk about the election with their household members in a fun way that gently nudged others to take part.

Figure 3.4 visually displays how the effect of the treatment increases for party guests as voting propensity decreases. As their voting propensity drops, the power of the treatment becomes stronger. It is those household members least likely otherwise to have voted who were most likely to be mobilized to participate due to the presence of the PATM box in their household. Previous GOTV research focused on low-propensity voters has found that getting these individuals to turn out is very difficult and very expensive. Making voting a celebration of community may be the key to unlocking full participation among all members of the public.

Postelection Survey Data

We also hypothesized that assignment to the treatment group would increase feelings of community identity and political efficacy. We explored

Effect of the treatment
among low & high household members

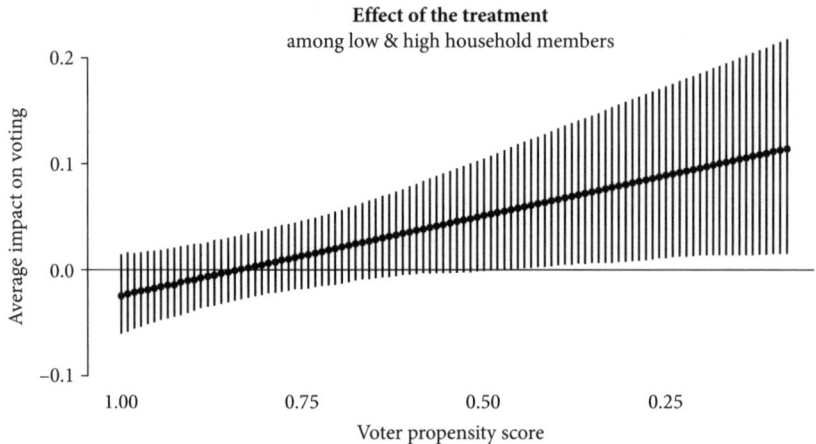

Figure 3.4: 2020 Baltimore Pilot, Effect of Assignment to Treatment on Guest Turnout, by Voting Propensity

these hypotheses with a postelection survey. Immediately following the pilot election, individuals who signed up to receive a box (including individuals randomly assigned to both the treatment and control groups) were invited via email to complete an anonymous online survey (see appendix for survey instrument). The invitation came from a member of our academic team, using a Black Girls Vote email address or a Baltimore Votes email address. Participants were thanked for their time with a ten-dollar Amazon gift card. The survey was in the field from June 22 to July 7, 2020. A total of 480 usable surveys were completed; 70 percent of participants were from a household that received a box, and 30 percent from households in the control group. Respondent age ranged from 18 to 77 (mean = 42.5); most (87.9 percent) respondents identified as female, 11.5 percent as male, and 0.6 percent individuals identified as nonbinary. Most (63.6 percent) identified as Black or as multiple races including Black; another large proportion identified as white, non-Latino (29 percent); and the remaining respondents identified as Asian only, Latino only, Middle Eastern or Arab, mixed race not including Black, or other. Of those providing a partisan identification, most (91 percent) identified as Democrats (including leaners). Reported turnout was very high among these survey respondents, consistent with the high turnout rates among party hosts found in the RCT. Among control group hosts, turnout was reported at 93.6 percent; among treatment group hosts, at 96.4 percent; the difference of 3.0 percentage points is not statistically significant.

While our survey found negligible differences in reported turnout for our party hosts, we did find evidence that participation in the program (having a box delivered to the household) affected political attitudes. In the full sample, individuals in treatment group households were more likely than individuals in control group households to report stronger identities as Baltimoreans, as shown in table 3.4. The total effect of the treatment compared with the control is a 0.197-point increase in identity as a Baltimorean ($p < 0.05$). The effect persists when we control for gender, education, race, and years lived in Baltimore (0.13-point increase, $p < 0.05$). Looking at our Black sample alone, we find similar results: The total effect of the treatment compared with the control is a 0.40-point

Table 3.4: Identity as a Baltimorean, by Treatment Group, 2020 PATM Pilot (Percentages)

Full sample	Control (%) (N = 141)	Treatment (%) (N = 339)
Not at all	4.26	3.54
Not very well	18.44	10.32
Very well	41.13	37.76
Extremely well	36.17	43.38
Black sample		
Not at all	6.52	3.72
Not very well	22.83	8.84
Very well	34.78	31.16
Extremely well	35.87	56.28
Non-Black sample		
Not at all	0.00	2.48
Not very well	9.80	13.22
Very well	49.02	51.24
Extremely well	41.18	33.06

Question wording: "How well does the term Baltimorean describe you?" Coded 0 = *not at all* to 3 = *extremely well*. Data collected June 22–July 7, 2020. The Black sample includes those respondents who selected Black as their sole race and Black in addition to some other race.

increase in identity as a Baltimorean ($p < 0.05$). This effect holds when gender, education, race, and years lived in Baltimore are included in the model (0.32-point increase, $p < 0.05$).[4]

We also asked survey participants a series of questions measuring feelings of political efficacy. The first question read, "When it comes to election policy, how much confidence, if any, do you have in each of the following parts of government to act in the best interest of the public?" Hosts in the treatment group consistently rated all levels of government (federal government, Maryland State legislature, governor of Maryland, Maryland State Board of Elections, City of Baltimore Board of Elections, and state elections officials) more positively than hosts in the control group. However, only differences in attitudes about the federal government reached statistical significance (full sample: $b = 0.28$, $p < 0.001$; Black sample: $b = 0.41$, $p < 0.001$). When all levels of government are treated as a scale, the effect of the treatment is positive and approaching statistical significance ($b = 0.03$; $p = 0.05$). Similarly, hosts in the treatment group tended to report slightly higher levels of political efficacy in response to other survey items, but the differences do not reach statistical significance.

General Election Efforts

Overall, the PATM pilot exceeded expectations in terms of both attitudinal and behavioral effects. Buoyed by this success, Black Girls Vote moved to expand the project to additional cities for the general election and beyond. Funds and community partnerships were secured to replicate in Baltimore City and the separate geographic area of Baltimore County, and to expand to Detroit and Philadelphia, for the November 2020 election. Note that while our analysis for the pilot focused only on the city of Baltimore, boxes were also distributed in Baltimore County. Thus, our effort in Baltimore City and Baltimore County in November 2020 should be understood as a return to those geographic areas, with the likely effect that recipients and community members were more familiar with the project than if the November 2020 effort had been their first exposure to PATM. In addition, PATM was conducted in the Atlanta metropolitan area for the January 2021 US Senate runoff election, in Richmond for the November 2021 gubernatorial election, in Detroit and Atlanta for the

November 2022 elections, and in Pennsylvania for the November 2024 election. In the remainder of this chapter, we focus on the replication in Baltimore City and expansion to Baltimore County; efforts in other cities (Detroit, Philadelphia, Atlanta, and Richmond) are described in chapters 4 and 5.

The randomization procedure and analysis plan for the November election effort in Baltimore mirrored those from the June pilot, but some changes were made. Delivery was still made by local partners, but now in a van wrapped with PATM graphics and information, including a QR code that facilitated sign-ups (figure 3.5). The social media presence of the campaign also ramped up. For example, during one day of the campaign, Lady Gaga allowed Nyki Robinson to take over her Instagram feed to promote the PATM project. The November 2020 effort in Baltimore included a slightly different box of goodies compared with the June 2020 box, including Herr's Old Bay chips, an Under Armour mask (Under Armour is headquartered in Baltimore), a jar of McCormick spices (also headquartered in Baltimore), Otterbein's cookies ("a Baltimore tradition since 1881"), and locally made hand sanitizer. The Under Armour mask alone (retail value thirty dollars) increased the desirability of the boxes, while the inclusion of it and sanitizer linked the boxes to the ongoing pandemic and the need for families to take cautionary measures. Boxes were delivered October 21–30. The RCT included 1,460 boxes and 2,204 individuals (848 hosts and 1,356 guests). We hypothesized that the effect of our treatment would be smaller given the increased salience of a general presidential election and that, as in the pilot, the effect would be isolated to low-propensity party guests. Results support these hypotheses, as shown in table 3.5.

Among party hosts, turnout is not affected by assignment to the treatment condition: Turnout is 92.5 percent among those in the control condition and 94.0 percent among those in the treatment condition; the difference of 1.5 percentage points is negligible and not statistically significant. In contrast, assignment to treatment increases turnout among low-propensity party guests by an estimated 5.2 percentage points, from 52.7 percent in the control group to 57.9 percent in the treatment group ($p = 0.09$). Looking at voter turnout for all low-propensity participants (including both guests and hosts), the effect is a statistically significant increase of 5.3 percentage points ($p = 0.05$), but there is no

Figure 3.5: Movement Team Delivering Boxes, and the Wrapped PATM Van

Table 3.5: PATM: 2020 Baltimore General Election RCT

	N	Control turnout (%)	Treatment turnout (%)	Difference
Everyone	2,204	78.9	79.8	0.9
Low-propensity voters	866	58.4	63.7	5.3*
High-propensity voters	1,338	91.7	90.4	−1.3
Hosts	848	92.5	94.0	1.5
High-propensity hosts	655	96.6	97.0	0.4
Low-propensity hosts	193	78.4	83.9	5.5
Guests	1,356	70.3	71.0	0.7
High-propensity guests	683	87.1	84.2	−2.9
Low-propensity guests	673	52.7	57.9	5.2*

Notes: Asterisks indicate differences that are statistically significant (one-tailed). Our analysis includes all household members, not just the individuals who signed up to participate. This increases our sample size from 848 (1,337 in treatment + 2,204 in control) to 2,204.

measurable difference among low-propensity hosts. These results are notable because they replicate the strong finding from the June pilot in a general (presidential) election. Since 2001, hundreds of GOTV RCTs have explored means of increasing voter turnout in local, midterm, and general elections. Those conducted in presidential elections are less likely than others to generate statistically significant effects; the impact of those GOTV efforts tends to be drowned out by other attention to the election by the media, political parties, and other political actors (Mann and Haenschen 2024). It's simply too noisy of a space to hear the effect of an RCT, especially one that is relatively small. When turnout is already expected to be high, any individuals not already voting in response to the high salience of the contest tend to be difficult to mobilize. Yet in the *very* noisy space that was the November 2020 election between Donald Trump and Joe Biden, we find a statistically significant effect of PATM on low-propensity household members of 5.2 percentage points. This is testament to the power of PATM.

Maryland is not a swing state. A Republican presidential candidate last won the state in 1988, and in the three races before 2020 the Democratic candidate won more than 60 percent of the vote. Thus, the two successful PATM efforts in Baltimore, including the pilot and the larger November 2020 effort, constitute significant evidence that the method works to increase voter turnout in lower- and medium-salience elections. The RCT results from the two efforts in Baltimore clearly support our hypothesis that PATM increased voter turnout. This is consistent with results from hundreds of GOTV projects over the last two decades that show that voter mobilization works, especially when the invitation to participate comes from a trusted source close to Election Day.

Conclusion

PATM effectively increased enthusiasm for voting and a community spirit of celebration around the Baltimore elections in June and November 2020, generating measurable increases in turnout. Often, participants hear about PATM from one of the project's local partner organizations or from a friend or neighbor, making it feel homegrown. The message about voting as a means of coming together as a community resonated with participants (see chapter 6). They felt that the box served as a reminder that voting is a community effort. Because these elections were held during the COVID-19 pandemic, many individuals were not able to participate in traditional political engagement events. PATM provided a space to continue to connect with others. The project generated excitement not only about voting but also about sharing an experience. PATM made them feel connected to others and made them feel proud to be Baltimoreans.

Participants also noted that the PATM materials served as a catalyst for conversations about voting with others, through verbal communication with members of their households, by sharing the contents of the box, or via social media. Black Girls Vote encouraged social media engagement as a part of the PATM experience, and our interview and focus group participants reported positive experiences engaging their networks about it in a way that cultivated a celebratory approach to voting.

The spirit of community celebrated by proclaiming, "I love Baltimore so I vote," persisted long after the elections were over. A year later, leaders of partner organizations told us they were still noting folks wearing the PATM T-shirts, and PATM signs were still visible in the windows of multiple Baltimore homes and businesses. This visible display of the lasting power of PATM illustrates the understanding of the project by Baltimore residents as something that was part of their community. This sense of local ownership, facilitated by the participation of local groups, the local items in the Baltimore boxes, and the use of a local printer whose graphics were recognized by Baltimoreans, created a highly successful PATM campaign.

Buoyed by the success of the Baltimore pilot, the PATM team garnered support to conduct a larger effort for the November 2020 elections in the city of Baltimore and added the separate geographic area of Baltimore County, as described in this chapter. In addition, funding was secured to support what we nicknamed the roadshow: efforts in the cities of Detroit and Philadelphia. Initial plans to also include Atlanta were eventually delayed to the January 2021 runoff elections for the two US Senate seats being decided that electoral cycle. These higher-salience elections presented very different contexts for a PATM effort. In the next chapter, we describe the implementation and results from those three roadshow efforts.

4

The PATM Roadshow

Baltimore is where Black Girls Vote was founded, and the original Party at the Mailbox (PATM) project likely benefited from the local name recognition of that organization, the partner organization Baltimore Votes, and the established trust that local organizations and individuals had in those two groups and their public leaders, including Nyki Robinson and Sam Novey. At the same time, we hypothesized that the power of the Voter Community Celebration Model to increase civic engagement through celebrations of community should work in other cities if the community connections in those cities could be effectively harnessed. In the heat of the presidential election of November 2020, funders impressed by the success of PATM in Baltimore supported an extension of the project to major battlegrounds of Detroit and Philadelphia. A few months later, we launched a last-minute PATM effort in Atlanta for the January 5, 2021, runoff election for two US Senate seats.

Could the project be successfully exported to new cities? In attempting to replicate the project, we faced the challenge of learning enough about those new locations, including which local community organizations would make effective partners. As with the model followed by Black Voters Matter (see chapter 1), PATM works through partnerships with small grassroots organizations. The partnerships and trust that those organizations already have with local residents bring legitimacy and power to the get-out-the-vote (GOTV) messaging. In addition, as demonstrated in chapter 3, PATM in Baltimore was successful because recipients of the boxes felt that the project belonged to and was meaningful for their local community. To replicate this effect in other cities, we would need to change the contents of the boxes to include local favorites, and we would need to find local, trusted messengers to promote the project to their networks and followers. Another approach (explored in chapter five) would be to later return to one of these roadshow cities as program credibility should grow during each iteration.

Another challenge was the pressure from funders to move the project to higher-salience elections. The power of any GOTV effort varies by election salience. Most effective randomized controlled trials (RCTs) are conducted in low- to medium-salience contests, where turnout is lower and there is more room for improvement. Most GOTV RCTs in high-salience, high-turnout elections are unable to generate statistically significant results because the few individuals not already voting in those elections are very hard to mobilize and the efforts being studied are drowned out by other messaging about the election. For example, a door-to-door mobilization effort in the Black and Latino community of South Los Angeles in the historic 2008 elections that included Barack Obama, while conducted by a trusted community organization with well-trained local canvassers, did not generate statistically significant results. Turnout in the control group in that RCT was 88.2 percent, compared with 88.5 percent in the treatment group (García Bedolla and Michelson 2012). As Kevin Arceneaux and David Nickerson note in their meta-analysis of multiple GOTV efforts, "Mobilization is most effective among those voters who are near the threshold of voting" (2009, 11). This threshold moves depending on the salience of the election. More relevant here is their conclusion: "In high-profile, competitive races, most registered voters will be above the threshold for voting and mobilization will not be cost-effective" (12). A more recent meta-analysis by Christopher Mann and Katherine Haenschen (2024) came to a similar conclusion.

The replication in Baltimore in November 2020 was conducted during a high-salience election, but the city and county of Baltimore, and the state of Maryland more broadly, were not swing regions. Maryland was not expected to deliver the margin of victory needed in the Electoral College in November 2020, as was the case in both Detroit (for Michigan) and Philadelphia (for Pennsylvania), or partisan control of the US Senate, as was the case in Atlanta in January 2021. The roadshow took PATM into contexts where it was going to be difficult to generate large, statistically significant effects on turnout. We anticipated few, if any, measurable RCT effects. These were battleground cities in battleground states. The PATM roadshow efforts were held in very different electoral contexts, alongside far larger and well-funded GOTV efforts.

Not only was PATM likely to be a smaller voice in these battleground locations, but the joy we hoped to inspire with the project conflicted with the broader narrative being messaged to Black voters in these hotly contested states about the threat posed by four more years of President Donald Trump and the importance of voting to remove him from office. PATM is about celebrating community and the positive emotions elicited when one comes out to vote to support one's neighbors and one's community. It is powered by linked fate and Black joy. In contrast, much of the messaging to Black voters and other traditional supporters of the Democratic Party during these elections was negative, focused on how Trump had fanned the flames of racial division in the United States and encouraged white Americans to dehumanize Black people (Stephens-Dougan 2021; Long 2022; Jardina and Piston 2023).

Despite these concerns, PATM moved forward in these locations. Given the rich data collected through our focus groups and interviews in Baltimore, we hypothesized that similar qualitative data from these high-salience electoral contexts would help us explore when and how PATM makes a difference, even if the turnout data from the RCTs failed to generate statistically significant effects. To preview our results, this is precisely what happened. PATM in Detroit and Philadelphia in November 2020 did not have statistically significant effects on turnout (we were unable to conduct an RCT in Atlanta in 2021, as detailed below) but did generate insightful qualitative data from individuals who signed up to receive a box and from their household members, which helped us refine our Voter Community Celebration Model.

In November 2021, November 2022, and November 2024, we varied the PATM program significantly, hoping to find ways to reduce the cost per vote and provide a model for increasing scale, using a variation of the boxes dubbed the *skinny sleeve*. We describe those results in chapter 5. Here, we focus on the original PATM model as piloted in Baltimore in June 2020.

As with the Baltimore efforts, we explore the effects of these roadshow programs using RCTs and survey, interview, and focus group data. These follow-up efforts allowed us to explore the effect of differences in election salience and geographic context and variations in how PATM was organized and executed. We also explore the different responses to and effects of the program in these locations to hypothesize what makes PATM effective and how to harness the power of voting as a celebration of community for future GOTV efforts. Overall, we find the following themes.

First, the local flavor of the program is key. Expanding PATM from the original city of Baltimore meant losing the authentic connection to Black Girls Vote and Baltimore Votes, well-known local organizations and the sponsors of very visible GOTV efforts in prior elections, including the 2018 Precinct Parties. The ability of PATM to reproduce this aspect of the program varied in the roadshow cities. At the same time, the local contents of the boxes (e.g., T-shirts for each city that featured icons of local culture, and variations in the included edible treats), and partnerships with local community organizations, encouraged recipients to see the project as locally driven.

Second, the effectiveness of a GOTV program based on the celebration of community is more potent in a geographically compact area where there is real-world visibility (e.g., visible posters in car and home windows) and saturation of the community with the GOTV messaging. In Baltimore, especially in the city of Baltimore, the PATM project was extremely compact, and neighbors out for walks or driving around town would see PATM posters and balloons at local homes. This emphasized the community nature of the effort. In contrast, the effort in roadshow cities was more geographically dispersed. This meant that many voters only saw PATM materials in their own homes or on social media rather than in neighbors' windows or on mailboxes.

The roadshow efforts differed from the pilot in multiple ways, partly because of the different local contexts (political, electoral, and otherwise) and also because the program was now more in the hands of local partners rather than under the daily supervision of Black Girls Vote staff. Robinson made multiple trips to these cities and consulted with local community leaders, but that networking did not embed her in the networks and culture of these cities in the same way she has been able to embed herself in the Baltimore community through the connections she has established over many years of living and working in the city, and she could not be in those cities every day. The original project in Baltimore was a cooperative project with Baltimore Votes, which means messaging was coming from two well-known local organizations and built on a relationship with the community from previous election cycle

activities. In contrast, Black Girls Vote did not have the same reputation in the roadshow cities. We anticipated that this might make it
challenging to replicate the success of Baltimore in other locations.

These roadshow efforts nevertheless generated important insights and
established relationships with local voters and community organizations
expected to make future PATM projects more effective, a theme
we return to in chapter 5 (we returned to Detroit and Atlanta for the
November 2022 election, and to Philadelphia for the November 2024 election). As we partnered with Black Girls Vote in these cities and collected
more qualitative data, we could better understand how PATM cultivates
celebrations of community. These celebrations had smaller effects on
turnout than in Baltimore but confirmed the basic mechanism: Black
voters came together to vote as celebrations of community, and PATM
encouraged those celebrations.

To the extent that the roadshow programs didn't replicate the Baltimore
findings, part of the explanation may lie in the degree to which the replications could not generate the same feelings of community celebration.
In June 2021, we spoke with 2020 Baltimore Votes communications and
program director Tasmin Swanson. Swanson was intimately involved with
the PATM efforts in Baltimore in 2020 and familiar with the roadshow
efforts that followed. We asked her to reflect on the different results and
speculate about what might be driving them, given her experiences with
the program. Swanson noted that there was more organic community
spread in Baltimore, while the roadshow efforts lacked the same sense of
community:

> One of the big differences in Baltimore was because deliveries were hap-
> pening in a couple of waves. Especially in the pilot, the boxes went out,
> people saw it—so there was way more community spread. Whereas in
> Atlanta, because of delivery logistics, we needed to get so many people
> signed up before the boxes reached Atlanta. It wasn't "Oh, my neighbor and
> all of the other people on my street have these posters up, and they have
> these shirts." It was more relying on influencer posts and advertising as
> opposed to community spread. We saw this in Philly and Detroit as well.
> Baltimore worked because it was a smaller city, and it felt more commu-
> nity oriented and organic. It was more paid marketing in the other places.
> (Tasmin Swanson, personal conversation, June 23, 2021)

In other words, the community that came together to celebrate voting in Baltimore with their PATM materials was inspired to do so because a first round of boxes went out to build up excitement about signing up and because it was a smaller city where other potential participants often saw early recipients sharing their posters and shirts. In Detroit, Philadelphia, and Atlanta, individuals were asked to sign up in response to online posts, including paid advertising; there wasn't the same sense of joining something that one's neighbors were already a part of. Swanson's impression was that it was this shared sense of community that was missing:

> It just was so different. Missing that strong community sense. Even look-ing at the social media, the types of pictures that were being posted in Baltimore were very different than the types of pictures that were being posted in Atlanta. They were very staged in Atlanta. "Here is my box. I am opening my box. I am on my couch." It was, they seemed staged. They didn't seem like they were sharing to celebrate. In Baltimore, it was actual people being excited about it, sharing it with friends, sharing it with family. . . . It seemed much more public.

The failure of the roadshow program to fully prime the spirit of commu-nity among recipients likely contributed to the lack of stronger results in the RCTs. If PATM works because it encourages voting as a celebration of community, then community members need to feel that they are, indeed, members of a community. They need to think about their shared community identity before they can decide to celebrate it.

In other ways, the roadshow program was stronger than the pilot. In most cities, delivery was still made by local partners, but now in a van wrapped with PATM graphics and information. The social media pres-ence of the campaign also ramped up. For example, as mentioned in the previous chapter, during one day of the campaign Lady Gaga allowed Robinson to take over her Instagram feed to promote the PATM project. Robinson also continued to organize Election Night virtual dance parties for all participants, regardless of whether they received a box. The NBA's Detroit Pistons and local apparel company Detroit vs. Everybody also provided local publicity in Detroit. Local and national media, includ-ing WXYZ television, the ABC affiliate in Detroit, and *Philadelphia* magazine all covered the project as well. In our postelection interviews and focus groups, we asked participants how they heard about PATM; respondents often noted that they heard about it on the local news. This heightened interest in PATM among celebrities and media reflects the high salience of those elections, but also the degree to which the program was seen as a positive, nonpartisan, local effort.

We turn now to descriptions of each city included in the PATM roadshow, details about the project in each location, and roadshow results.

Detroit 2020

Detroit has the largest Black majority of any major city in the US, at 77.1 percent, according to 2020 US Census data. This was not the case for many years of the city's history. Historians first mention enslaved Black people in Detroit in 1736, while the first census of the city, conducted by the French in 1750, lists 33 enslaved people among the city's 483 inhabitants (including both enslaved Black people and Pawnee Indians); the number of enslaved people rose rapidly over subsequent years (Boyd 2017). The 1820 Census recorded 1,355 white people and 67 Black people in Detroit; in 1830, these numbers had increased to 2,096 and 126, respectively (Boyd 2017, 26). Before the Civil War, Detroit was a choice destination for Black people fleeing enslavement due to its proximity to the Canadian border.

Things shifted rapidly between 1915 and 1920 due to the Great Migration and World War I. During the Great Migration, Detroit again became a popular destination due to the job opportunities at the Ford Motor Company. The story of Black Americans in Detroit cannot be told without mention of Henry Ford. When Ford decided to hire Black workers and give them opportunities to work in jobs historically reserved for white workers, it represented "a quantum leap forward for black workers" (B. Bates 2012, 2). As Beth Bates notes, "By rejecting the notion that better jobs were for white men only, Ford raised expectations and hope about what was possible, suggesting a corner had been turned in the ongoing black struggle for inclusion as full-blooded Americans. In this regard, Ford's policies sparked a transformation in the lives of black workers and their families, helping lay a foundation for a labor-oriented civil rights agenda, and, ultimately, providing a base for the formation of the urban black middle class" (2012, 3). Working for Ford inspired thousands of Black Americans to move to Detroit—the city's Black population increased by over 600 percent between 1910 and 1920. The sudden, rapid growth of the city's Black population cannot be over-emphasized. It grew from 5,741 in 1910, to 40,838 in 1920, to 120,000 by 1930, an increase of 2,000 percent that also increased the Black propor-tion of the city's population from less than 1 percent in 1910 to nearly 8 percent (B. Bates 2012, 16). Many came from the South, part of the Great Migration to the North and Midwest by Black Americans fleeing racism and Jim Crow and seeking new opportunities made possible by the jobs left vacant as men left to fight in Europe during World War I. Thanks to Ford's hiring practices, the percentage of Black workers at Ford in 1920 exceeded their share of the population: Blacks represented 3.3 percent of the population but at least 10 percent of Ford's workforce (Boyd 2017, 109).

Detroit also has a history of violence and discrimination against Black people. During the Spanish-American War, racism spiked, generating an average of two lynchings of Black people every week between 1889 and 1903 (Boyd 2017, 86). In addition to racism and violence, Black residents of Detroit also often faced challenging economic conditions. Between 1900 and 1910, Black workers, especially men, were pushed out of their jobs and replaced by immigrants from Europe. During the Great Migration, racist housing policies including restrictive covenants and real estate codes meant Black people were squeezed into the city's East Side, where ghettos developed due to the limited and deteriorating hous-ing stock (B. Bates 2012, 32). Beth Bates also notes, "Another way blacks were kept in their 'place' was through the brutality of Detroit's largely native-born, white police force" (2012, 6). Black residents were often charged higher rents than white families, despite being forced to live in lower-quality housing (Boyd 2017, 97). Many new arrivals hoped moving to Detroit would bring economic prosperity; instead, "newcomers often found residential segregation, high rents, social ostracism, and racial discrimination" (Kornweibel 1976, 308). A surge of newcomers in the summer of 1941 made things even worse.

White homeowners fled to the suburbs when open-housing ordi-nances were approved after World War II, further increasing the share of the (remaining) population that was Black. Residents who moved to Detroit during the Great Migration often settled in a neighborhood called Black Bottom, which developed into "a thriving enclave" of Black-owned homes, churches, and businesses. In the early 1950s, however, the neighborhood was razed to build a freeway and park "in one of the most controversial episodes of mass gentrification in Detroit history," replacing Black residents with mostly white residents (McGraw 2017). By 1990, Detroit was a majority-Black city (Boyd 2017).

Detroit is also a heavily segregated city. A recent analysis of 2020 US Census data by scholars at Brown University found that the Detroit metropolitan area was the third most segregated city, looking at segregation between Black and white residents, with a dissimilarity index of 74.5. Dissimilarity indexes measure the degree to which two groups are relatively distributed across a city or metropolitan area, and range from 0 to 100. A dissimilarity index of 0 indicates total integration, and a dissimilarity index of 100 indicates total segregation, with all members of each group located in completely different neighborhoods. Detroit's Black-white dissimilarity index for 2020 is topped only by those of Newark, New Jersey (with a score of 76.6), and the Milwaukee, Wisconsin, metropolitan area (75.1) (Diversity and Disparities, n.d.).

Despite these economic and housing challenges, Detroit is a city built on a strong, positive Black community identity. Detroit is the largest Black city in the United States, and between 1954 and 2020 the community continually elected Black political candidates to represent them in Congress (McGrady 2022). After the November 2022 elections, there was no Black representative from Detroit in the US Congress for the first time in seventy years. This resulted in a significant outcry from Black community leaders in Detroit, who blamed changes to the political environment including redistricting, the role of big money in politics, and lower voter turnout (One Detroit 2023b). At the time of our 2020 RCT, however, Detroit was still positioned as a solidly Black political stronghold that had fought for Black political representation both locally and nationally. Black identity and duty to the community are strongly ingrained in the hearts of Detroit's residents, who remain committed to uplifting one another in the face of political and social struggles. And, as noted above, the city has had more than a few such struggles. More recently, in 2008, Detroit was rocked by a whistleblower lawsuit against Black Mayor Kwame Kilpatrick. Kilpatrick was sentenced to twenty-eight years in prison on two dozen charges of racketeering and

Table 4.1: 2020 Census Demographic Data for Detroit, Michigan

Race	
White alone	14.4%
Black or African American alone	77.1%
American Indian and Alaska Native alone	0.4%
Asian alone	1.9%
Native Hawaiian and Other Pacific Islander alone	0.0%
Two or more races	2.4%
Hispanic or Latino	7.7%
White alone (not Hispanic or Latino)	11.0%
Income	
Median household income (in 2020 dollars), 2016–2020	$32,498
Per capita income in past twelve months (in 2020 dollars), 2016–2020	$19,569
Persons in poverty	33.2%

Source: "QuickFacts: Detroit City, Michigan," US Census Bureau, accessed February 3, 2025, https://www.census .gov/quickfacts.

conspiracy, and the state was forced into state-managed receivership by the governor (Spence 2011; Williams 2020). Economic challenges led the city to declare bankruptcy in July 2013, and two years later, the first white mayor since 1974, Mike Duggan, took office. Detroit struggled with crime, unemployment, underperforming schools, and thousands of vacant and dilapidated houses in subsequent years. The last is partly a reflection of the city's shrinking population since the 1970s and high unemployment rates. Average household incomes are low, and a third of city residents live in poverty (table 4.1).

In Detroit, PATM partnered with forty community organizations to distribute 2,000 boxes, 531 of which were part of the RCT. The Detroit RCT included 531 hosts assigned to treatment and 457 to the control group ($n = 988$). Adding household members increases the size of the overall Detroit RCT to 2,340. Boxes were delivered October 23–31. In addition to the voting information materials, the Detroit box had an Under Armour mask, a Detroit Pistons baseball cap, and local goodies including Better Made BBQ chips, a Faygo pop, and a Sander's choco-late bar shaped like Michigan's lower peninsula (figure 4.1). Our focus in Detroit was on majority-Black neighborhoods, a community that

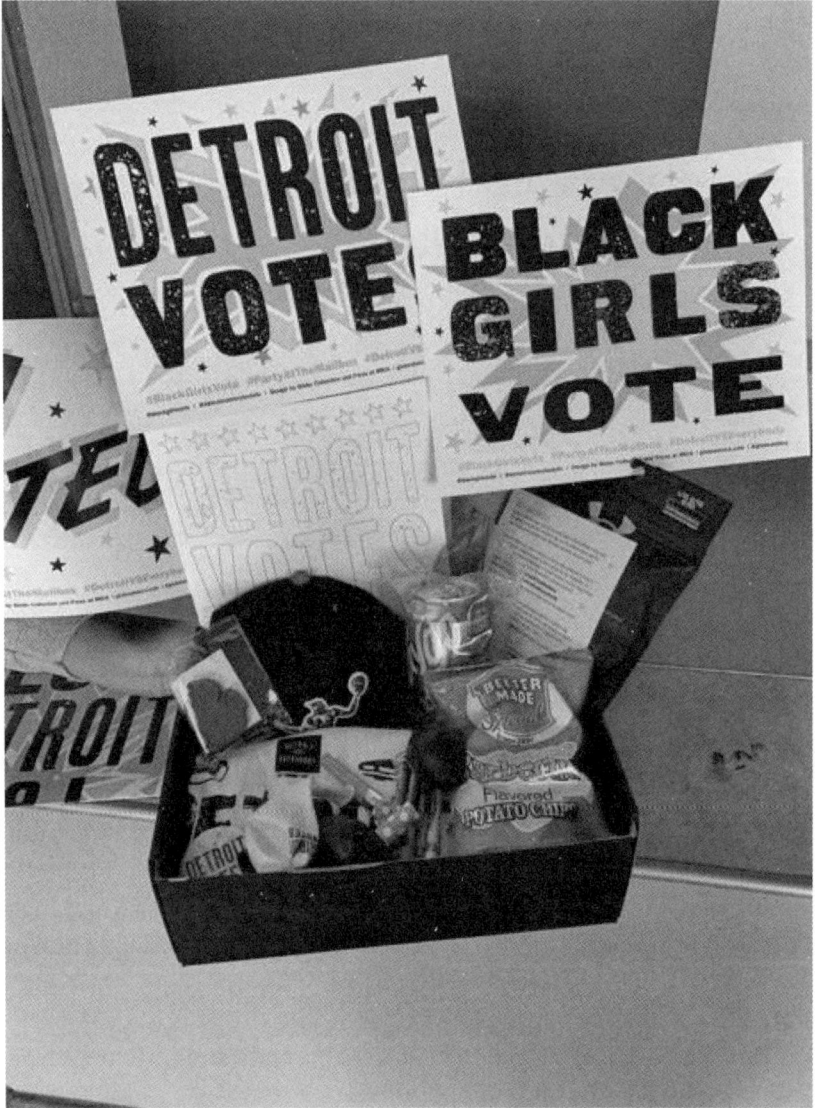

Figure 4.1: The 2020 PATM Box for Detroit

was hard-hit by the COVID-19 pandemic. This was particularly true in October 2020. The second day that PATM was in the field delivering boxes (October 24), Robinson learned that the city was on the verge of a total shutdown to fight the spread of the virus, and she spurred her team into overdrive to ensure that boxes could be safely delivered

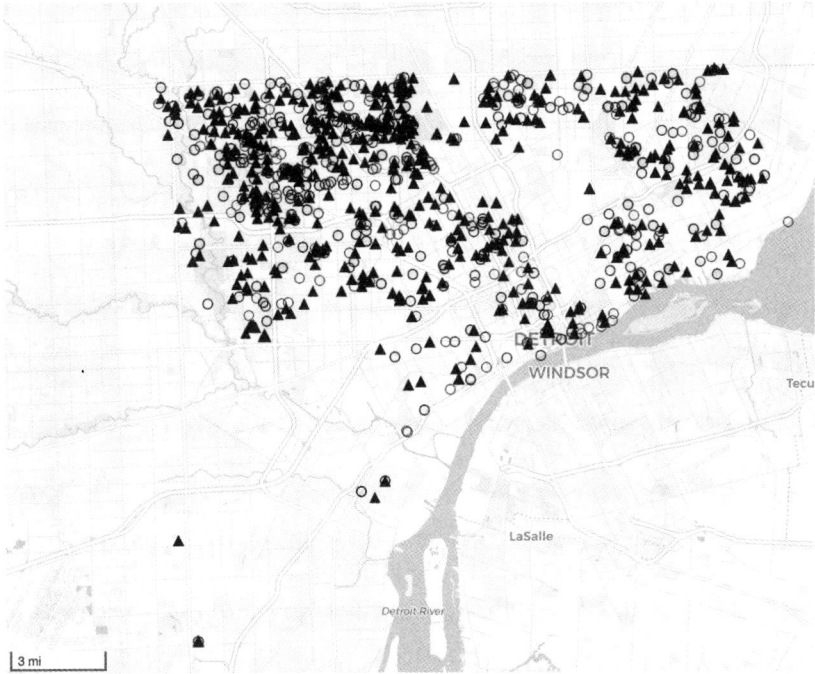

Figure 4.2: Map of Treatment and Control Households for PATM in Detroit,
November 2020
Note: Treatment households are triangles; control households are circles.

before Election Day. The geographic spread of the effort is shown in
figure 4.2.

Reflecting the high salience of the election in Detroit, and the strong
interest in Black voter turnout by multiple organizations, PATM inter-
sected with efforts of multiple other entities. For example, on National
Vote Early Day (Saturday, October 24), PATM partnered with the Detroit
Pistons, Michelle Obama's When We All Vote initiative, More Than a Vote,
Lyft, and Michigan Secretary of State Jocelyn Benson to host an event at
the Henry Ford Detroit Pistons Practice Facility (WXYZ Detroit 2020).
In addition to live entertainment, refreshments (cider and donuts), and
the chance to get autographs from Benson, Detroit Pistons head coach
Dwane Casey, and Pistons legend Earl Cureton, PATM boxes packed
by Pistons players were available for the first 150 participants. The event
also offered participants the opportunity to submit their ballots in a drop

box. A free bus shuttled residents from the neighborhood to and from the event, and Lyft offered a code for free rides.

The Vote Early Day event with the Pistons is just one example of the intense effort put into turning out Detroit voters in November 2020. The Democratic presidential campaign of Joe Biden reportedly spent $32.5 million in ads in the city, while Republican President Donald Trump spent $9.7 million. Biden and his vice-presidential candidate, Kamala Harris, visited Detroit multiple times. Leaders of Black congregations were joined by Democratic candidates almost every Sunday, and churches took steps to make voting more convenient for their parishioners. Community organizers, business owners, and members of the Divine Nine Black fraternities and sororities worked to turn out voters with text messages, phone calls, and in-person and virtual events (Gray 2020).

These efforts reflected the math of the election, particularly for the Democratic Party, and the understanding that turnout in a city where 77 percent of residents are Black, given that Black voters overwhelmingly prefer Democratic candidates, could be decisive. In 2016, Democratic presidential nominee Hillary Clinton won 95 percent of the vote in Detroit, winning 234,871 votes to Trump's 7,692. Detroiters cast 41,625 fewer votes that year compared with 2012, with an overall turnout rate of just 48.61 percent, contributing to Trump's victory in the state by just 10,704 votes. In 2020, turnout in Detroit increased to 50.88 percent; Democrats won 94 percent, winning 240,936 voters to Trump's 12,889 and contributing to Biden's narrow victory in the state (50.6 percent to 47.8 percent) by a margin of 154,188 votes.

As expected, given these widespread GOTV efforts in the city, there is no statistically significant turnout difference between the PATM treatment and control groups, even among low-propensity party guests (table 4.2). Given the very high electoral salience of battleground cities in battleground states for a presidential election, we were skeptical that we would detect measurable differences in turnout in Detroit. The baseline turnout rates, even for low-propensity voters, were extremely high, leaving fewer individuals on the cusp of participation for mobilization. After the election, we collected 255 surveys, using the same method as in Baltimore. Participants were compensated with ten-dollar Amazon gift cards. Unfortunately, participation was low and relatively slow (surveys were completed from November 11 to December 5, 2020), possibly due

Table 4.2: PATM: Detroit, November 2020 RCT

	N	Control turnout (%)	Treatment turnout (%)	Difference
Everyone	2,340	81.0	78.2	−2.8
Low-propensity voters	1,234	77.0	75.7	−1.3
High-propensity voters	1,106	85.1	81.0	−4.1
Hosts	988	82.9	81.4	−1.5
High-propensity hosts	537	83.7	80.1	−3.6
Low-propensity hosts	451	82.1	82.8	0.7
Guests	1,352	79.4	75.9	−3.5
High-propensity guests	783	86.4	81.9	−4.5
Low-propensity guests	569	73.6	72.0	−1.6

Notes: None of the differences shown here are statistically significant. Our analysis includes all household members, not just those who signed up to participate. This increases our sample size from 988 (1,300 in treatment + 1,040 in control) to 2,340.

to the postelection context of battles over the vote results. Participants included an equal mix of treatment and control hosts. The survey data show no statistically significant differences in reported identities or feelings of political efficacy, either in the full sample or looking only at Black respondents (see appendix for details).

The lack of a statistically significant estimate for effects on turnout does not mean that the November 2020 Detroit program was not successful. PATM resonated with local residents and built a baseline of familiarity with the project. In November 2022, we returned to Detroit with the skinny sleeve version of the boxes, and in a lower-salience election, and successfully increased turnout among targeted Black women voters (see chapter 5). If the lack of Detroiters' familiarity with Black Girls Vote or PATM in November 2020 mitigated the project's ability to generate statistically significant increases in turnout, the networking and publicity from 2020 may have contributed to higher levels of familiarity in 2022. This speaks to the importance of GOTV projects and community organizations that are consistently visible and active year-round and across multiple electoral cycles, rather than helicoptering in for a single election, an argument often repeated by those working with historically marginalized communities. Qualitative data from the November 2020 round also speak to the success of the program (see chapter 6).

Philadelphia

Philadelphia had a sizable Black population even before the Civil War, estimated at 15,000 in 1830 and growing to 22,000 by 1860, leading to the development of a vibrant Black community and the city's status as a major stop on the Underground Railroad. During the Great Migration, the Black population in the city grew dramatically, from 63,000 in 1900 to 134,000 by 1920, and 220,000 by the end of the 1920s (Wolfinger 2013). Philadelphia has been home to several recent community-led initiatives and social justice movements aimed at addressing issues of police brutality, economic inequality, and systemic racism. The Black Lives Matter movement has been active in the city since its founding in 2013, with local activists leading protests and calling for reforms to the criminal justice system. Overall, Philadelphia's history of Black activism is testament to the power of community-led initiatives and the resilience of those who fought and continue to fight for social justice in the city. Despite the many such successes achieved over the years, the challenge of increasing voter turnout remains a persistent one, particularly among low-propensity voters.

Philadelphia is a racially diverse city; in 2020, the largest proportion of residents of the city (41.4 percent) were Black, compared with 34.1 percent who were white non-Latino, 15.1 percent Latino, and 7.4 percent Asian (table 4.3). It is also one of the most racially segregated cities in America (as is Detroit). Aseem Shukla and Michaelle Bond (2021), using US Census data, found that "almost no matter which groups you look at, and using multiple ways of measuring segregation, Philly is one of the most stubbornly divided metropolitan areas in a rapidly diversifying and increasingly integrated country." Philadelphia's Black-white segregation is second only to Chicago's among big cities and is fourth highest in the nation for large metropolitan areas, and the city is more segregated than 94 percent of counties with at least 10,000 people and more than a negligible (smaller than 5 percent) Black population (Winch 2000; Shukla and Bond 2021).

The 2020 election in Philadelphia was, as in Detroit, one of extremely high electoral salience. Press and pundits alike marked Philadelphia as a key city for the 2020 race, and this was reflected in the number and intensity of GOTV campaigns, campaign spending, and media

Table 4.3: 2020 Census Demographic Data for Philadelphia, Pennsylvania

Race

White alone	39.3%
Black or African American alone	41.4%
American Indian and Alaska Native alone	0.3%
Asian alone	7.4%
Native Hawaiian and Other Pacific Islander alone	0.0%
Two or more races	4.3%
Hispanic or Latino	15.1%
White alone (not Hispanic or Latino)	34.1%

Income

Median household income (in 2020 dollars), 2016–2020	$33,831
Per capita income in past twelve months (in 2020 dollars), 2016–2020	$29,644
Persons in poverty	23.1%

Source: "QuickFacts: Philadelphia City, Pennsylvania," US Census Bureau, accessed February 3, 2025, https://www.census.gov/quickfacts.

coverage of the race. In 2016, Clinton had been favored to win the state, given Pennsylvania's history as a state that leans Democratic and Barack Obama's victory in 2012 by 5.4 percentage points. Instead, Trump won the state by less than 1 percentage point, eking out a victory by 44,292 of 6.2 million votes cast overall—the first time a Republican presidential nominee had won Pennsylvania since 1988.

In 2020, Democrats invested considerable effort in winning back the state, which FiveThirtyEight's election forecast had named the most likely tipping-point state (the state most likely to provide the margin of victory needed to win the election) (Silver 2020). Democratic presidential nominee Joe Biden worked to mobilize Black voters before Election Day, traveling to the city the Sunday before the election and speaking at a Souls to the Polls event at the Sharon Baptist Church in West Philadelphia and a drive-in rally at FDR Park in South Philadelphia, both in heavily Black neighborhoods.

Participation in the 2020 election reached record highs, with more than 90 percent of eligible Philadelphians registering to vote (a thirty-five-year high). Turnout on Election Day was 68 percent, higher than for any presidential election since 1984. Of more than 749,000 votes cast, Biden won

604,175 (81 percent) to Trump's 132,870 (18 percent). Compared with 2016, Biden won 20,000 more votes in Philadelphia than Clinton, while Trump gained about 24,000 votes. The presidential race wasn't the only reason for the intense interest in the election. Democrats and Republicans broke spending records in their battle for control of the state legislature, where a change of just a few seats would determine partisan control of the chamber (Caruso 2020).

In Philadelphia, PATM partnered with sixty community organizations, including She Can Win, Unity in the Community, the National Coalition of 100 Black Women (Pennsylvania Chapter), the Urban League of Philadelphia, Make the Distinction, the Achieving Reunification Center, the Laborers District Council of the Metropolitan Area of Philadelphia and Vicinity, ICARE Academy, New Voices for Reproductive Justice, and Parkway Northwest High School's Peace and Social Justice Academy, among others, to help get the word out about the program and to distribute 5,150 boxes, including to the 2,209 households in the treatment group. The control group consisted of 1,599 households (figure 4.3). Overall, there were 9,447 individuals in the Philadelphia RCT. Boxes were delivered from October 22 to November 1. In addition to voter information materials, posters, a T-shirt, and an Under Armour mask, the Philadelphia boxes had local treats including Tastykake Butterscotch Krimpets, Utz potato chips, and Peanut Chews (figure 4.4).

Partner organizations promoted PATM to their members and to the general public, including through social media posts and stories in traditional media such as newspapers and television news broadcasts. One illustrative example comes from an interview on ABC6, the local Philadelphia affiliate, which featured comments from Robinson and Jasmine Sessoms, the founder of She Can Win, a nonprofit that trains and recruits women of color to run for office. In the news segment, Sessoms told ABC6 viewers that she asked locals, "Hey, did you vote? If you did, let's celebrate; if you didn't, let's find out why and how can I get you to vote." The segment reiterated to Philadelphians that PATM "want[s] your civic duty to be a celebration" and that the box was intended to create a spirit of celebration in the city, noting the inclusion of "local goodies like Peanut Chews and Tastykakes," as well as a T-shirt designed by a Temple University student (A. Johnson 2020).

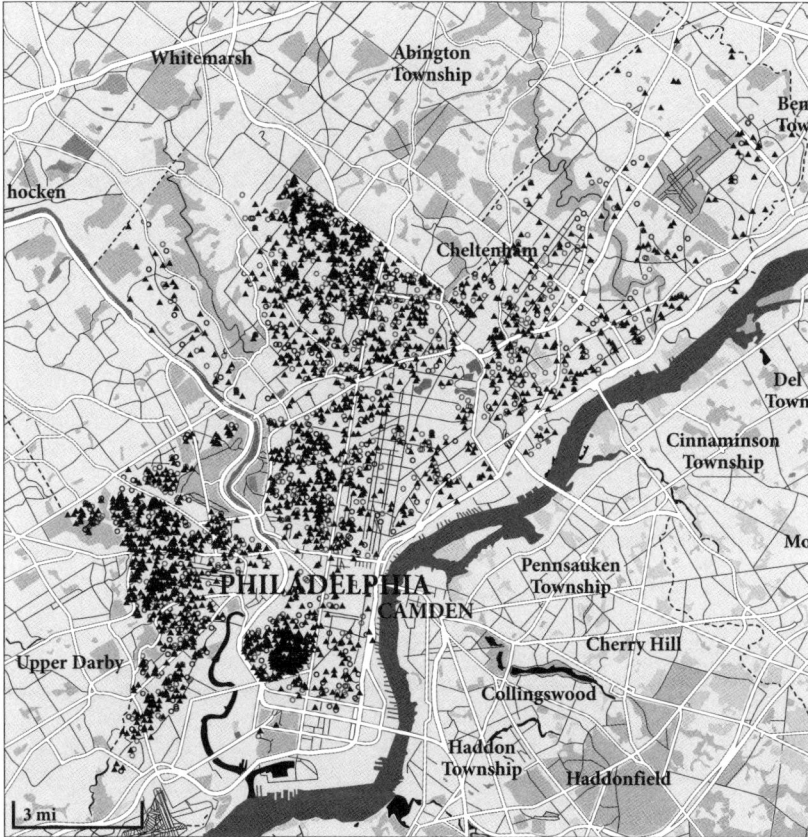

Figure 4.3: Map of Treatment and Control Households, PATM in Philadelphia, November 2020
Note: Treatment households are triangles; control households are circles.

As in Detroit, the rollout of the PATM project in Philadelphia in October 2020 was not without hiccups. During our distribution efforts, on the afternoon of October 26, two Philadelphia police officers fatally shot Walter Wallace Jr. in the predominantly Black neighborhood of West Philadelphia. Videos of the incident quickly circulated on social media, and the community responded with protests against police brutality and racism. Over the next few days, fifty-seven law enforcement officers were injured in clashes with protesters, and hundreds of people were arrested for assaulting police and for burglary. Eventually, Pennsylvania

Figure 4.4: The 2020 PATM Box for Philadelphia

Governor Tom Wolf deployed the National Guard to the city. The city later settled a wrongful death lawsuit brought by Wallace's family for $2.5 million (Diaz 2021).

The protests, and a temporary curfew, made delivery efforts more difficult for the PATM teams on the ground. Additionally, because the media was largely focusing on these protests, rather than on the election or GOTV efforts like PATM, the sign-ups on our interest lists were very slow to start, with only about three hundred sign-ups or fewer per

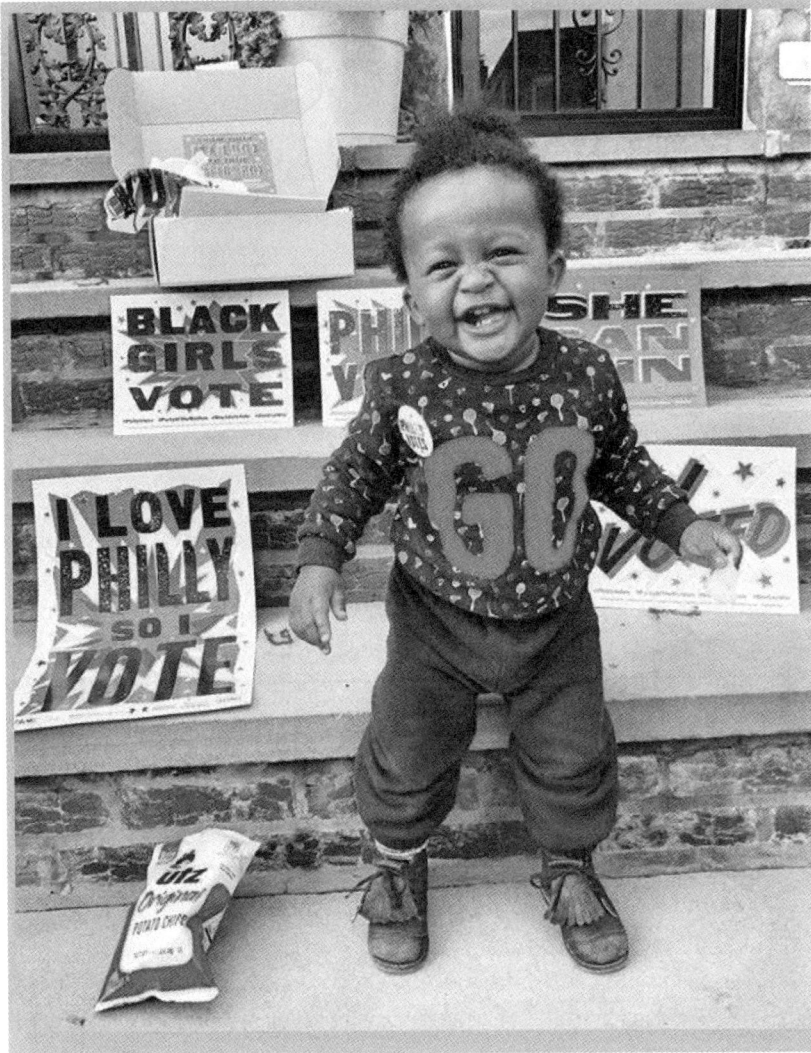

Figure 4.4: (*continued*)

day. This meant that even when boxes were ready for distribution, they had nowhere to go. Things turned around following a three-minute interview on Philadelphia's very popular morning news show *Good Day Philadelphia* (FOX 29) on October 26, 2020; the segment generated over one thousand registrations on the PATM website and helped

Table 4.4: PATM: Philadelphia, November 2020 RCT

	N	Control turnout (%)	Treatment turnout (%)	Difference
Everyone	9,447	79.5	75.2	−4.3
Low-propensity voters	2,956	60.3	57.3	−3.0
High-propensity voters	6,491	87.2	84.0	−3.2
Hosts	3,808	91.1	91.3	0.2
High-propensity hosts	3,147	93.5	93.3	−0.2
Low-propensity hosts	661	78.7	82.0	3.3
Guests	5,639	71.3	64.7	−6.6
High-propensity guests	3,344	81.3	75.3	−6.0
Low-propensity guests	2,295	54.6	50.6	−4.0

Notes: None of the differences shown here are statistically significant. Our analysis includes all household members, not just the individuals who signed up to participate. This increases our sample size from 3,808 (5,592 in treatment + 3,855 in control) to 9,447.

bring the total sign-ups for that day alone to over twenty-three hundred. While the events that followed Williams's death slowed early dissemination of PATM information through traditional media, and limited our early distribution process, we were ultimately able get every box out to Philadelphia hosts and their household members (guests) before the election. The PATM team was on the ground for a few extra days in Philadelphia to ensure maximum impact of the program.

As expected, PATM did not generate statistically significant effects in turnout, as shown in table 4.4. After the election, we collected 558 surveys, using the same method as in Baltimore. Participants were compensated with ten-dollar Amazon gift cards. Unfortunately, again, participation was low and relatively slow (surveys were completed from November 11 to December 6, 2020). Participants included an equal mix of treatment and control hosts. The survey data show no statistically significant differences in reported identities or feelings of political efficacy. This is the case for both the full sample and the subset of Black respondents (see appendix for details). However, as with Detroit, the 2020 effort in Philadelphia may have seeded the field by raising awareness of Black Girls Vote and PATM. In November 2024, we returned to Philadelphia with a different version of the project and successfully increased turnout among targeted Black households (see chapter 5).

Atlanta 2021

Atlanta is often called "the cradle of the modern Civil Rights Movement." It is the birthplace of Dr. Martin Luther King, Jr., and the Southern Christian Leadership Conference (SCLC) (Brown-Nagin 2011). The city's history of Black activism stretches back far before then, to the 1880s, when Black washerwomen established a labor organization and then went on strike for better wages and more autonomy in their work. Subsequent strikes from 1892 to 1906 protested segregated streetcars (Myrick-Harris 2006). Over time Black Atlantans shifted from a strategy of incremental progress informed by Booker T. Washington's politics of respectability to embrace W.E.B. Du Bois' strategy of "bare-knuckled power politics," generating a racial solidarity that they successfully exercised to fight for their rights (Driskell 2014, 3). Much of this activism was led by Black women, who embraced "activist womanhood" in their push for the rights of their children and their neighborhoods (Driskell 2014).

In the 1940s, Black Atlantans advocated for civil rights through massive voter registration campaigns, won through legal battles the right to participate in primary elections, and successfully pressured city leaders to hire Black police officers. In the 1960s, Black college students in Atlanta conducted sit-ins to push for desegregation of restaurants and lunch counters, Ethel Mae Mathews pushed for school desegregation in her role as president of the Atlanta chapter of the National Welfare Rights Organization, and civil rights groups in Atlanta including the SCLC and the Student Nonviolent Coordinating Committee, headquartered in Atlanta, advocated for Black rights including passage of the Civil Rights Act of 1964 and the Voting Rights Act of 1965 (Brown-Nagin 2011). By the early 1970s, Atlanta symbolized the achievements of the civil rights movement: it had a Black representative in Congress and seats in state and local government. It has had a Black mayor since 1974. It is home to multiple historically Black colleges and universities, including Clark Atlanta University, Spelman College, Morehouse College, and the Morehouse School of Medicine. "On the strength of black political power and accounts of good race relations, coupled with an economic boom, Atlanta advertised itself as a 'mecca' for African Americans. The black-themed popular magazines *Essence* and *Ebony*, printed stories proclaiming that Atlanta provided an ideal environment for black achievement and advancement" (Brown-Nagin 2011, 436).

After Joe Biden's victory in November 2020, and amid ongoing false claims of voter fraud, much of the nation's attention shifted to Georgia. Due to the state's unique electoral laws, multiple races had yet to be decided. In most elections in the United States, the candidate who receives the largest proportion of votes is declared the winner, even if no candidate receives a numerical majority of the votes. This is known as plurality voting. In Georgia, however, if no candidate receives at least 50 percent of the vote, the state schedules a runoff election between the top two vote getters, a system known as majority voting. Georgia shifted from plurality voting to majority voting in the 1960s to disenfranchise Black voters and protect white supremacy—requiring a winning candidate to win a majority of the vote reduces the political power of a minority group, and the change in Georgia was deliberately made by white supremacists seeking to maintain political power (Kousser 1999).

In November 2020, Georgians weighed in on two races for seats on the US Senate—a special election to fill a two-year vacancy, and a regular election for a six-year seat then held by Republican David Perdue. The special election was triggered by the retirement in December 2019 of Republican US Senator Johnny Isakson. Georgia Governor Brian Kemp appointed Republican Kelly Loeffler to the seat, and a special election was scheduled for November 2020.

In that first round, in November 2020, neither race generated a clear winner. For the short seat, Democrat Raphael Warnock won 32.9 percent of the vote and Loeffler won 25.9 percent, while Republican Doug Collins won 20 percent and Democrat Matt Lieberman (son of former US Senator and vice-presidential candidate Joe Lieberman) won 2.8 percent of the vote. For the full seat, Perdue led with 49.7 percent of the vote, while his challenger, Democrat Jon Ossoff, won 47.9 percent, and Libertarian Shane Hazel won 2.3 percent. To summarize, while Warnock and Perdue would have won in a state with different electoral rules, in Georgia they went on to runoff elections against Loeffler and Ossoff, scheduled for January 5, 2021.

The race was front-page national news for multiple reasons, adding to the salience of the race for Georgia's electorate. Warnock is the senior pastor at Atlanta's Ebenezer Baptist Church, once led by the Reverend

Martin Luther King Jr., and Warnock was endorsed by high-profile Democrats including former President Barack Obama and former gubernatorial candidate Stacey Abrams. Then-President Donald Trump had endorsed Loeffler's Republican opponent in the first round, Collins, and had publicly asked Kemp to appoint Collins to the vacant seat. After Collins was knocked out, Loeffler pursued and eventually obtained Trump's endorsement.

In addition to these high-profile endorsements, the race was salient because of the effect their outcome would have on the partisan balance of the US Senate. Outcomes from other races in November 2020 left the chamber with fifty Republicans and forty-eight Democrats (including two independents who caucus with the Democrats), and a White House that would be controlled by Democratic President Biden and Vice President Harris. In the event of a tie vote in the US Senate, the tie is broken by a vote cast by the vice president. Thus, if Democrats won both US Senate runoffs, they would have the power to out-vote Republicans (with tie-breaking votes cast by Harris).

Hoping to replicate the strong results from the Baltimore pilot (results from November 2020 were not yet available), funders urged PATM to go to Georgia to boost Black turnout for the runoff election. As with the races in Detroit and Philadelphia in November 2020, there was some concern that we would be unlikely to detect a statistically significant effect in such a high-salience environment. Timing was also very short, which made the logistics of this PATM round particularly challenging, as did the calendar. The decision to conduct an effort in the city for the runoff was made in early November 2020, just after the general election. Targeted neighborhoods were selected in early December, and by mid-December, even as fundraising to fill the budget continued, partner organizations were selected and PATM leadership began publicizing the effort and the sign-up website. These efforts were complicated by the holiday season (Thanksgiving, Christmas, and New Year's Day). These challenges notwithstanding, box delivery started on Friday, December 18, and four thousand boxes went out to Georgia voters before the runoff.

All eyes of the nation were on Atlanta as we were in the field. Georgia was the focus of intense national attention through December 2020 and in the days leading up to the January 5, 2021, runoff. *The New York Times*

Table 4.5: 2020 Census Demographic Data for Atlanta, Georgia

Race	
White alone	40.4%
Black or African American alone	49.8%
American Indian and Alaska Native alone	0.4%
Asian alone	4.8%
Native Hawaiian and Other Pacific Islander alone	0.0%
Two or more races	3.2%
Hispanic or Latino	4.9%
White alone (not Hispanic or Latino)	38.0%
Income	
Median household income (in 2022 dollars), 2018–2022	$77,655
Per capita income in past twelve months (in 2022 dollars), 2018–2022	$60,778
Persons in poverty	17.7%

Source: "QuickFacts: Atlanta City, Georgia," US Census Bureau, accessed February 3, 2025, https://www.census
.gov/quickfacts.

reported, "The runoff race has made Georgia the epicenter of American politics. President Trump and President-elect Biden have traveled back to the state. Vice President Pence and Vice President-elect Kamala Harris, too. One data-tracking firm puts the amount of money poured into the state by late December at close to $450 million" (Burch 2021). The salience of the runoff elections was also heightened due to continued pushback from Trump about the November 2020 results. His legal and rhetorical efforts to call those results into question, including his lies about the election being stolen in Detroit and Philadelphia, were a backdrop to GOTV efforts in Atlanta. In the end, Georgia voters went to the polls just a day before the violent insurrection of January 6, 2021, when Trump supporters stormed the US Capitol. The nation's focus was not just on Georgia but on Georgia's Black voters. According to 2020 US Census data, the state is 33.0 percent Black. That percentage is 49.8 percent in Atlanta—the largest of any racial group (table 4.5).

Outcomes in the two January 5, 2021, runoff elections were extremely close. Democratic challenger Ossoff ousted Republican incumbent Perdue by a margin of just over 55,000 votes in a race with 4.5 million ballots cast. In Fulton County, where part of Atlanta is located, the margin was much less narrow, with Ossoff winning 71.7 percent of the vote. The second race was a special election to determine whether Loeffler should stay in the seat vacated by Isakson for the term ending in 2022 or be replaced by Democratic challenger Warnock. Warnock won the race by about 93,000 votes, a larger margin than Ossoff's over Perdue but still a narrow victory in a high-profile race. *New York Times* columnist Nate Cohn credited strong Democratic voter turnout, and especially turnout among Black voters, for the two Democratic victories (Cohn 2021), as did political analyst Dave Wasserman, who tweeted in response to Cohn's piece, "Black runoff turnout was phenomenal and the Trump base just couldn't keep up."[1]

The high level of Black voter turnout in January 2021 was widely attributed to the efforts of former gubernatorial candidate Stacey Abrams and her organizations, Fair Fight and Fair Fight Action. Abrams rose to the national stage in 2018 when she unsuccessfully ran against Georgia's then–Secretary of State, Brian Kemp, in an election clouded by claims of voter suppression, as detailed in chapter 1. Abrams was not a newcomer to politics in 2018: She served in the Georgia House of Representatives from 2007 to 2017, including as minority leader from 2011 to 2017. In 2016, she founded the New Georgia Project, which focused on boosting voter registration in the state. After the election, Abrams worked to fight voter suppression, especially in Georgia and Texas, through her organizations. More than eight hundred thousand new voters were registered in the state between November 2018 and November 2020, most of whom were under age thirty and 49 percent of whom were people of color (NPR 2020). Abrams credited that number to the hard work of a consortium of multiple organizations.

Another major player in the state is Black Voters Matter, cofounded in 2016 by LaTosha Brown and Cliff Albright. In the weeks before the January 2021 election, Black Voters Matter conducted a statewide bus tour with their wrapped "We Got the Power" bus, making stops around the state to meet with voters and share information about absentee and early voting. The group also conducted car caravans, set up church booths, conducted door-to-door canvassing, and sent out text message blasts and robocalls. Black Voters Matter also works behind the scenes to boost Black political power, including lobbying for free postage for absentee ballots and filing lawsuits to challenge election administration procedures they claim are discriminatory.

Figure 4.5: The Atlanta 2021 PATM Box Contents

These and other groups were actively mobilizing Black voters in Atlanta long before PATM came to the state in late 2020. Black Girls Vote coordinated with many local organizations to get out the word about the PATM boxes and boost enthusiasm for voting in the runoff election. These multiple efforts to encourage voters to participate meant that many individuals in the PATM RCT who were randomly assigned to control (and did not receive a box) were likely receiving a large volume of messages about the importance of Black turnout in the January 5, 2021, runoff election from multiple organizations.

As in other cities, the contents of the box reflected the city. In addition to a T-shirt, posters, and other educational materials, they included a can of Coke, HotLanta hot sauce, RAP Snacks chips, a branded face mask from the Atlanta United FC soccer team, hand sanitizer, peach-shaped chocolate, saltwater taffy, balloons, and a coloring book and crayons (figure 4.5).

Mirroring efforts in other cities, the roadshow in Atlanta publicized the sign-up website and collected information from voters hoping to receive a box. Some sign-ups and box distributions were also conducted on the ground, an option made necessary by the short time frame in which the project was conducted. PATM partnered with local organizations in Atlanta to give local credibility to the effort and to ensure that large numbers of eligible voters heard about the program and went to the PATM website to request a box. The leading local partner was CivicGeorgia, an advocacy organization working to increase civic engagement in the state since 2017. Speaking to local media in the run-up to the January election, CivicGeorgia founder Kevin Shanker Sinha noted that the group was proud to partner with Black Girls Vote for the PATM effort: "Party at the Mailbox is a creative, fun, and safe way to get people motivated to vote. We are proud to be part of the movement of Georgia GOTV organizers showing the world what happens when we strategize and mobilize" (Thomas 2020).[2]

In total, we received 4,667 entries on our PATM box interest list. After we cleaned the lists, removing people who were deemed ineligible (e.g., people who lived outside Atlanta, who already received a box through a nonrandomized event like a church-based giveaway, or who got an unrandomized VIP box used to promote the event) and removing all but one person per household, we matched the voters to the voter file. This left us with a pool of 1,198 hosts and 2,535 guests. Volunteers kept lists of which addresses received a box, but unfortunately some paper records of sign-ups and deliveries were accidentally discarded by local organizers before they could be shared with the research team. This means that we have incomplete information about who signed up to receive a box and who received one at an in-person event (there were promotional events held throughout the city where people received an unrandomized box, and in the cleaning process we would remove these people from the analysis and also ensure that their household didn't receive another box). Without reliable records about box sign-ups and distribution, we cannot conduct a robust RCT analysis. However, we have some information: thousands of individuals signed up to receive a box via the online PATM form, and for those individuals, we know whether they were randomly assigned to the treatment or control group. We used that list to recruit participants for our postelection survey, interviews, and focus groups, which we used to gather insights into how the program was received in the local community.

Our initial protocol called for qualitative data after the election to be collected from individuals who signed up to receive a box. We followed this plan for the November 2020 elections in Baltimore, Detroit, and Philadelphia. Recall that our pilot results found that the effect of PATM was centered on party guests—not the individuals who signed up to receive a box but low-propensity members of their households. After the November 2020 results in Baltimore confirmed the pilot findings, we altered our postelection process to also gather survey and qualitative data from those household members. When email messages were sent in January 2021 to individuals in Atlanta who requested a box to ask if they wanted to complete the survey or join a focus group, we asked them to share the invitation with other members of their households who were also registered voters. Thus, our Atlanta analysis allows us to dig deeper into how the program was perceived by those household members and how it affected their attitudes and reported behavior.

Overall, we collected 596 surveys (513 hosts and 83 guests) between January 19 and February 8, 2021; half of the participants were from households randomly assigned to receive a box (treatment group), and the other half were from households that were not (control group). Respondent age ranged from 18 to 79 (mean = 37.6); most respondents (84.8 percent) identified as female, 14.6 percent as male, 0.2 percent as nonbinary, and 0.2 percent as transgender female. Most (86.5 percent) identified as Black or as multiple races including Black; another 9 percent identified as white, non-Latino; the remaining respondents identified as Asian only, Latino only, Middle Eastern or Arab, mixed race not including Black, or other. Of those providing partisan identification, most (86 percent) identified as Democrats (including leaners).

None of the participants from the control group should have received a box, but about 9 percent of our control group survey respondents reported receiving one. Similarly, 34 percent of those who were assigned to receive a box said that they did not. This illustrates how unreliable an RCT analysis would be, given our lack of information from the ground. At the same time, we still can glean insights about PATM from self-reports in the survey data. Black Atlantans who reported that they received the treatment reported stronger feelings of political identification with their city ($p = 0.01$), as voters ($p < 0.05$), and as Americans ($p < 0.05$), as shown in table 4.6. Guests across each

Table 4.6: Identity Strength, PATM, 2021 Atlanta Survey: Black Sample

	Control group average	Treatment group average	Difference
Identity as an Atlantan			
Everyone	2.00	2.20	0.20*
Hosts	2.14	2.18	0.04
Guests	1.32	2.31	0.99*
Identity as an American			
Everyone	2.12	2.41	0.29*
Hosts	2.14	2.39	0.25*
Guests	2.00	2.59	0.59*
Identity as a voter			
Everyone	2.53	2.76	0.23*
Hosts	2.63	2.77	0.14*
Guests	2.00	2.68	0.68*
Agree that the government in Atlanta cares what people like me think			
Everyone	0.60	0.64	0.04
Hosts	0.62	0.64	0.02
Guests	0.48	0.63	0.15*
Agree that people like me have a say in what the federal government does			
Everyone	0.68	0.73	0.04*
Hosts	0.70	0.74	0.04
Guests	0.59	0.64	0.05
Agree that the government in Washington cares what people like me think			
Everyone	0.44	0.47	0.03
Hosts	0.45	0.47	0.02
Guests	0.41	0.42	0.01

Notes: Identity survey items are coded 0 (not at all) to 3 (extremely well). Efficacy items are coded on a scale from 0 to 1, with higher scores indicating higher levels of political efficacy. Differences noted with an asterisk are statistically significant. Data was collected January 19–February 8, 2021. Results for the full sample can be found in appendix table A9.

identity measure reacted more strongly than hosts. The difference in treatment effects between host (0.99 points) and guest (0.04) status is 0.95 points ($p = 0.00$) in identity as an Atlantan. That is, that the treatment increased identification as an Atlantan 0.95 points more among guests compared to hosts. Similarly, the effect among guests on identity as a voter and identity as an American is 0.54 points greater ($p < 0.05$), and 0.34 points greater ($p = 0.04$) than the effect among hosts. Treated participants also reported stronger feelings of political efficacy, a finding we saw earlier in the Baltimore pilot survey data, although not consistently across all levels of government or across both hosts and guests, and of relatively modest effect sizes. This suggests that the effect of PATM on turnout is not due to increased feelings of political efficacy but instead that the mechanism is likely the primed feelings of community. Individuals whose households received a box were more likely to feel like members of their communities, and as voters; they then were more likely to vote as expressions of those identities.

Generally, it is challenging to document effective GOTV efforts in a presidential election. The two successful PATM efforts in Baltimore, including the pilot and the more considerable November 2020 effort, constitute significant evidence that the method increases voter turnout in lower- and medium-salience elections. At the same time, the null RCT results in Detroit and Philadelphia indicate that it may not work as well in very high-salience elections or that the model may need to be changed to be effective in high-salience contexts. Previous GOTV RCTs targeting majority-Black communities in a presidential election, November 2008, also did not find effects on turnout (García Bedolla and Michelson 2012).

At the same time, that we cannot document shifts in voter turnout in these two instances is not necessarily incompatible with the idea that the project worked to influence hearts and minds in those cities, especially given the later successful PATM efforts in Detroit and Philadelphia in subsequent elections. We used interviews with voters and organizational leaders and focus group discussions to explore how the project was received and remembered by members of the treatment and control groups in each city. These data help pinpoint the aspects of the program that resonated with voters and are likely to be essential to successful future PATM efforts.

Conclusion

After the very successful pilot, interest in and visibility of PATM surged. Funders were more likely to want to support the effort, but also persistently nudged Robinson to find ways to bring down the estimated cost per vote. As noted earlier, the initial cost-per-vote estimates were relatively high, reflecting the cost not just of materials and delivery but also of labor and investments in community partners. Building the PATM program from the ground up in roadshow cities, and generating partnerships with local community organizations, was time consuming. The vast majority of this labor was performed by women and people of color. (We invite readers to review the lists of individuals thanked in our acknowledgments section for some insight into the large number of people who made PATM possible.) Regardless, funders and potential funders were skeptical of these high costs, while also excited about the possibility of using PATM to influence high-salience elections in Detroit, Philadelphia, and Atlanta. While most GOTV efforts tend to be more effective in lower-salience elections, funders were less interested in supporting efforts in cities that were not the sites of high-salience contests deciding partisan control of major political institutions. We generated a healthy increase of 5.3 percentage points among household members of box recipients in Baltimore, where the November 2020 election was a lower-salience event compared with the battlegrounds of Detroit and Philadelphia, and we did not replicate our results in those two cities. Similarly, we could not replicate our results in Atlanta in January 2021, partly because of the loss of data by local organizers.

While we did not generate measurable effects from the PATM efforts in these high-salience elections, that does not mean that PATM didn't help push some voters over the cusp from abstaining to participating. There is simply too much background noise in these contests—mailers, television and radio advertisements, social media posts, and in-person events—that muddies the different levels of mobilization delivered to individuals assigned to our treatment and control groups (e.g., Malhotra et al. 2011; Gerber et al. 2017; Bergh and Christensen 2022; Green and Gerber 2024; Mann and Haenschen 2024). Theoretically, PATM was part of that noise and helped some individuals decide to vote; our lack of statistically significant results reflects the reality that we can't isolate those effects from the overall noisy GOTV environment. Moving forward, larger-scale efforts reaching more voters and including reinforcing messages may generate measurable results regardless of election salience. For example, recipients of PATM boxes might later receive postcards reminding them about the upcoming election, or recipients might be incentivized to join online or offline conversations or events designed to further emphasize the theme of community celebration. In an election where much of the messaging to communities of color, and to Black communities in particular, was about how four more years of Donald Trump would do further harm to those communities, our message about celebration and Black joy may have moved some individuals to vote who needed something positive to vote for.

We do not mean to suggest that only battleground federal elections are important contexts for voter mobilization. Many important campaigns occur at the local and state levels, and in contests with far less GOTV activity. We expect that cultivating celebrations of community in these sorts of elections, where an even stronger link could be made between participating and the effect on one's neighborhood, should be very effective. Just as campaign contributions can make a larger impact in a smaller race, so too should a PATM-themed effort have a larger impact in a race where that invitation to vote is the only one, or one of very few, that a low-propensity voter receives.

In subsequent elections, we shifted strategies to test whether we could generate significant effects with a streamlined process and smaller package. This began with a pilot effort using a skinny sleeve in addition to our classic box, at a lower cost point per package, and delivering packages via the US Postal Service rather than using the PATM van. Our first effort using this strategy was in Richmond, Virginia, for the 2021 gubernatorial election. While the skinny sleeve increased turnout slightly, the classic box appeared to have no effect. These results raised more questions than they answered, leading to additional tests of the skinny sleeve in Atlanta and Detroit for the November 2022 midterm elections, and in Philadelphia for the November 2024 presidential election. We also explored different methods of choosing participants, moving from a sign-up model to one using randomized selection from voter files. We turn to details of those efforts, and what the results tell us about the Voter Community Celebration Model, in chapter 5.

5

Skinny Sleeves

The Party at the Mailbox (PATM) packages were enormously popular with recipients. Social media posts and feedback we collected in our interviews and focus groups made this very clear. Recipients used the posters and balloons to decorate their front doors, mailboxes, and cars. They wore their T-shirts in social media posts and around their communities, including when they went to the polls to vote. They shared the coloring books and crayons with their younger household members (and used those items to start conversations with their children about voting, as we detail in chapter 6). The local snacks—Berger Cookies in Baltimore, Tastykakes in Philadelphia—emphasized the local nature of the PATM project. The boxes were, as advertised, a party in a box, and participants in each city used those contents to celebrate.

At the same time, assembling and delivering the boxes was logistically challenging, especially as the project grew in size and in geographic scope. Some items were donated, such as the Under Armour face masks, while other items had to be purchased. Vendors had to be paid to design the local T-shirts and signs, and to assemble and deliver the boxes. This precluded the project from enjoying any meaningful degree of economies of scale. In other words, as the project grew, the price per box remained relatively stable and relatively high in terms of cost per vote. While PATM's financial supporters were excited about the positive results in terms of increasing turnout, they were less enthusiastic about the cost-per-vote estimates and encouraged PATM to find ways to reduce those costs. Internally, PATM leaders hoped to find a way to take the program to more cities in future elections, which meant they needed to find a way to reduce the logistical challenges of box assembly, delivery, and the collection of names and contact information from potential participants (party hosts).

Innovations to the program in November 2021 and November 2022 addressed these concerns. First, PATM moved away from the strategy of signing up hosts; instead, potential participants would be chosen randomly from lists of registered voters. Second, PATM shifted away from face-to-face deliveries with the wrapped van. While this was a fun part of the process, and one we heard very positive feedback about from our interview and focus group participants, it was also logistically challenging, especially in cities with larger geographic footprints (e.g., the Atlanta metropolitan area). Instead, packages would be delivered via the US Postal Service. Finally, PATM shrunk the box, from the original (*classic*) box to a *skinny sleeve*: a smaller number of items packaged in a padded envelope rather than in a cardboard box. This reduced the cost per package, and postage costs for the skinny sleeves were lower than for the classic boxes. The skinny sleeve was piloted in Richmond, Virginia, for the November 2021 gubernatorial election. We conducted a follow-up project in three cities from the roadshow: Detroit and Atlanta in 2022 and Philadelphia in 2024.

Richmond

The city of Richmond has long been a focal point of Black political organizing and behavior. Black communities here date back to the antebellum period when enslaved Black people living in accommodations at tobacco factories—and away from their owners—formed close ties that survived the Civil War and Jim Crow segregation (Hayter 2017). In 1871, Richmond's Jackson Ward was created to concentrate Black political power, one of the first Black urban districts in the United States. This neighborhood in the northern part of downtown Richmond was once known as the Harlem of the South, and as the birthplace of Black entrepreneurship. In 1978, it was registered as a National Historic Landmark District (Feliciano and Kargbo 2021).

One notable early example of a Black community organization active in the city is the Richmond Crusade for Voters, founded in 1956 in the wake of the US Supreme Court's historic *Brown v. Board of Education* decision ending segregation in public accommodations, and the subsequent resistance of white residents in Richmond to desegregate public schools. As detailed by Julian Maxwell Hayter in *The Dream Is Lost: Voting Rights and the Politics of Race in Richmond, Virginia*, the Crusade paid the poll taxes for Black voters, empowering the Black community to gain seats, and political power, in the city. Hayter notes, "The Crusade's struggle for political power would not have been possible without the organizational and political will of Richmond's black women. . . . The Crusade's first meetings took place in Ethel T. Overby's home, and by the late 1950s Overby and the Crusade transformed people's homes into a type of cottage industry for voter mobilization activity. . . . Black women held positions of *actual* influence within the Crusade, helped transition from protest to politics, and led the way into elected office" (2017, 8; italics in original). PATM in Richmond thus follows a long tradition in the city of Black women leading the fight for civic engagement and political power.

Building on the rich history of Black political organizing in Richmond, the 1965 Voting Rights Act (VRA) played a crucial role in further empowering the Black community and transforming the political landscape on a national scale. The VRA is one of several landmark pieces of legislation passed in the mid- to late 1960s as a culmination of the civil rights movement. The VRA's two key provisions are in section 2 and section 5. Section 2 restates the Fifteenth Amendment and affirms the right of Black citizens to vote; it curtails the use of poll taxes and other barriers to voting participation in Black communities. Section 5 includes preclearance requirements for states and counties with histories of disenfranchisement, requiring any changes to voting procedures to be precleared by the Department of Justice. Virginia was one of five full states included in the original law as passed in 1965, a sign of the history of depressed Black participation in the state.

In 1969, white residents in Richmond moved to dilute Black political power by annexing parts of nearby Chesterfield County, an affluent white suburb next to Richmond. The fight against this dilution of Black political power went all the way to the US Supreme Court, where local activist Curtis Holt Sr. failed in his effort to undo the annexation but won a ruling that at-large elections were unconstitutionally diluting Black political power. The legal costs for Holt's case were paid by white residents of the annexed area who feared that integration would mean Black students in attendance at their schools (Hayter 2017, 129).

In *City of Richmond v. United States* (1975), the court noted that "the predominant (if not sole) motive and desire" of the annexation plan "was to acquire 44,000 additional white citizens for Richmond in order to avert a transfer of political control to what was fast becoming a black-population majority" (quoted in Hayter 2017, 146–147). Two years later, in 1977, the new district election system led to the first Black-majority city council in the city's history as well as the city's first Black mayor, Henry Marsh (Hayter 2017, 148). In 1989, Virginians elected Doug Wilder, the first time a Black American was elected governor of a state. In a special election in February 2023, Richmond voters elected Democrat Jennifer McClellan to a seat in the US House of Representatives, the first Black woman elected to Congress from Virginia.

Wilder's election notwithstanding, the state has a long history of resistance to the VRA and protection of minority voting rights. As Anita Earls and colleagues note, "In fact, Virginia's record of legislative redistricting was one of the primary reasons cited for the need to extend the VRA in 1982" (2008, 767). It used redistricting processes and rules about voting procedures, election schedules, and the structure of elected bodies to depress Black electoral power and representation (Earls et al. 2008). For decades, these policies and procedures were consistently challenged by Black citizens and organizations, often successfully.

Decisions by the US Supreme Court in 2013 (*Shelby County v. Holder*) and 2021 (*Brnovich v. Democratic National Committee*) eliminated many of the VRA protections that generated these successful legal decisions. In *Shelby County v. Holder*, the court ruled that the coverage formula used to determine which geographic areas were subject to section 5 preclearance was unconstitutional. In its decision in *Brnovich v. Democratic National Committee*, the court reduced the ability for plaintiffs to sue using section 2, ruling that voting rules that impose burdens on voters that result in racial disparities in how difficult it is for citizens to vote, but that were not enacted with discriminatory intent, are not violations of the VRA.

In 2021, Virginia lawmakers approved the Voting Rights Act of Virginia, which was modeled after the VRA and reinstated many of the protections of the federal VRA that had been weakened by the Supreme Court (McClellan 2023). At the time, Democrats controlled all three branches of the state government. Lawmakers also repealed the state's photo ID law and loosened restrictions on ballot drop-off boxes and absentee voting. After Republicans won the governorship and control of the House of Delegates in 2021, they moved to roll back these expansions on convenience voting, but those efforts were blocked by the Democrat-controlled state senate. Virginia remains one of four states where the constitution permanently disenfranchises citizens with felony convictions, a policy that blocks many Black citizens from access to the ballot. In 2021 Democrat Governor Ralph Northam signed an executive order automatically restoring voting rights to tens of thousands of felons who were no longer incarcerated. These changes to voting laws took effect the same year that PATM went to Virginia. In 2022, new Republican Governor Glenn Youngkin rescinded Northam's executive order.

In addition to this legal context, our PATM effort in Richmond took place during a high-salience electoral context: the gubernatorial election between Democrat Terry McAuliffe and Republican Glenn Youngkin. Ralph Northam, the Democratic incumbent, was unable to seek reelection, as the Virginia constitution prohibits governors from holding office for two consecutive terms. As is generally true in US politics, the race was more competitive than would have been the case if an incumbent were running for reelection. In addition, coming on the heels of the 2020 presidential race, the 2021 gubernatorial contest in Virginia was a high-salience election because it was seen as a potential indicator of broader national trends, such as whether Republicans could rebound after Donald Trump's failure to win a second term in office.

Trump rallied for Youngkin, calling him a "fantastic guy" and claiming that without a Republican in power, the Democrats would destroy the suburbs. Harking back to the fears around integration in Richmond stoked by Holt in 1969, Trump made the link between the election and the impact on local schools: "If you vote to keep the radical Democrat machine in power, they'll totally ruin that very special place where you live and they'll wreck the schools" (Elwood 2021). Reflecting the high salience of the race, turnout in the election was far higher than in previous gubernatorial elections, with a 15 percentage-point increase in the percentage of registered voters who cast ballots (from 40 percent to 55 percent), the highest rate of turnout in decades. Youngkin won by a narrow margin of 50.58 percent to 48.64 percent.

For this round, PATM piloted two innovations. One was to use public lists of registered voters to randomly choose who would receive a box rather than compiling lists of interested voters via an online form. We selected Richmond ZIP codes where the population was at least 60 percent

Black according to the 2019 five-year American Community Survey. We then limited our list of registered voters to Black women with a high propensity to vote (based on their voter history) and between one and four other registered voters living in their households. These selection criteria were based on results from earlier iterations of the PATM project, as described in chapters 3 and 4, where we found that the boxes had the largest effect on low-propensity guests (household members) who lived with a high-propensity host (box recipient). We expected that sending sleeves to higher-propensity women would lead to spillover effects among their lower-propensity household members. After this list of potential participants was identified, we randomly selected some of those individuals to receive a box or sleeve, while randomly assigning others to the control group. As with the classic PATM boxes, we then tracked participation in the election by box recipients (addressees) and their household members, comparing them with potential recipients who had not been selected and their household members.

This change in how participants were selected dramatically reduced the cost of the project, particularly in terms of staffing time to promote the sign-up form and screen submissions. At the same time, we were less successful in postelection attempts to recruit interview and focus group participants because registered voters had not opted in by providing us with their contact information. Thus, our evaluation is limited to the RCT and does not include the rich qualitative data from the previous PATM activations.

A second set of innovations was meant to lower the cost per vote of the project. This included testing smaller packages and changing the delivery method. Voters randomly assigned to the treatment group were further randomly divided to receive either the classic box of informational materials and celebratory materials, or a smaller package in a large, padded envelope (what we called the skinny sleeve). This reduced the cost per package from twenty-seven dollars per box for the classic box to thirteen dollars for the skinny sleeve. The skinny sleeves included a T-shirt, a button, two pieces of taffy, stickers, a temporary tattoo, three signs, and a poster—far fewer items, but with a similar mix of celebratory and informational items (figure 5.1). The delivery method also differed in Richmond: Packages were delivered via the US Postal Service instead of via the PATM van. This also reduced costs significantly, and more so for

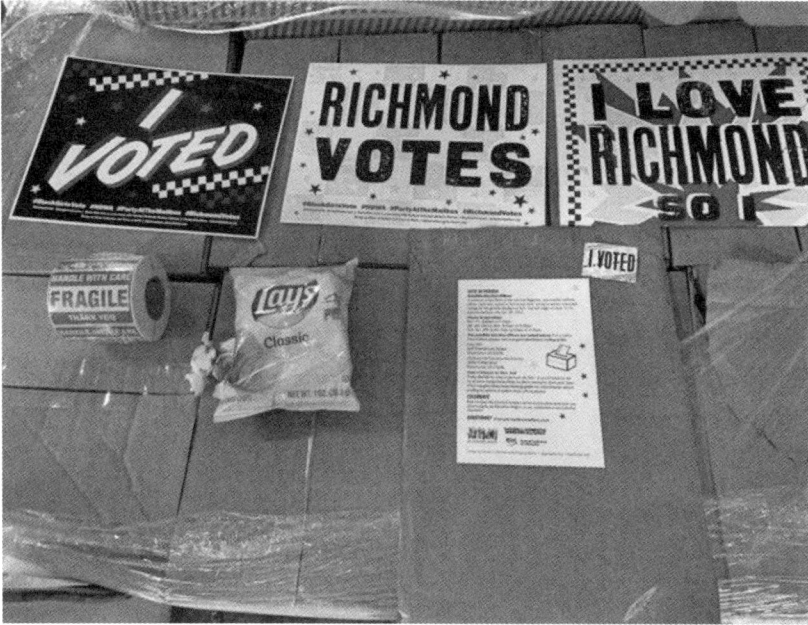

Figure 5.1: The Skinny Sleeve

the skinny sleeves, which required less postage. Because the boxes and sleeves were unsolicited, we added a sticker with a QR code to the outside packaging, allowing recipients to learn more about PATM before opening the package. The sticker read, "Let's celebrate democracy together, Richmond! This box was sent on behalf of Black Girls Vote and the National Domestic Workers Alliance. We thank you for being a registered voter! Enjoy what's inside, post the fun on social media, and share with your family, friends, and neighbors!"

Receiving an unexpected package in the mail is very different from receiving one you hoped to receive by filling out an online form. In previous rounds, individuals became interested in PATM after hearing about it from friends, social media, or local political news coverage. They signed up for the program because they wanted to get a box, but even if one never arrived (if they were randomly assigned to the control group), they knew about the program and, as indicated by our qualitative data, were excited to be part of something going on in their local community. If a box did arrive, it was a happy occasion that led to online unboxing videos and sharing with household members and on social media. In contrast, registered voters in Richmond who received a box may not have known about the program before the delivery. Perhaps they scanned the QR code or searched for online information about PATM after receiving it (forty-nine unique visitors scanned the QR code) and then felt like they were part of a community or a larger group, but as noted earlier, we do not have qualitative data that would allow us to test for that. If individuals in Richmond did not receive a box (if they were randomly assigned to the control group), they may never have heard of PATM at all.

Results in Baltimore (see chapter 3) found no effect on turnout by hosts, but we hypothesized that in Richmond there might be a small effect among party hosts (i.e., those who received a box addressed to them) because it was a personalized get-out-the-vote message. We hypothesized that recipients would feel thanked for their previous turnout behavior, and that the packages would cue their identities as voters and as members of the Richmond community. At the same time, we expected smaller effect sizes overall compared with those generated in Baltimore because the program was shallower: The boxes were not accompanied by significant media coverage or visible community participation. Without the publicity arranged in previous PATM rounds to generate sign-ups, or the partnerships with local groups, there was little sense that this was something that Black people in Richmond were doing together as a community. Fewer people knew about the program, and the excitement that was built around the deliveries in Baltimore did not happen in Richmond. This also meant that we did not expect spillover effects into the community or members of our control group, as those individuals likely would have little to no knowledge that packages were being delivered.

Of 6,634 total hosts randomly pulled from the voter file, two-thirds ($n = 4,489$) were randomly assigned to the control condition, while the remaining third was split randomly into two treatment conditions: classic box ($n = 1,076$) and skinny sleeve ($n = 1,069$). The classic box was very similar to the boxes used in previous PATM rounds but was delivered by the US Postal Service rather than via an in-person delivery from PATM program members. The skinny sleeve was smaller, likely delivered into mailboxes and mail slots rather than left on doorsteps, and also delivered via the Postal Service. We consider "hosts" those we addressed

Table 5.1: PATM: Richmond, November 2022 RCT

	Hosts (recipients)	Guests (household members)
Control group turnout	81.4% (3,656/4,489)	49.4% (3,619/7,322)
Sleeve group turnout	83.3% (890/1,069)	48.5% (859/1,771)
Sleeve vs. control	1.81 percentage points ($p = 0.07$)	−0.92 percentage points ($p = 0.75$)
Box group turnout	80.8% (869/1,076)	46.8% (830/1,774)
Box vs. control	−0.68 percentage points ($p = 0.69$)	−2.63 percentage points ($p = 0.97$)
Sleeve vs. box	2.49 percentage points ($p = 0.13$)	1.71 percentage points ($p = 0.30$)
Treatment (sleeve or box) vs. control	0.56 percentage points ($p = 0.29$)	−1.78 percentage points ($p = 0.96$)

Notes: Our hypotheses for PATM projects are directional, and we typically use one-tailed tests of statistical significance. One exception to this rule is the "sleeve vs. box" comparison in this table, where we test for differences between treatments. This p value is two-tailed.

the materials to, and "guests" others in their households, although we cannot be certain whether the packages were received or opened by their intended recipients or by other household members (or, indeed, if they were swiped by porch bandits, a possibility we return to later).

As shown in table 5.1, the skinny sleeve outperformed the classic box but only affected hosts. Hosts who received a sleeve were 1.81 percentage points more likely to turn out compared with hosts in the control group; this difference is marginally statistically significant. Hosts who received a sleeve were 2.49 percentage points more likely to vote compared with hosts who received a box; this difference is not statistically significant. Among guests, effect estimates are null. Sending sleeves to high-propensity Black women in Richmond increased their turnout slightly, but there is no effect on household members as observed in previous PATM rounds. In Baltimore, statistically significant effects were isolated to party guests (household members who did not personally request a box), with negligible effects on party hosts (individuals who requested a box; see chapter 3). We concluded that receiving a box had no marginal effect on hosts beyond any background boosts to turnout that might have resulted from the feeling of belonging to the effort via signing up for the program or knowing about PATM more generally, sentiments that were shared in the qualitative data.

Results from the Richmond effort thus complicated our findings and theory in several ways. One possibility is that the random deliveries isolate the community-building effect. Black women received an unexpected package and, if they opened it, learned about a community celebration of voting and of Black women as powerful participants in US elections. This boosted their turnout even above the already very high participation rate (81.4 percent) of those who did not receive a package. However, this theory does not explain why only the skinny sleeve was effective, while the classic box was not. Returning to the point noted earlier, it may be that the classic box was more likely to fall victim to porch bandits given that it may not have always been delivered inside a mailbox. It is also possible that recipients were more suspicious of an unexpected box and received but did not open these unsolicited packages. In an August 2022 *Slate* interview, Black Voters Matter cofounder LaTosha Brown noted that some people hostile to the work she was doing to mobilize Black voters harassed her by sending unmarked boxes from Russia to her house (J. Johnson 2021). A second possibility is less encouraging: The statistically significant effect of 1.81 percentage points is only due to chance, and the skinny sleeve cannot reliably boost turnout among recipients. Without qualitative data or tracking data for the box and sleeve deliveries, we are unable to explore further or dismiss these competing post hoc explanations. As noted later in this chapter, our replications in 2022 in Detroit and Atlanta, and in 2024 in Philadelphia, helped refine our understanding of when and how the skinny sleeve PATM model can increase participation.

As we looked to further explore the power of the skinny sleeve, we considered ways to strengthen its effectiveness. One insight from earlier iterations of the PATM project, especially the Baltimore pilot, was that the geographic density of the project meant that all members of the community, not just individuals randomly assigned to the treatment group, saw the PATM posters, balloons, and T-shirts all around them. We observed the impact that seeing PATM materials in the neighborhood had on community members (even those who did not receive a box) in Baltimore. Moving forward, we sought to reproduce this experience by ensuring that targeted neighborhoods received the treatment in a more concentrated way. We increased the density of the project in 2022 in two ways: by randomizing assignment to treatment and control by precinct, rather than at the household level, and by centering the project on a well-publicized in-person voting festival held in each of the two cities. Both treatment and control precincts were equally distributed around each festival, meaning that the festival itself was not randomly assigned to one group or the other. This design does not allow us to test the impact of the festival itself (but see chapter 1 for a review of these kinds of festivals and their impacts on voting). Instead, we hoped that these festivals might boost the impact of receiving PATM materials.

The two panels of figure 5.2 show the maps of both locations. Treated households are marked with triangles while control households are marked with circles. The address in the middle of each panel is the location of the polling place party or festival. The clumped pattern reflects the fact that households were randomized at the precinct level. The effort in Richmond was much more spread out geographically. It was also randomized at the household level. In Richmond, it was possible that neighbors on the same street could be assigned to any condition (i.e., box, sleeve, or control), whereas in Atlanta or Detroit we worked to replicate the neighborhood atmosphere created in earlier PATMs in Baltimore by clustering our assignment to treatment or control by precinct. We also limited the geographic scope of the projects to much smaller areas: The farthest two households in Detroit were 3.12 miles apart, and the farthest two households in Atlanta were 2.58 miles apart—both much smaller geographic areas than in Richmond, where the farthest two households were 9.35 miles apart. This means that the efforts were far more concentrated in Atlanta and Detroit compared with Richmond. Additionally, no party was involved in the Richmond efforts.

Detroit and Atlanta, November 2022

Following up on the Richmond results, we conducted a test for the midterm November 2022 elections using only skinny sleeves randomly sent to high-propensity Black women voters—a similar type of pool to that used in Richmond. One key difference is the focus on two pre–Election Day voting parties at local polling places: the Votelanta Music Festival at Dome in Atlanta and the Detroit Votes Concert at the Northwest

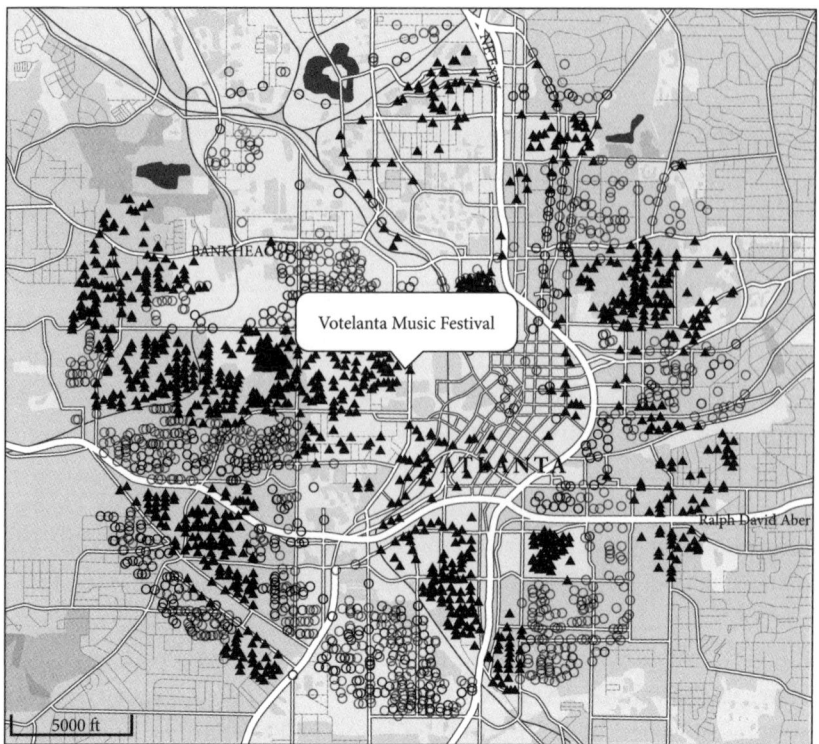

Figure 5.2: Maps of Treatment and Control Groups Around the Voting Festival
Locations (Top Panel: Atlanta; Bottom Panel: Detroit)

Notes: Maps (Atlanta and Detroit) show treatment households as triangles and control
households as circles. In the middle of each panel is the location of the polling place
party or festival.

Activities Center in Detroit. Both events were designed to promote voting and to be festive, including music and free food. As detailed later in this section, the two programs differed from each other in terms of headliners, funding, scale, and location.

Aiming to deliver about 4,000 skinny sleeves in each city, we limited our RCT to areas immediately surrounding those parties within the smallest geographic circle possible that would accommodate an RCT with that many packages. In other words, the geographic areas for the RCTs around each party were determined by how small of a circle we could draw around each venue that contained a pool of about 8,000 households. In Atlanta, we selected all active (in the voter file), high-propensity Black women within a circle 2.58 miles in diameter. The pool included 8,006 hosts and 6,161 guests (registered household members). In Detroit, the pool was within a circle 3.12 miles in diameter and included 7,832 hosts and 7,771 guests (see figure 5.2). We conducted identical efforts in both cities. Targeting these cities in 2022 meant we were returning to cities from earlier PATM projects: Detroit in November 2020 and Atlanta in January 2021 (see chapter 4). Those earlier efforts had generated null RCT results, but we hypothesized that returning to the cities for a subsequent election would generate stronger results due to the increased familiarity (brand recognition) that PATM would now enjoy. We used skinny sleeves instead of classic boxes, reflecting the ongoing desire to reduce the cost of the program and also the encouraging results from the skinny sleeve in Richmond in November 2021. While the midterm elections were high-salience elections in many cities, including Atlanta, the election in Detroit was expected to be a much lower-salience race, allowing for us to further explore the degree to which PATM works in different electoral contexts.

Detroit

Conditions in Detroit in November 2022 were ideal for a PATM RCT given the low level of competitiveness for the races at the top of the ticket: the Twelfth and Thirteenth Congressional Districts. Both safely Democratic seats, the Twelfth was and is held by Rashida Tlaib; the Thirteenth was an open seat but safely Democratic, and the likely winner was Democratic nominee Shri Thanedar. Turnout was expected to be slightly lower than usual due to the lack of a Black candidate for either seat (Tlaib is Palestinian American and Thanedar is Indian American). Thus, while Detroit has the largest Black majority of any major city in the US, at 77.1 percent according to 2020 US Census data, it was expected to not have a Black representative in Congress for the first time since 1955 (Spangler and Hendrickson 2022). Also on the ballot in November 2022 was the gubernatorial race between incumbent Democrat Gretchen Whitmer and Republican nominee Tudor Dixon, who was endorsed by former President Donald Trump. In the months before Election Day, Whitmer was widely expected to easily win reelection; political forecasters such as FiveThirtyEight rated the race safely Democratic. Michigan did not have a US Senate race in 2022. Overall, the election was expected to be relatively low salience, with Democratic incumbents and nominees likely to win and no Black candidates in high-profile races that might boost Black voter turnout. Turnout for the November 2022 election was 34 percent, a decrease from the 41 percent in the previous gubernatorial election four years earlier.

In contrast with the challenges faced in Detroit for the 2020 activation of PATM, the 2022 round proceeded smoothly. In 2020, box delivery coincided with a spike in the COVID-19 pandemic, which raised the specter of a citywide shutdown that would have precluded further deliveries, and sign-ups were relatively sluggish until some last-minute earned media drove traffic to the PATM website (see chapter 4). In contrast, in November 2022 no such logistical challenges were present.

Atlanta

The election in Atlanta in November 2022 was again (as in January 2021) one of extremely high salience. At the top of the ballot was the US Senate race between two high-profile Black candidates: incumbent Raphael Warnock, who first won the seat in the runoff election of January 5, 2021, and Herschel Walker, a well-known former football player endorsed by Trump. The Warnock–Walker race was that election's second most expensive contest in the country (topped only by the Pennsylvania race for US Senate between Republican Mehmet Oz and Democrat John Fetterman), with much of the spending coming from outside the state. Also as in 2021, partisan control of the US Senate was at stake. Pundits predicted that Republicans were likely to pick up at least one seat and regain the majority. In addition, both political parties saw winning the Georgia Senate seat as an important measure of their national strength, given the closeness of races there in 2020 and 2021. Georgia voters in November 2022 also saw a rematch between Republican Governor Brian Kemp and Democrat Stacey Abrams, whom Kemp narrowly beat in 2018 in a race marked by charges of voter suppression, particularly of Black voters (see chapter 1).

Over 2.5 million Georgia voters cast their ballots before Election Day, an indication of the salience of the race. On this point, Georgia's Secretary of State Brad Raffensperger (2022) said in a press release, "Georgia voters came out in near Presidential-level numbers. . . . County election directors handled that demand with the utmost professionalism. They navigated a whole host of challenges and executed seamlessly. They deserve our highest praise." Overall, turnout in the November 2022 election in Atlanta was very high. The city occupies two counties in Georgia where overall turnout was 57.19 percent (55.99 percent in Fulton County and 58.97 percent in DeKalb County).

PATM 2022

The efforts in both Detroit and Atlanta were centered on getting people out to vote, specifically getting people out to vote early. For Atlanta, the party that served as the focus was the Votelanta Music Festival (figure 5.3), and for Detroit, it was a Detroit Votes Concert with food and local musicians (figure 5.4). Both locations also served as early-voting polling places, but because of the timing of the events (the Atlanta event started at six o'clock in the evening, while the Detroit event started earlier, at three in the afternoon), only voters in Detroit could choose to vote early while attending the event.

The Votelanta Music Festival was organized by the People's Uprising—a fairly new nonprofit group in Atlanta with roots in the 2020 aftermath of the death of George Floyd. This event had headliners like Gucci Mane and Omeretta the Great, both of whom have national profiles but have roots in Atlanta. Gucci Mane is one of the pioneers of trap music, a subgenre of rap music that takes its name from local Atlanta slang. In 2016, *The New Yorker* called Gucci Mane "one of the greatest rappers

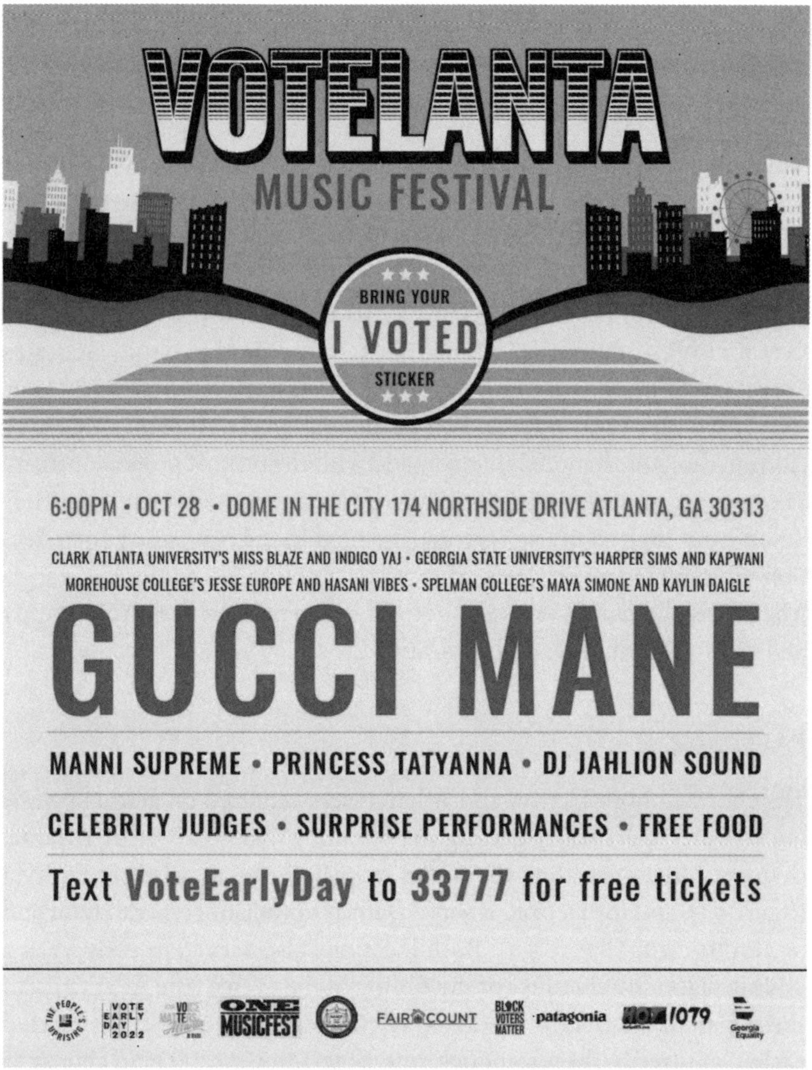

Figure 5.3: Votelanta Music Festival Flyer

Atlanta has ever produced" (Sanneh 2016). Rapper Omeretta the Great, born and raised in Atlanta, came to national prominence after appearing on *Love & Hip-Hop Atlanta* and after her song "Sorry Not Sorry," about what parts of Atlanta are the "real" Atlanta, went viral (Reyes 2022). The Atlanta festival had over four times the budget of the Detroit efforts and was held in a much larger venue. The free music festival was put on by the

Figure 5.4: Detroit Votes Concert Flyer

People's Uprising, ONE Musicfest, and Vote Early Day. Other local partners helped fund the event, including Atlanta Votes!, Equality Foundation of Georgia, the Atlanta NAACP, Pro Georgia, Patagonia, Fair Count, Black Voters Matter, Hot 107.9, Pizza to the Polls, and Well-Dunn. Students from local colleges and universities performed at the event for a chance to win an exclusive session with a major music label (Kyles 2022).

In contrast, the Detroit Votes Concert had a more local feel and was situated at a polling location in the heart of Detroit's Black community (see figure 5.2). All of the performers were local acts, including the Detroit Youth Choir and local high school bands. The efforts were headed by the Human Fliers, Detroit Votes, and students from Detroit Public Schools. The Human Fliers is a company in Detroit that grew out of a grassroots movement to teach business skills to local youth: Vaughn Arrington's youth block club in Detroit's Red Zone (Lewis 2022). This is the area between Seven Mile and Eight Mile commonly associated with gang violence. Arrington created a place in this community for young people to come together and learn about finances, marketing, and speaking with customers, and where he could inspire young people to become entrepreneurs. Human Fliers specializes in person-to-person marketing and on-the-ground campaigns. Arrington's nonprofit, Team Strength Detroit, focuses on uplifting young people living in poverty. Arrington and his group are an embedded, trusted part of the community in Detroit (Veasey 2023). His leadership of the event contributed to the local feel of the Detroit Votes Concert.

Leading up to the Detroit Votes Concert, community members partnered with local churches and had members commit to bring groups of attendees to the center to join the celebration. Human Fliers involved local college students in knocking on over 145,000 doors in Detroit—twice the number they had originally hoped to achieve. They taught people how to vote and about Vote Early Day for months leading up to the election. Arrington said that "the young people walked away with a feeling of urgency, appreciation, and inclusiveness. I think that each one of them feels as though they can lead change independently. There's absolutely no doubt that these young people have been impacted and that they know how important their voices are" (Veasey 2023). The community-centered approach to the Detroit event was reflected in the participation of local talent, including event host Coco the Comedian, known locally as the first lady of comedy. Michigan's Attorney General Dana Nessel and Lieutenant Governor Garlin Gilchrist II also attended. Nessel told crowds at the event to "vote! And vote like your democracy depends upon it, because it does."

In keeping with the theme of celebration of community that the Voter Community Celebration Model is based on, Human Fliers released a short (four-minute) video after the election showing Arrington and the young volunteers from the effort celebrating their work to increase turnout: dancing, bobbing for apples, face painting, and making their own cotton candy. Comments from program leadership echoed the theme of engaging young people, as exemplified by the inclusion of coloring books and crayons in the PATM packages. The video was joyful, but also emphasized the importance of voting and supporting democracy. Program director Simone Minus commented, "It showed the kids, like wow! When I become 18, this is my responsibility" (Veasey 2023). The youth involved in the Human Fliers effort to engage voters in the November 2022 election had fun, but they also learned about the process of and importance of casting a vote. Recall that in the planning stages of the PATM project in Baltimore, we sought to emphasize civic engagement as a collaborative effort. The PATM boxes contained engaging materials for children, such as coloring books and stickers. The children's items were included intentionally, as family plays a significant role in shaping Black political thought and consciousness. These items not only encourage family conversations but also create a celebratory atmosphere surrounding the political process that could have a lasting impact on future generations of Black voters (see chapter 6). While the party in Detroit was intended to encourage eligible voters to cast a ballot, it involved local youth from the earliest stages of planning to also build voter identification for future elections.

We expected that those who received PATM materials (i.e., randomly assigned to the treatment condition) would also be tempted to attend one of these parties given their proximity to those locations. While we lack data to test this assumption, we did find an average treatment effect among the entire sample for hosts in Detroit—where the festival was smaller, more intimate, and arguably somewhat more community-centric. The efforts in Detroit looked and felt similar to those original grassroots efforts in Baltimore. A local organization planned the event and emphasized the joy in voting and being part of the community. The skinny sleeve itself made people aware of the election and the festivities surrounding it. The party made people feel like part of something bigger than themselves. While we can't say definitively that the polling-place party helped boost the impact of the treatment in Detroit, this is one explanation for why our results differ from location to location.

Results

The PATM skinny sleeve RCT in Detroit in November 2022 increased turnout among the entire sample (table 5.2) by about 1 percentage point, although this result was not statistically significant ($p = 0.119$, one-tailed).

Table 5.2: PATM: Detroit, November 2022 RCT

	N	Control turnout (%)	Treatment turnout (%)	Difference
Everyone	15,603	53.5	54.4	0.9
Low-propensity voters	4,140	28.9	29.1	0.2
High-propensity voters	11,463	62.3	63.7	1.4
Hosts	7,832	62.8	64.8	2.0*
Guests	7,771	44.1	44.0	−0.1
High-propensity guests	3,631	61.1	61.3	0.2
Low-propensity guests	4,140	28.9	29.1	0.2

Notes: Our analysis includes all household members, not just those who signed up to participate. This allows our total sample size to increase from 7,832 (3,923 in control + 3,909 in treatment) to 15,603 (3,890 household members in control + 3,881 in treatment). Note that in this analysis, we have no low-propensity hosts. An asterisk indicates a statistically significant effect at $p < 0.05$, one-tailed.

The effects are focused on hosts (those who received materials personally addressed to them), for whom turnout increased by 2 percentage points ($p = 0.035$, one-tailed). Early PATM efforts using the classic box and the sign-up model showed the most promise among low-propensity voters or party guests (see chapter 3); in contrast, the skinny sleeve and random mailings used in later iterations of the project showed the most impact among high-propensity addressees (hosts). Recall that in Richmond in November 2021 the skinny sleeves increased turnout among hosts by an estimated 1.81 percentage points ($p = 0.07$, one-tailed). The Detroit results thus replicate the Richmond results, and with a stronger level of statistical confidence (reflecting the larger size of the RCT).

As shown in table 5.3, turnout in Atlanta was 76.7 percent among those Black women voters randomly assigned to not receive a PATM package, compared with 74.7 percent of those who were mailed a skinny sleeve. The differences observed are not statistically significant, suggesting that the intervention did not affect voting decisions. These results helped us refine our understanding of when and where PATM is effective and highlights the need for continued experimentation and innovation. Looking back at the differences in the early-voting festivals, the underlying levels of election salience, and the implementation of the two November 2022 skinny sleeve iterations, we conclude that PATM may be most effective in lower-salience contexts (as in Detroit for this same election), and when the packages are accompanied by community organizing that ties the

Table 5.3: PATM: Atlanta, November 2022 RCT

	N	Control turnout (%)	Treatment turnout (%)	Difference
Everyone	14,167	58.7	57.4	−1.3
Low-propensity voters	3,790	16.1	15.4	−0.7
High-propensity voters	10,377	74.0	73.1	−0.9
Hosts	8,006	76.7	74.7	−2.0
Guests	6,161	35.8	34.6	−1.2
High-propensity guests	2,371	65.6	67.1	1.5
Low-propensity guests	3,790	16.1	15.4	−0.7

Notes: None of the differences shown here are statistically significant. Our analysis includes all household members, not just the individuals who signed up to participate. This increases our sample size from 8,006 (4,000 in treatment + 4,006 in control) to 14,167. Note that in this analysis, we have no low-propensity hosts.

packages to a more general spirit of community celebration. We return to these overall findings at the end of this chapter and detail which aspects of PATM still need to be evaluated.

Philadelphia, November 2024

In November 2024, PATM returned to Philadelphia for the general election. This RCT differs from the ones conducted in Richmond, Detroit, and Atlanta in three important ways. First, we did not design this study to be concentrated around any particular festival or event. Second, we conducted a head-to-head comparison between the two methods used in previous iterations to create lists of participants: sign-up (opt-in) lists and random assignment from the voter file. We refer to those who opted in as "warm" households and those randomly selected as "cold" households. Finally, we only selected Black women from both of these lists and randomized their households into either treatment or control. We used what we learned about the power of party "hosts" to spur their household members to political engagement and sought to supercharge this RCT by specifically focusing on this group. We also hoped to learn more about the effect of returning to a city a second time, building on our results in Atlanta, Baltimore, and Detroit. We did not detect a statistically significant effect of the PATM programming in Philadelphia in November 2020 but hoped that we might do so by returning in 2024.

The sign-up list was publicized by Black Girls Vote from October 24 to 30, 2024, and a total of 329 usable sign-ups were collected. We randomized those 329 Black women into treatment (162) or control (167) from our sign-up (opt-in) sheet and used a rolling protocol to select the remainder of our participants from the voter file. That is, we randomized the order of the voter file so that the organization could send out the remainder of their sleeves randomly. After the treatment list from signups was determined, households were chosen from that randomized list to equal the number of remaining PATM skinny sleeves. Of the 13,259 households with likely Black women in the voter file, 2,675 received a sleeve, while the other 10,584 were set to the control. We then included their household members in our analysis, which increased the size of our RCT from 13,588 (party hosts in both treatment and control) to 33,998 (13,588 party hosts + 20,411 party guests). Overall, there were 6,762 people in the treatment and 27,236 people in the control group. Skinny sleeves were mailed on October 31, 2024, five days before Election Day.

The RCT generated small, marginally significant effects among Black women mailed a PATM package, increasing turnout by 1.5 percentage points ($p = 0.045$) from 77 percent to 78.5 percent (table 5.4). Among

Table 5.4: PATM: Philadelphia, November 2024 RCT

	N	Control turnout (%)	Treatment turnout (%)	Difference
Everyone	33,999	64.8	69.3	+4.5*
Hosts	13,588	77.0	78.5	+1.5*
Guests	20,411	57.0	62.8	+5.8*
Cold households (hosts and guests)	33,279	64.6	68.5	+3.9*
Cold hosts	13,259	76.7	77.3	+0.6
Cold guests	20,020	56.8	62.2	+5.4*
Hot households (hosts and guests)	720	84.1	83.6	−0.5
Hot hosts	329	95.7	98.1	+2.4
Hot guests	391	73.3	72.6	−0.7

Notes: Our analysis includes all household members, not just the individuals who signed up to participate (hot households) or to whom a skinny sleeve was addressed (cold households). An asterisk indicates a statistically significant effect at $p < 0.05$, one tailed.

household members (party "guests"), turnout increased from 57 percent in the control group to 62.8 percent in the treatment group, a statistically significant effect of 5.8 percentage points ($p < 0.001$). Grouping everyone together (hosts and guests), the effect is a 4.5 percentage point increase ($p < 0.001$), from 64.8 percent in the control group to 69.3 percent in the treatment group, another large and statistically significant result.

Most participants in the RCT were randomly selected from the voter file, and we refer to them here as "cold" households to note the lack of previous contact with PATM. In contrast, "hot" households are those who opted into the program by visiting the PATM website to request a package. The vast majority (almost 98 percent, $n = 33,279$) of participants in this RCT are "cold," while the remaining 2.1 percent ($n = 720$) are "hot." Not surprisingly, given the small number of hot participants, the effects are focused on "cold" households. Overall, turnout among cold hosts and guests increased from 64.6 percent in the control group to 68.5 percent in the treatment group, a statistically significant effect of 3.9 percentage points ($p < 0.001$), and particularly among cold guests, for whom turnout increases from 56.8 percent to 62.2 percent (a difference of 5.4 percentage points, $p < 0.001$).

Examining these results in combination with those from previous PATM RCTs, we confirm several findings. This was not the first PATM effort in Philadelphia; as we found in Baltimore and Detroit, PATM was more successful when returning to a city for a second time. This was in a high-salience electoral context, a context in which we previously had found more negligible effects. The overall effect was relatively large, and driven by increases in turnout among household members of high-propensity Black women who were randomly selected from the voter file to receive a PATM sleeve. This builds on our previous PATM RCTs using skinny sleeves and random selection to confirm that this is an effective way of increasing Black turnout, albeit not among those to whom the packages were addressed. Instead, the sleeves were likely used by recipients to talk about the election with members of their households. We did not embed a qualitative element in this RCT, so we cannot know for sure what recipients felt or did, but our robust design and large effect sizes give us clues that this may be the case. That the effect was concentrated in "cold" households further suggests that the unexpected nature of the arrival of the sleeves matters. Highly engaged Black women in "hot" households were extremely likely to vote (95.7 percent) in the control group, leaving little room for improvement, and other members of their households were also very likely to vote (73.3 percent in the control group). This suggests that those Black women who opted-in to PATM were already highly motivated to vote and to mobilize their household members to vote. In contrast, Black women chosen randomly had a lower base level of turnout (76.7 percent) as did their guests (56.8 percent). For these women, receiving the PATM sleeve in the mail was likely received as a welcome surprise—something that made them feel seen and appreciated, based on qualitative data from previous PATM RCTs. The sleeves gave them the means to start effective conversations with household members about voting, increasing turnout among those household members by 5.4 percentage points—a huge effect given the electoral context.

Qualitative Data

Due to the design of this leg of the project, we couldn't collect much qualitative data from targeted individuals. Scaling up PATM to include more people at a lower price point meant fewer connection points between our research team and targeted voters. Our interaction was unidirectional—we sent a skinny sleeve, and they received it. However, we included a QR code on the mailed packages in Atlanta and Detroit and on the PATM website where folks could provide feedback. This did not generate much participation, so we can't reliably glean any new revelations from these data. On that feedback form, we included questions about how the packages made people feel, as well as an open-ended question about why they felt that way. While not statistically robust, these data points give us a glimpse into what it was like to receive one of these mailers.

Fourteen individuals in Detroit completed our survey. Half of those respondents (50 percent, $n = 7$) said that they received a sleeve, while 14.3 percent ($n = 2$) declined to answer and the other 35.7 percent ($n = 5$) said that they did not receive a sleeve. We asked those seven individuals who said they received a mailer about their emotional response, specifically asking them to identify the top three emotions they felt in response to the PATM sleeve. In line with our Voter Community Celebration Model (see chapter 2), for an effective program PATM ought to elicit positive feelings among community members, as this response is the mechanism that drives increases in turnout. The sentiment expressed by the group was overwhelmingly positive. All participants expressed positive emotional reactions to receiving the mailer. Four out of the seven individuals indicated that the mailer had made them feel "excited." Other emotions listed among respondents who received the sleeve in Detroit were "proud" (mentioned twice), "appreciated" (mentioned twice), "like a part of my larger community" (mentioned twice), "surprised" (mentioned twice), "happy" (mentioned once), and "connected" (mentioned once). None of the participants in Detroit mentioned negative emotional reactions to receiving the mailer.

The respondents in Detroit expressed feeling valued and appreciated when they received the PATM mailer, and they specifically mentioned the Detroit-specific items and snacks. One respondent was particularly moved by the inclusion of a Detroit vs. Everybody shirt with iconic Detroit symbols, and they stated that receiving the mailer made them "almost cry" and felt that it was "very special." The respondents also appreciated the unexpectedness of the gift and the feeling that their opinions and voices as Black voters were being considered during a critical time. Additionally, respondents mentioned feeling proud to be voters and members of the Black community in Detroit. Overall, the feedback from recipients of the PATM sleeves in Detroit was positive and indicated that the mailer had a meaningful impact on them.

In Atlanta, twenty-seven people filled out one of our surveys. Of these, 22 percent ($n = 6$) personally received a skinny sleeve, 55.6 percent ($n = 15$) said that neither they nor anyone in their household received a sleeve, and the remaining 22.2 percent ($n = 6$) declined to answer this question. We asked the six people who said that they received a mailer how it made them feel and asked for the top three emotions that they experienced. Again, the overall sentiment in Atlanta was positive—five of the six respondents said that it made them feel "surprised." Five of those respondents mentioned another positive emotion coupled with being surprised. These respondents reported that the sleeve also made them feel "connected" (mentioned three times), "appreciated" (mentioned twice), "excited" (mentioned twice), "proud" (mentioned twice), "like part of my larger community" (mentioned once), and "enthusiastic" (mentioned once). On the other hand, and as we initially feared, one person reported feeling "anxious" and "suspicious."

We asked those respondents to share why they felt these emotions. Several respondents said the packages made them feel appreciated. One Black woman who took the survey, in her forties, said, "I've never received anything like this before and it shows that someone is thinking and appreciate what the people are doing." Another Black woman, this one in her twenties, said "It was very different and great to receive acknowledgement." Another woman surveyed, who is in her sixties, said that it made her feel "proud to be an African American female voter." Two other women reiterated that the sleeve made them feel "excited" about voting and that it was a surprise, as they weren't "expecting anything." Finally, a thirty-two-year-old woman put their anxiety and suspicion about receiving the sleeve in context. She told us in her survey response that she "never received any package like it before and with all the craziness going on, it made me suspicious." While we can't be certain what "all the craziness going on" was a reference to, we hypothesize that it might have something to do with the foreign interference mentioned earlier by the cofounder of Black Votes Matter, who had mail sent to her house from Russia, or the FBI report released just a month earlier entitled "Foreign Actors Likely to Use Information Manipulation Tactics for 2022 Midterm Elections" (FBI 2022). Overall, while the reactions to PATM mailers (sans sign-up) were generally positive, future efforts need to exert some caution when sending out cold mailers.

We also wanted to know how people felt about attending the linked festivals in Detroit and Atlanta. We were not able to gather any additional information from the Detroit party, but we were able to send some of our team members to the party in Atlanta. They mingled at the Votelanta Music Festival and passed out postcards (figure 5.5); individuals could scan a QR code to fill out a survey and express interest in participating in a focus group. This effort led to a small number of people completing a survey $(N = 23)$; of those twenty-three, four individuals personally received a PATM skinny sleeve, and one said that someone in their household received one $(n = 5)$. We asked partygoers to tell us, in their own words, how receiving the package made them feel. Respondents told us it made them feel a range of positive emotions including happy, proud, excited, hopeful, surprised, enthusiastic, and appreciated. We asked respondents to tell us why they felt those emotions in reaction to the package, and one person said, "It's my voice and my choice"; another

PARTY AT THE MAILBOX

Thanks for showing up to the Votelanta Music Festival!

Black Girls Vote is celebrating amazing people like you who show up and vote to make Atlanta great. We appreciate you!

PLEASE: Scan this code to tell us what you think

We want to know how you feel about our work to celebrate voting and how we can improve our program

It will take ~10 minutes

People who answer the survey will have a chance to win a $100 Amazon gift card

You can also ask to participate in a focus group (Zoom), for which we will thank folks with a $50 Amazon gift card

Scan the code!

BLACK GIRLS VOTE

Figure 5.5: Postcards Handed Out at Votelanta Music Festival

said they felt surprised because the sleeve was "unexpected." One respondent said that it made them feel happy because they "love packages," and another said that it made them feel appreciated and that "it was such an exciting event to be a part of." These numbers are far too small to run any statistical analyses, but the postcard effort generated enough interest to conduct a focus group attended by six Atlantans. When asked how they felt about voting, perhaps unsurprisingly, many spoke of voting as a duty—this is a theme we captured in our other focus groups around the country (see chapter 6). In this context, they talked about a documentary film by Greg Palast entitled *Vigilante: Georgia's Vote Suppression Hitman*, which "investigates Gov. Brian Kemp's plan to stop people of color from voting and documents his family's connection to the state's historical racism and slavery" (Palast 2022), and talked about their own (or their family's) experiences with voter suppression. Gemma, a twenty-five-year-old Black woman who works as a medical social worker, talked about her excitement around voting and how it's a community event: "And I get excited, like, you know, when it's time to vote, I get, you know, all pumped up. The sorority I'm in, we go all out when it comes like to social action. So, I just get very excited around that time."

At the same time, voters acknowledged that they sometimes feel a variety of negative emotions around voting: frustrated, hopeless, or even scared when it comes to recent elections. Several participants lamented the choice of candidates when compared with past elections, a sentiment captured well by Anne, a thirty-five-year-old Black woman. The first time she voted, for Barack Obama, she felt hopeful, but by 2022 that hope had faded to cynicism:

> The first time I voted was the first time for Barack, and that was like such a positive experience feeling very hopeful, and you know, changing just all of that, and just comparing that to now. . . . I vote but sometimes it feels like there's no hope. Like, because, like she said, like nobody is taking it serious. So, you have, you know, people with no qualifications because I feel like [inaudible] you know, pretty close to it. And now it's just like . . . Whoever did whatever, even if it were by two years ago, it doesn't matter. Like, you know, you want to be up there and run? You can. So, I feel responsible doing it. But if I felt like okay, is everybody gonna go vote? And it's everybody listening to this? To all of this mess, and being able to see the truth?

And it's just like . . . Okay, well, I did my part. So, it definitely doesn't feel like it did with Barack.

A similar theme emerged in a conversation about anxiety between our focus group moderator and participants John and Cara. They said that those feelings arose from just trying to get to the polls to vote and standing in line, and they were present all the way to the other end of the process, considering the outcome of the election:

JOHN: Yeah, maybe anxiety. I mean, because, you know, from, from the outcome to the actual physical process of going and standing in line and all that sort of thing. It's, you know, it can take time.

MODERATOR: Was one part more anxious than others? Was waiting in line more anxious or was it sitting in front of the TV for three days to see the results? What created that anxiety?

JOHN: More of the results? I mean, yeah, it's the whole, it's just the whole thing. And it's gotten real simple, at least for me, it's gotten much easier to just walk in and vote and walk out almost now, you know.

CARA: Yeah, I'm an early voter, just because I don't ever want to get in, get to the point to where I go to my precinct, and there's a long line, because I might have a zillion things I need to have done that day. And so, anything to get in the way to where I'm like, man, I'm so pressed for time, I have to leave. So, for me, it's easier to go during the early voting times when I can literally walk in and walk right out. And it's nothing.

These participants felt embarrassed about the way their state was portrayed in national news. Participants said that they did not feel that politicians like Marjorie Taylor Greene (a Republican member of the House of Representatives serving the Fourteenth Congressional District in Georgia) and candidates like Herschel Walker represent them as Georgians. Cara said that she felt like "Georgia is the laughingstock of the US to a certain degree." Anne mentioned fear, specifically around national politics and the general sentiment held by other Americans:

I think, for me, like, just viewing what happened on January 6, like two years ago was low, like that was very low, just for our nation. So, I think we have seen pretty close to rock bottom, and we are, we're slowly like trickling back up. But I also feel like, you know, to quote Jay-Z, women lie, men lie, numbers don't lie. So, when people don't acknowledge numbers, it is frightening, because that is a fact. That's not an opinion. That's not, you know, a spectrum, there's not something to argue about. The number is the number. So, it was crazy to me how many grown adults were just like, he [Joe Biden], he didn't win. And it was wild, that, you know, they could stand up there and say that when the numbers were the numbers, and it's like when the other side loses, we don't, I don't want to say we, but when the other side loses, they don't do that. It's just come on, like . . . Okay, this wasn't our turn. But it just seems like there are a lot of, hate to say crazy, but just crazy people saying crazy things that are blatantly untrue. And it scares me that a huge portion of the population is agreeing with them. That is scary. That scares me as a Black person.

This comment from Anne paints a clear picture that when it comes to voting in the Black community, there are competing emotions at play. Voting as a celebration of community is *not* always the default. However, voting as a communal act came up throughout the conversation. For instance, Anne spoke about the importance of voting for her community regardless of whom you vote for:

My family and friends, we talk about the act of voting versus like, which party you're with or whatever. But amongst ourselves, we are . . . We all have the same smarts, we're all sharing the same means, like . . . Did you see what he said? And what she said? And been like, you know . . . So, we're just talking about, you know, sharing your stickers, your voting stickers, and, you know, asking, "Did you vote? When are you going to vote?" But I feel like my community's . . . my community and my family . . . like we're all on the same page without really saying it.

The takeaway we are left with is that while membership in the community is, perhaps by default, important to the act of voting in Black communities, celebration often needs to be primed. This is especially the case in high-salience elections where negative national influences are at work on the local level, competing with the joy that can naturally be felt in other contexts.

We also learned from the focus group that the festival in Atlanta was a fun experience, and according to our team, the event was well attended (around thirty-five hundred people). Given that the headliner is in a music genre that typically plays extremely late (other concerts in this genre typically start near the closing time of this event), some participants felt that the event stopped early—but still after the headliner got to perform. This was exacerbated by the fire marshal showing up toward the end of the event, although the event was not actually shut down any earlier than planned and advertised. However, given that our theory is based on celebration and community, these perceptions should be considered when interpreting the results of our RCT. Additionally, none of our focus group participants (all of whom were partygoers) received a PATM sleeve in the mail. The overall sentiment of the conversation with these partygoers is in stark contrast to the sentiment expressed among people who received a PATM box or sleeve (see the discussion earlier in this chapter and in chapter 6).

Discussion

Overall, we have learned that while it is possible to scale up the PATM program, it is far more effective when it is linked to community celebration and embedded with local leadership. The evidence from our RCTs is that community celebration is a key factor in driving voter turnout among Black communities. We learned from Richmond that the skinny sleeve was more cost effective than the classic box, and when they are sent out at random, the skinny sleeve may be less prone to being stolen or may appear less suspicious—although this new format does not eliminate suspicion altogether, as we learned from the Atlanta mailer survey.

The community celebration organized at the early-voting location in Detroit, with local musicians and food, appeared to have a greater impact on turnout than the music festival in Atlanta, which did not have early voting available. This is likely for multiple reasons. First, the Detroit event created a greater sense of belonging and a shared commitment to voting and civic engagement among people of all ages. Like Nyki Robinson's involvement in Baltimore, Vaughn Arrington's involvement in Detroit may have helped in emphasizing the community aspect of the voting celebration. Celebrating community participation in the democratic process is not only fun, but it also reinforces the idea that voting is a collective act and a way to make a difference in one's community. Our results suggest that future efforts to mobilize Black voters should prioritize community building and celebration in addition to traditional mobilization techniques. In addition, having the party at an early-voting location may have given people the opportunity to vote while they attended the party, minimizing the anxiety that some experience around voting and maximizing the fun and celebratory atmosphere, as well as the convenience.

We have also learned that the impact of our program can vary depending on the location, the level of competitiveness of the election, and the type of event we organize. Our efforts in Atlanta did not yield statistically significant results, despite the use of the skinny sleeve and the presence of a voting festival. This suggests that the impact of the program is highly context dependent and that a one-size-fits-all approach is unlikely to be effective. Both 2022 cities and PATM efforts were anchored by a voting music festival, but the Atlanta event was much larger and had a less local feel compared with the event in Detroit. The emotions experienced by individuals in these two cities varied as well, which likely also affected turnout. Detroiters, in a less salient election and without the weight of the future of the country on their shoulders, experienced more positive emotions when thinking about voting, while Atlantans were weighed down by the negative Warnock–Walker campaign. Future efforts to mobilize Black voters should consider the unique characteristics of each community and adapt their strategies accordingly. This might involve tailoring messages and outreach efforts to the specific concerns and interests of each community, as well as organizing events that resonate with local cultural practices and traditions.

In contrast, the 2024 effort in Philly was for a high-salience election in a battle ground city in a battleground state. There was no local celebration linked to the PATM packages. Yet, we boosted turnout among both Black women and their household members who were randomly selected from the voter file to receive a skinny sleeve of celebratory PATM materials. Given results from previous rounds, including qualitative data, we attribute this to the positive emotions elicited by the receipt of an unexpected package that sparked Black joy, and the opportunity it provided recipients to engage with household members in a positive way.

Overall, our PATM program has shown promise in increasing voter turnout among Black voters, but we have also learned that the program is not a panacea. It generated statistically significant increases in turnout in some contexts, and negligible results in others. Continued experimentation and innovation are necessary to further refine and improve the program. As we move forward, we hope to learn more about the factors that drive voter turnout in Black communities and to develop more effective strategies for mobilizing this important constituency. In the next chapter, we take a deep dive into the qualitative data collected in each city during the PATM project, and in particular into how voters in each city talked about voting as a duty to their ancestors and their communities. In the concluding chapter, we provide overall takeaways from PATM and examine how best to mobilize Black voters with celebrations of community.

6

Voting for Duty, Voting for Joy

As detailed in chapter 2, rational choice models of individual turnout decisions find that voting is irrational unless one considers the benefits that accrue to individuals due to the satisfaction they gain from exercising their citizen duty, known as the D term. The D term has since been repeatedly revisited and expanded, and other factors have been added to the equation, but civic duty remains a strong predictor of turnout, as illustrated by the familiar "voting is your civic duty" phrase that circulates every election season. In Black communities, the D term is also understood as a duty to one's ancestors who fought for the right to vote, as well as the duty to show up for one's community. The Voter Community Celebration Model (VCCM) explored in this book further adds to that equation—it is not just showing up to vote as a means of fulfilling duty to one's community, but the celebration of community that one expresses through showing up. VCCM puts back into the equation the Black joy that continues to lift up and sustain Black communities, and links it to the duty that many Black Americans feel compels them to vote. In this chapter, we share the sentiments of Party at the Mailbox (PATM) participants where they express, in their own words, the sense of community celebration that embodies VCCM and supports the theoretical underpinnings of the PATM program.

The interview script and focus group guiding questions focused on how individuals viewed themselves in relation to their communities and how they viewed PATM (see appendix for scripts and additional participant demographics). We were broadly concerned with how PATM was perceived by participants, including whether it was seen as generating the intended feelings of community and celebration. We do find these themes in the data. In this chapter, we focus on how the qualitative data support the power of PATM as a celebration of community. We also share findings in the data focused on the idea of *voting as a civic duty* and the various ways in which participants understood that phrase.

Qualitative Methodology and Data

After the elections in Baltimore, Detroit, Philadelphia, and Atlanta in 2020 and 2021, we collected qualitative data via semistructured interviews and focus group conversations. All conversations were conducted remotely using Zoom. Participants were recruited through an email message sent from a Black Girls Vote email address (or a Baltimore Votes email address, for the June 2020 pilot). Invitations were distributed to individuals who had signed up to receive a box or who were representatives of a partner organization. The interview team and focus group coordinators invited batches of ten randomly selected people from each list to participate until we met our participation goals. Each participating voter received a fifty-dollar Amazon gift card; representatives from local partner organizations were not compensated. Overall, we spoke to ninety-four individual voters and forty-four organization representatives and conducted seventeen focus groups that included ninety-two people (table 6.1). In this chapter, we use these qualitative data to explore how PATM was received by and affected our target communities.

Given historical (and justified) caution in Black communities about participating in research studies (Zinn 1979; also see chapter 1), we took deliberate steps to ensure that interviewers and focus group coordinators had cultural competency and would make participants feel comfortable. Our qualitative data collection team included twenty-one faculty and

Table 6.1: PATM Qualitative Data

	Total interviews (voters, organization leaders)	Focus group participants, groups	Dates of data collection
Baltimore primary 2020 (*pilot*)	36 (22, 14)	25, 3	July 2–29, 2020
Baltimore general 2020	30 (22, 8)	8, 2	December 8–28, 2020
Detroit 2020	19 (12, 7)	24, 5	December 18, 2020–January 16, 2021
Philadelphia 2020	24 (16, 8)	11, 3	December 18, 2020–January 18, 2021
Atlanta 2021	29 (22, 7)	24, 4	January 22–February 9, 2021
Total	138 (94, 44)	92, 17	July 2, 2020–February 9, 2021

graduate and undergraduate students from local colleges and institutions, including historically Black colleges and universities. Interviewers were recruited and trained by the evaluation team before data collection, and each city's team of interviewers was coordinated by a local scholar with expertise in conducting interviews, local politics, and history. All focus group discussions were moderated by Black women. Most of the interviews were conducted by the seven Black women and four Black men on the interview team; the team also included one Latino man, two Latinas, two white women, and one Asian American man.

The interview script and focus group guiding questions focused on how individuals viewed themselves in relation to their communities and how they viewed PATM (see appendix for scripts). We were broadly concerned with how PATM was perceived by participants, including whether it was seen as generating feelings of community and celebration. These qualitative approaches allow us to fully test VCCM (see chapter 2). To preview our findings, we do find these themes in the data.

Most individuals we spoke to had lived in their current city for at least ten years, with ninety-two participants reporting they have lived in their respective city all their life. They expressed deep ties to their neighborhoods and reported active engagement in social activities in their communities and pride in their city's culture. These relationships with their communities reflect the participant pool: Individuals were generally hosts who had requested a PATM box, and most were high-propensity voters. Overall, 134 (72 percent) of our 186 individual qualitative data participants were women, including 82 Black women (61 percent), 6 Latinas (4 percent), and 46 white women (34 percent). Of our 52 male participants, 23 were Black (44 percent) and 29 were white (56 percent).

Qualitative Data Results

VCCM is rooted in the strong, positive location-based identities held by many Black residents of majority-Black cities in the United States. For Black citizens, regional or metropolitan identities (e.g., being from the South or from a particular city) are particularly salient (Trépanier 1991; J. Cobb 1994; Thompson and Sloan 2012). The historical and present marginalization of the Black community creates a context where the act of voting becomes linked to personal identity with the collective. It highlights the group's position in society and the importance of the steps taken by elders in securing voting rights for the group. Therefore, Black voter mobilization has often been classified as duty based. The PATM project brings Black joy and pride back into the equation as something that sustains the community, propels it to act, honors the work done in the past, and celebrates the work done in the voting booth.

Pride in Community Belonging

In Baltimore, Detroit, Philadelphia, Atlanta, and Richmond (and many other cities), being from that city is a source of pride, often with a recognition of the cultural contribution Black communities have made in fostering the individuality of each location. Additionally, these locations are some of the few cities where Black families have lived for several generations (Robinson 2014). Atlanta, for example, tops the list of places where young Black people would like to live, and the Black population of the city has grown due to the New Great Migration (the reversal of the Great Migration) that began in the 1970s and is currently influencing the politics of the South (Grant 2020). As political scientist Keneshia Grant observes, "Many people describe Atlanta as the epicenter of the 'new' South and Black achievement" 2020, 159). In a 2021 national survey of Black adults, about half (52 percent) said that "where they currently live is very or extremely important to how they think about themselves" (Cox and Tamir, 2022). We heard this place-based pride in our interviews and focus groups. For example, in the following exchange from a Detroit focus group that included our moderator and two Black women in their forties, the moderator opened the conversation with a few icebreakers, including asking what it meant to participants to be a Detroiter. The responses from Alicia and Colleen illustrate their community pride:

> MODERATOR: What does it mean to you to be a Detroiter? Anybody can chime in.
> ALICIA: I'm proud to be a Detroiter.
> MODERATOR: Okay. So, it's pride.
> COLLEEN: I definitely think pride is a huge part of it. I feel as if in very few cities do you go to and find people who rep their city all the

time. Like, we're always proud to claim that we are Detroiters. And it's because, you know, I think about the history of our city. And that's really huge for Detroiters, and even the connection to neighborhoods, like, just like you started this conversation with, you know, where in the city, do you live? People always ask that, people always ask, which high school did you attend, like, those are, you know, those connections are important. And, and the city itself, even though it's big, it's small, like you always figure out like, I'm almost certain before we get off this call, someone is gonna figure out some connection I have, even though I don't think we all know each other. And so, I just think that just the connectedness and the pride that we have is, is what it means to be a Detroiter. And to really understand the history that we have and represent is a big part of who we are as citizens of this city.

This pride in being a Detroiter, that feeling of connection with other people—these are the foundational attitudes that support the theory of voting as a celebration of community. When Black residents of these neighborhoods are invited to celebrate those identities and celebrate their communities through voting, they respond because they feel proud to be residents of those communities and they feel that it is an identity to be celebrated. The PATM packages' ability to prime those identities with their contents and messaging is a crucial aspect of why we believe PATM increased civic engagement among those who received packages or otherwise engaged with the PATM project.

Previous literature has discussed the association between Black political participation and strong community-based attitudes. Throughout the 1970s and 1980s, scholars attempted to uncover why Black participation remained high even following the 1960s civil rights movement. Some early researchers posited that experiences of racial subordination and exclusion served as a catalyst to collective electoral participation, also known as compensatory theory. Other scholars posited a competing theory, ethnic community theory, in which Black communities are aware of and acknowledge previous experiences with disenfranchisement (McClellan 2023). This perspective is rooted in understanding how identity shapes community cohesion. Ethnic community theory (Olsen 1970; William et al. 1975; Guterbock and London 1983; Ellison and London 1992;) holds that community-based Black participation stems from a consciousness of one another that develops among community residents and encourages cohesiveness throughout the group, especially in the face of pressures from outside groups. Subsequent explorations of these two theories have found stronger support for ethnic community theory than for compensatory theory (Bobo and Gilliam 1970; Ellison and Gay 1989; for more information, see chapter 2).

PATM participants from Detroit whom we spoke to frequently mentioned the importance of community and the special nature of their identity as Detroiters. Harking back to the famous 2014 hip-hop song "Detroit vs. Everybody," Detroit boxes included a Detroit vs. Everybody cap from a local company of the same name. Detroiters feel the city is an island unto itself, a special community separate from the rest of the state of Michigan. In their focus group discussion, participants talked about their strong identities as Detroiters, their love of community, and how voting was not only a duty to their ancestors and the historic battle for the Black franchise but also a means of helping their city and their neighbors. In this excerpt, our moderator has just asked participants whether voting is a duty or a choice. The comments from Tonya, Nora, and John, three Black residents of Detroit, all speak to this theme. All agreed that voting is a duty (a topic we later delve into more deeply). More relevant to VCCM, they discussed how voting was about helping that community.

> TONYA: Okay. Come on, you know, voting. So, I used to be one of those people who I don't vote. That used to be me, right? Until things have to happen personally, in my life, before voting became a duty, like when I started, started teaching school, in Grosse Pointe, that that changed me because I graduated from Detroit Public High School, before we barely had had any resources, and to go to a place that they had an abundance of things. That was just a shocker . . . And so, I think it's a, I think it's a duty, and almost, it's more than a duty! Please start talking about, you know, the resources for housing and education, and all these things. And you start to realize, like, everything that's being . . . our people are going through, and our communities are impacted by comes from policy and politics.
>
> MODERATOR: Okay, it sounds like you're saying that when you vote, you're thinking about the community. Would you say that's accurate?
>
> NORA: Yes.

MODERATOR: Okay. So, Nora says yes. John and Emma, are you thinking about the community, when you're voting? Yes. Okay.
... Okay. Okay. So, let's talk a little bit about community. So, for some folks, like you all mentioned, the places where you were from born and raised. They define the neighborhood as community for others, like, you know, I'm, I go to a school and that's my community. For others, it's, I'm a Black woman, and that's my community. How do you all define community for yourselves?

NORA: Community for me will be my neighborhood, the area that I'm in, like I'm from 7 Mile to Lahser [areas in Detroit], you know, Evergreen to Lahser, 7 Mile to 8 Mile—my little square. I will consider that my community and I'm ... that's what I would consider as my community. So, when we work together, we look out for each other. For the elderly, I definitely do that check on them, whatever they need, you know, I consider that as a community. Somebody who's communicating, I'm letting them know about the things that's going on in the neighborhood. We're looking out for each other. If we see something to get involved, instead of turning a head, you know, somebody breaking into a house, call the police.

MODERATOR: People you live in close proximity with, people that live on your block, or a few blocks. Okay, what about others?

NORA: Community! Help with the kids ... Stuff like that.

JOHN: I think for me, community may be a little broader than that. Community for me, is, you know, what Nora said would be more of a neighborhood for me. Yeah, my community is probably the East Side of Detroit. So, when I vote, or when I'm, when I'm thinking about elections, or whatever, I'm voting for my community, and my community is really what will benefit, you know, the East Side of Detroit which will really benefit all of Detroit. However, when I really think of community, I think of the East Side.

As illustrated in this excerpt from one of the Detroit focus groups, Black Detroiters see voting as a means of helping their community, whether that means their neighborhood of nearby city blocks or the wider community of the East (or West) Side of Detroit. Nora compares voting to checking in on elderly neighbors, looking after each other's children, or calling the police if one sees a burglary in progress. The duty to vote is about being there for those who can't vote or for children whose schools need better resources. Voting isn't just about a duty to honor ancestors from the past—although this was a theme of our postelection conversations with voters—but also a duty to be there for one's community in the present and to improve the future. In the context of ethnic community theory, focus groups illuminated how and why Black community consciousness is present, and participants gave examples of how it operates day-to-day.

Emotional Reactions and 2020 in Context

Reviewing the transcripts from these conversations is like taking a time machine back to 2020, a period marked by the depths of the COVID-19 pandemic, which was having an inordinate impact on Black communities; by the Black Lives Matter protests sparked by the murder of George Floyd, in addition to other episodes of police violence against Black people; and by the distinct sense that America was at a crossroads of racial reckoning. Many observers referred to the period as one characterized by a dual pandemic of COVID-19 and an awareness of systemic racism, especially police brutality against Black people. Amid these pandemics, Black residents of these cities might have desperately needed something to celebrate. Our focus group and interview guiding questions specifically asked participants to reflect on how they and their families had been affected by COVID-19 and how they felt about Black Lives Matter. Their responses—particularly when discussing family and friends who died, and the ongoing threat of being killed by law enforcement—are chilling.

Yet these same people also had hope and joy. Hope that the election would make a difference. Hope in the election of the first woman, a Black woman, to be vice president. Hope in the ability of their votes and those of other members of their communities to generate change. Joy in celebrating Kamala Harris's victory. Joy in being part of a community in a city that they loved, even as they noted the challenges facing that community. Joy in being part of a historic movement—the PATM project— that was honoring the power of the vote and celebrating their city.

Throughout the interviews, feelings of joy and hope remained present. This is consistent with previous scholarship on Black emotions and community. Black joy has always served as an act of "resistance, resilience, and reclamation" (Nichols 2023). From enslaved women participating in outlaw parties (Camp 2002) to Black social media groups resisting subjugation by building online communities (Lu and Steele 2019), hope and joy have consistently been important factors in Black political participation. Our focus group and interview results are consistent with the findings in this previous literature. Community members told us that PATM served as a channel to highlight or remind residents of the best aspects of their community.

Many Black voters in the cities we worked in spoke of having a duty to vote; while their understanding of the root of that duty and how it influenced them varied, it was a constant theme underlying their decisions to vote. But the conversations we had about PATM were more about the joy of voting—participants noted that PATM generated a unique, celebratory perspective to their civic participation that was particularly welcome during the dark times of 2020, and one that they were sharing with their housemates and neighbors. As Amber, a twenty-eight-year-old woman from the pilot project, commented in her interview, "Receiving the Party at the Mailbox box was just, like, I don't know, that really nice moment of, like, remembering that voting is actually like a really important and like can be . . . I dunno, it came with a lot of joy for me this year. . . . I live in a house with several roommates, so it was also just like a very sweet experience for like, five of us to be at dinner like going through this very nice box with like, beautiful letterpress signs and little snacks and different, different mementos." We heard similar feedback from other voters who received PATM materials for the Baltimore pilot. The boxes were shared with housemates and friends, as well as on social media, and used as a means of celebrating the election. Recipients posted the balloons and signs on their doors, in their home and car windows, and on their sidewalk mailboxes. When they walked around their communities, they saw neighbors doing the same. When they went to vote, they wore their PATM shirts proclaiming, "BALTIMORE VOTES." The June 2020 news cycle was dominated by COVID-19 lockdowns and concerns about police violence against Black people; in this context of a double pandemic, the PATM boxes brought neighbors together to celebrate their city and their election.

Individuals who were in the control group of the pilot project also felt part of the celebration, and in many of the same ways. While they didn't have their own signs or T-shirts, they were able to join in the fun via social media and as they took walks around town. In chapter 1, we shared this quote from Juliette, a woman in her forties from the pilot project who didn't get a box but noted in her conversation with our interviewer that social media posts about PATM still made her feel like part of her community's voting experience:

> INTERVIEWER: How would you describe your experience, if you had one, with the Party at the Mailbox efforts overall?
>
> JULIETTE: I didn't personally receive a box in my mailbox. . . . I had such a fun time following along with people on social media who did and I thought, this year in particular, the idea of really celebrating what it feels like to vote from home and, you know, to be encouraged and to see people have a reason to publicly post on social media to talk about their voting experience is not something that I had ever seen in the city, in such a way. Like there's a handful of people will go, go vote, they'll post the . . . post a picture like with their "I voted" sticker. But this I think encouraged a lot more people to talk about their voting experience and to share publicly that they were voting. And that, to me, is so important, the idea of normalizing voting. Like it's not just a certain kind of person who votes—everyone can vote. And I think that's what this campaign showed in a way that I haven't seen in other years on social media.

Juliette said that PATM normalized talking about voting and encouraged her to share her voting intentions and behavior on social media. The boxes were a catalyst to raising the subject, an observation shared by many of our participants.

Another illustrative example comes from this exchange between our interviewer and Rahul, a fifty-year-old Black man from the pilot, who also did not receive a box but experienced the program through his neighbors, who posted signs, wore the T-shirts, and kept voting on his mind as he moved around the city:

> INTERVIEWER: Okay. So, in that case, did you see other people who participated or who did get a box and, in your opinion, how successful do you think the campaign was at getting other people out to vote?

RAHUL: I did see it because, you know, I like to walk for exercise, get fresh air and all that stuff. So, you know, I'd be out in the city walking and you would see in people's windows "Party at the Mailbox" or "Black Girls Vote" if I remember correctly. So, I would see people with the signage in their window. Now, I didn't see a lot of people with the T-shirts, but I did see whatever—since I didn't get the box, I don't know what was all in it—but I did see the signs in the windows. Yeah, I definitely saw signs in windows, and that was in different parts of the city.

INTERVIEWER: So, from those signs in the windows or even from like, if you saw any presence on social media of people sharing . . . in your opinion, were there any like community-building effects that happened based on this initiative?

RAHUL: I don't know about community-building but if somehow you forgot about voting, or didn't take voting seriously, but you've constantly seen it, it means you say, "You know, maybe I need to take this more seriously or maybe I need to get out on Tuesday and vote." I just think that it, it kept voting, how to say, how should I say it? It kept it on your mind, if you know what I'm trying to say. You didn't like . . . It was like you couldn't forget it. You know, it's kind of like a commercial that keeps telling you . . . We'll use football for a second: You know, up until the Super Bowl, you know, you're bombarded with commercials, you know, even if you're not a football fan, you know, on a particular Sunday the Super Bowl is going to be played. Because you've seen eight billion commercials already. And that's how I thought about Party at the Mailbox, you know, I was like, okay, even if I'm not gonna vote, I know on this Tuesday, voting's going on. So, I think that was a good thing. It kept it on people's minds. And just didn't brush it under the rug.

For Rahul, the signs in people's windows kept voting on his mind and made him take it "more seriously." He likens the ubiquitous presence of the signs to that of Super Bowl advertisements, making it nearly impossible even for those generally not interested in football (or politics) not to know the date of the event, and possibly making it less likely that they would choose to forgo the event that everyone was talking about.

Multiple voters commented about the presence of signs in their neighborhoods and mentions of PATM on social media. They saw people in their PATM T-shirts taking photos as they went to drop off their ballots. Even if they didn't receive a box, they felt the presence of the PATM program in their communities, and it made them happy. Repeatedly, our interview respondents used words like "joy" and "celebration" to describe PATM. They shared the boxes with their housemates and neighbors. They said they felt like they were a part of something larger than themselves. They see voting as a duty—many noted that Black people had to fight for the right to vote, and so now it is their duty to exercise that right. Unique to PATM, compared with other GOTV campaigns, is that the PATM project and materials made voting fun.

Most of the hosts were already politically active, and likely voters. PATM did not increase their individual likelihood of voting. But the boxes helped motivate others, including members of their households. One of our respondents, Sean, a fifty-year-old Black man, noted that he usually urges his husband to vote by reminding him, "Do you realize what our ancestors went through to have this right, blah, blah, blah." But when the PATM box came, Sean's husband was excited. It made voting "fun." And while Sean said he is a regular voter and would have voted even if he hadn't received the box, he noted that he used it as his "own little marketing tool" to reach out on social media and remind his friends to participate.

Bianca, a Black woman who participated in one of our pilot project focus group conversations, took this a step further. She described taking the signs with her friends to make their very own GOTV caravan:

What we did was we actually used the signs. I didn't get mine until Friday night, very late, but that Saturday we decorated our cars with the signs and actually drove through, even though I live in Waverly, we drove through the Ashburton area. We actually had someone with the loud PA system just screaming and reminding people to get out and vote. So, we actually just did a caravan and we used the free stuff to decorate our cars and we wore the shirts, which I thought was, it wasn't my idea, a pretty ingenious way to kind of get everybody's attention. Even my neighborhood in Waverly, if I had put the signs up, very few would have seen it just because of where my home is located. So, to be able to just to drive through the community, and you could see people come to their doors and there were some people out in their yards and stuff. I enjoyed that part of it.

Wearing their "I love Baltimore so I vote" PATM shirts, and with their cars adorned with PATM signage, Bianca and her friends took the GOTV message to a neighboring Black community. We don't know how those Ashburton neighbors felt about the impromptu car caravan, but what is clear from Bianca's description is that she and her friends enjoyed themselves considerably. The PATM box motivated them to spread the GOTV message and have some fun.

The interviews conducted after the pilot also clarified the trust that Baltimore residents have in Nyki Robinson and her organization, Black Girls Vote. Multiple studies have emphasized the importance of GOTV campaigns having a long-standing relationship with members of historically marginalized communities, rather than being seen as only showing up at election time, to maximize the effectiveness of the campaigns (Grumbach et al. 2024). Black Girls Vote is seen as a trusted, constant presence in the city. Our interviewer's conversation with Linda, a thirty-nine-year-old Black woman from the pilot project, illustrates the power of Robinson's reputation.

> INTERVIEWER: Okay, so this next section, I want to ask you some questions about local organizations that you might have had interactions with recently. So, do you . . . like what . . . do you have any organizations working in Baltimore that come to mind? Like just when you think of local organizations, would you—are there any that you would list?
> LINDA: Umm I do like what Nykidra does . . . Black Girls Vote.
> INTERVIEWER: Mm hmm.
> LINDA: It is a . . . it's a statement. It's a phrase that everyone is familiar with. And . . . she doesn't just do it one political season, it's a continuing . . . It's all the time . . . Her presence is all the time.

Linda sees Black Girls Vote as a consistent presence in the neighborhood, not an organization that just shows up the week before an election and then disappears until the next election. In contrast, consider this exchange that our interviewer had with Raquel, a fifty-year-old Black woman, where Raquel mocks the election-season attempts by candidates to appeal to Black voters by showing up in their places of worship:

> The only time I really see people out talking, out trying to, you know, say, "I'm this or I'm doing this, I'm doing that," is election time. And then after election time, I don't see them anymore. You know, whether it's on the news, on the radio, or when you're going up to vote, and you stand in the line and they're trying to talk to you to persuade you to get their vote. Me personally, no. After that I really don't see those people. It's a running joke with me and a couple of friends. We're like, "Yeah we go to church during election time to see all the candidates." Then soon as the election is over you don't see the candidates at church [anymore] [*laughing*]. "Yeah, I'm up with y'all, I'm praising with you!" [*impersonating the candidates*] and then after they lost the election or won the election, you know . . .

These factors all likely contributed to the success of the PATM pilot effort (see chapter 3). The boxes brought a spirit of joy to the city, even among members of the control group who didn't personally receive a box. The effort was led by a trusted community organization that residents knew had a long-standing commitment to the city and was not going to disappear after the election. This latter factor—that the GOTV message came from a trusted source—is a best practice for increasing turnout, particularly in historically marginalized communities of color (García Bedolla and Michelson 2012). As with the Party at the Polls efforts that inspired PATM, the celebration of community and democracy motivated the prosocial behavior of voting.

The celebratory spirit of the PATM project was also shared by interview and focus group participants in the November 2020 effort in Baltimore County. This comes up in the conversation between one of the authors and Kelly, a Black woman who moved to Baltimore in 2017:

> MODERATOR: So, I wanted to know if you can maybe just describe your experience with the box. Like maybe what did you do with the box? And did you post anything on social media? . . . How did your household feel about the box? Just, you know, things of that nature?

KELLY: Yeah. So, I remember, like, I wasn't anticipating actually getting a box because I kind of submitted my entry a little bit later, then I remembered to. But then I got a text message from [the PATM delivery crew] . . . because it was hand-delivered, which I thought was really cool, because, you know, one saves money on the postal fees, and it helps the postal workers who were already overwhelmed with everything. But I was excited to get the box. I opened it, it was . . . I thought it was packaged really well. I really like all the contents and all the information that was in there. My husband and I were very excited about it. Because I thought it . . . had a bunch of things that represented Baltimore really well. And I thought that was really cute, but I really liked all the different activities and again, the information that was all provided in the pamphlets and stuff. So, we walked through everything, and it was fun. And, you know, it made me excited for voting. You know, we did absentee ballots this year. So, it was kind of . . . I had serious, you know, FOMO because I didn't get the sticker—a cool "Maryland voted" or "I voted" sticker this year, but I got something from Party at the Mailbox, you know, that box and there was, it made me feel a little bit better. So, I did post to social media, because, you know, that was one of the things I was asked. And I thought that was fun.

As shown in her response, Kelly was excited about the box; it made her and her household excited about voting. She describes going through the contents as "exciting" and "fun" and as making her feel good. Again, as in the pilot, the celebratory mood the boxes aimed to generate resonated with the participants in the PATM project in November. Our interview with Josie, a Black teacher who works in the city of Baltimore and lives in Baltimore County, hits on these same themes.

INTERVIEWER: How would you describe your overall experience with the Party at the Mailbox efforts? . . . You can talk about what your experience was like as a volunteer, and you can just talk about your experience as a voter.

JOSIE: Oh, so is it like a scale or just like it was incredible?

INTERVIEWER: Or just like, yeah, just in general, like maybe like, if you want to do like a scale of one to ten. . . . How did you feel about your box and the social media campaign around it? And then we can get into . . . more specific questions too.

JOSIE: So, definitely a ten all around. And it goes for the box and just the voter engagement. Because everyone that I've encountered or you know, that's been around, was so energized, like really cared about our duty as, you know, individuals to make sure we vote. I feel like what the box . . . catered to even if it's just everybody in the household. Like there was something for the kids in the coloring books, the T-shirt for someone to wear. And like now, like with the masks, right, that's so needed. And the hand sanitizer, the holidays are coming up so they can have a container of cinnamon right in there. Right. Oh, it was great.

INTERVIEWER: I used my cinnamon to make cookies. It was perfect. And how successful do you think the campaign was in actually getting people out to vote?

JOSIE: Oh very successful! . . . Of course, I don't have like, you know, data to prove it. But based off like social media like even reposting and even when they went to vote like: Oh, I have my shirt. Right? Or dropping it bounced off in the mailbox. . . . Like it was a big push, I really think it helps.

INTERVIEWER: That's great to hear! From the research so far, it seems very successful. So, I can at least back it up on the on the data side. Seeming very successful. And do you think that it had any other effects outside of voting? More specifically, like do you think that there was a community-building effect from it?

JOSIE: Absolutely. Absolutely, like people coming together as a community to, you know, to encourage each other in every aspect, like, okay, get involved, be aware, like how can I help you? You know, definitely saw communities coming together, even being out there with the voter engagement.

PATM not only celebrated community, but it built community by celebrating the election and celebrating Baltimore. Clara, another November 2020 PATM participant, hit on this point more directly. A Latina in her late thirties who grew up in Baltimore but moved away to attend college, she had just moved back to Baltimore a few months before the primary to take care of her father during the pandemic and was working remotely:

> INTERVIEWER: How did participating in Party at the Mailbox make you feel?
>
> CLARA: I mean, it made me feel like part of a community, especially with like-minded people. When I was like, searching #PartyAtTheMailbox, and I was seeing, like, what was done before and like, should I even waste my time signing up for one of the boxes. And I saw, like, the different stories and captions that people had, especially on Instagram, like, it made me think, like, okay, these people are, like, legit, like, it's a worthy cause. And, you know, I'm, I'm here, I'm telecommuting, I'm not doing anything else, let me just, you know, join in, you know, their mission and their values by signing up for the party at the mailbox. And it was, you know, it was a really good talking point, like, when the two volunteers, or staff I don't know, dropped off the box. To my house, yeah, to my house. And it was like, a good . . . a good way for me to talk, talk to my dad about it. And, you know, he was like, 'Well, why are they doing this?' And, you know, and so I would explain it and, and he was impressed. He's like, they came all the way out to Baltimore County. I was like, Yeah, I mean, it's not hard. But, you know, like . . . they know that people are dedicated to the cause and getting the right people in office to continue their work. So . . .
>
> INTERVIEWER: That's really encouraging to hear, too. I think one thing that I really enjoy about the project is that we do do personal drop-offs. And I think just something like that was just a nice . . . little cherry on the sundae was that it would give, you know, relief . . . to our mail workers. But it was just like, a way also to kind of show voters that we genuinely want to give them something for really doing their . . . exercising their right and their duty as voters. So yeah, that was really encouraging to hear. My next question is that, um, how do you think maybe community members felt about Party at the Mailbox? And just maybe, to hear like, either, if there were other people in your neighborhood that might have heard about it? Or like your friend as well?
>
> CLARA: Yeah, I mean, my, my cousins live on [——] Street in East Baltimore. They're the ones, the same ones that told me about it.

Oh, yeah. All on their street, everybody has the poster. Not everybody, but like, most of the houses had the poster in the window.
So, you know, I know in that community, it's definitely something
that's discussed and like a common you know, talking point.
And . . . if you don't even talk to your neighbor, but you see it in
the window, that's like it's a safe house, or that's a like-minded
person. You would feel okay if something were to happen about
like knocking on the door, or like, I don't mean to sound like old
timey but like, knocking on the door to ask for like a cup of sugar.
You know, I think it really strengthened the sense of community
downtown, especially in East Baltimore, where I know there's a lot
of like, transplants from Harford County and Baltimore County.
So, yeah, I'm sure it's a definite . . . it's a refreshing, you know, way
of life there, you know, to see that it . . . Oh, there's also a sense of
community and in the city! Everybody has these posters in their
window.

According to Clara, the posters in windows made people feel connected.
Seeing those posters in most of the houses simultaneously built community and celebrated community. The box also gave Clara an opportunity
to talk to her dad about voting, reinforcing the point made by many
others that the box was a catalyst for talking to friends and family about
the election. These points were made repeatedly by our interview and
focus group respondents. Jaedyn, an older Black woman who participated in one of the Baltimore focus groups, called the use of signs and
balloons in her neighborhood a form of "communicating through our
porches." Even without personally interacting with their neighbors,
PATM box recipients felt like they were communicating enthusiasm for
their community and for voting.

Another illustrative example of these themes of celebration and community comes from a conversation from the November 2020 effort in
Baltimore that our interviewer had with Rhonda, an Afro-Latina woman
originally from Nicaragua.

INTERVIEWER: All right. So, we're gonna ask you about the Party at
the Mailbox now. So, how would you describe your experience, if
any, with the Party at the Mailbox effort overall?

RHONDA: So, I participated in Party at the Mailbox for the primary. And then I request, and I requested for this general election, but I didn't get a kit, which is fine. Like, I know that, you know, it was limited supplies, and all of that, but I think that overall, it was an awesome initiative. I think it added some like positivity and like hope, to the general feel of elections and whatnot. So, I love like, when I got it, the first time for election, general election, you know, putting it up in my mailbox with the balloons and like taking pictures, and my kids like love the coloring book that was supplied by Party at the Mailbox. So, the T-shirt, and I mean, just like it was just like, everything was so cool. Like the Berger Cookie was just felt like, wow, like celebration, like, and I'm like part of something bigger, too. It's not just this, like, this one box. But like, there's all these other people that are getting this and experiencing this. And we're liking this experience as a collective. And that was pretty awesome. Powerful.

Rhonda didn't get a box for the November election (although she got one for the June pilot), yet she still felt part of "something bigger," something "powerful." She felt like part of a collective group celebration. Similarly, Amanda, a twenty-one-year-old woman from Baltimore, told our interviewer that getting the box didn't influence her decision to vote, as she always votes, but it felt like she was being recognized for her participation. Amanda said getting the box and wearing the shirt made her feel "more pride in being politically active in Baltimore."

In both rounds of the PATM project in Baltimore, participants repeatedly echoed the themes of community and celebration. When we asked community members in Baltimore about the boxes, many of them recalled not just the specifics of what was physically in the box but also how the project made them feel. The boxes were about community: They were from a trusted local organization with a year-round presence and were filled with local items that reminded recipients of their pride in Baltimore. Items were shared within households, on social media, and with the neighborhood through the wearing of T-shirts and the posting of signs in car windows and on street-facing home windows and front doors. It made recipients feel like something they were doing together as Baltimoreans. The boxes were also about celebration: They recognized the commitment to voting of those who signed up and helped them think of the election in a fun way, with snacks and balloons. PATM made the election about celebrating voting and celebrating Baltimore.

These themes continued in successive iterations of PATM in other cities. One example of how Black voters we spoke to see voting as a celebratory act comes from a story shared in a Detroit focus group by Twyla, a Black woman in her early thirties. She shared the story of voting for the first time as a college sophomore, to elect the first Black president of the United States, and how that event felt both historic and celebratory:

> I was, I believe a sophomore in college. And so, I lived in a dorm. So, everyone was excited to vote, you know, we were so excited. We were excited to make sure we register, we walk to our voting location, we waited in line. And so, just that the night of how everybody was celebrating, and it was that our generation, in which I feel as if it was important that we got out to vote, made a difference, and my grandparents and you know, be alive, to also celebrate that, you know, that milestone in history. So, from that time from that period on, I was just like, "Oh, I'm always going to vote." Because it was just so exciting, like the excitement behind it, the lead up to it, and then be able to say I was part of, you know, helping a Black man get into office, whether, you know, people are doing the electoral vote or all that I get. Okay, well, it's part of that popular vote, you know, for him and I, you know, got my brothers, they were younger than me and got them to vote, stuff like that. So, it just is important to me, because of that aspect. Like I just enjoy that time in my life. Like, I'll never forget that and like how everyone, like, all my college, everybody, in college where we live in the same boat, and we always just so excited running up and down the halls, you know, just exciting moment.

For Twyla, voting for Barack Obama was celebratory. While she understood that her vote (as part of the popular vote) likely didn't matter due to the Electoral College, she still was excited to be part of this exciting moment in history. That feeling stuck with her; twelve years later, her feeling that voting is exciting and allows her to be part of something larger than herself comes through in her story.

That the boxes were themed by city added to their power to harness feelings of community and communal city pride. As noted earlier, this was a key component of PATM from the beginning, as Robinson believed cueing local pride would boost PATM's ability to increase turnout. Focus group and interview participants repeatedly noted the local flavor of their boxes, even if they had been randomly assigned to a control group and didn't receive one, as illustrated by comments from Alice, a Black mother of two in her thirties who lives in Detroit and did not get a box, and Pamela, a Black woman in Atlanta who did. Alice noted, "It was like all like Detroit-related things. So, it kind of made you feel proud of your city as well and made you feel proud for voting." Pamela said the unique Atlanta flavor of her box was especially noticeable for her because she had a friend in Baltimore who had received a box, which allowed the two friends to compare contents. Pamela noted, "It was really cool. I got a box, it was really cool, I was very excited about it. I posted on social media and some of my friends were asking about it. One of my friends who lives in the Baltimore area was jealous, because she said that was better than the stuff that they got in their box. . . . I thought it was really cool to have so much local stuff. . . . Just knowing that these local businesses were out there and around was really nice to have that as well." A Black woman participating in one of our Atlanta focus group discussions, Barbara, said the box felt like "a welcome to Atlanta gift box." Similarly, Adrian, a twenty-six-year-old Black woman in Atlanta, said, "It felt like Atlanta in a box."

The power of PATM, shared by our focus group and interview participants, was that it made voting fun. For example, Ayanna, a Black woman in Atlanta, rated the program a perfect ten: "The idea of the box, I would give it an absolute 10. Especially during the pandemic, a lot of people don't want to go out. They're worried about their health. So, they can celebrate right at home. My own little watch party." This summarizes the idea of the original PATM box perfectly—the contents were designed to allow individuals to celebrate voting in their own homes, safely, during the COVID-19 pandemic. Although most of the voters we spoke to said they think of voting as a duty and consider themselves committed voters, they said PATM made voting less boring and more of a celebration. Consider this comment from Alice, the Black mother from Detroit quoted earlier. Note that Alice did not receive a PATM box (she was in the control group); nevertheless, she was very enthusiastic about the program and its likely impact.

ALICE: I think that when things like Party at the Mailbox are done, it just keeps you more excited about voting and, you know, spreading the information, especially [to] the youth. That for me, I don't know, it's just so many different things coming at them right now. That there's something like this is perfect. I think right up there.

INTERVIEWER: Do you think that the Party at the Mailbox campaign was actually getting people out to vote?

ALICE: I think that it was successful. I think that any type of thing that can get, I mean, like when you add music to it, and you make it seem like a party and you, you know, make it seem fun as well as getting the information. I think things like that are beneficial for all age groups. Because some people just don't understand and they just don't know what they don't know. And I think the Party at the Mailbox was successful with that.

For some of our focus group and interview participants, requesting a PATM box was also about being part of history, and they didn't want to be left out. Elizabeth, a Black woman who participated in a Philadelphia focus group, describes the contents of the box as "history-making things." She continued, "I think that that box was a history-making thing. And I saw it on my friend's Facebook timeline. She did a little unboxing and I was like, 'Oh, I want one of those.'" For Elizabeth, being part of PATM felt like being part of a movement. A Black man from Atlanta, LaShawn, said the program "was another opportunity for people to feel like they were a part of something. . . . It made people feel as if they were a part of a special club." Another example of this sentiment comes from Faith, a forty-two-year-old Black woman who participated in one of our Philadelphia focus groups:

Like I knew we were in this place, like a historical movement happening. And it was just really cool to like, have the element of fun behind it. Because it's been a lot of work, you know? Yeah. And I just thought it was great. And because we actually worked at . . . I go to the community college, and I was on the committee that was getting people registered to vote and stuff like that. And so, we had, we received a couple boxes to give out to people and then to help to get them to sign up for it. And it was just really like the way people received the boxes, how excited they were. And that care and they were like, wait, really, they're not going to spam me and we're like, no! [inaudible] Like let's do this together. Let's eat some chips and have some fun, [have a] watch-party later or whatever. So, it was just the energy that having these boxes, we were showing people and they were signing up for them right there. It was cool to be a part of that, it really was . . . and then to hear people be like, "I really got a box." Like yeah, we weren't lying. Like, no, it was just cool. And it felt like and, you know, the paperwork on it said it was happening in other cities. But it also felt very local at the exact same time, you know, it felt very local because you had those like local items in there like the Tastykake and stuff like that. I just thought it was just some good energy amongst all this muck that was happening, you know, and you see people's spirits kind of like . . . shoulders relax and be like, oh, we're gonna get that? We're like, yeah, are you registered to vote? Let's go!

Adrian, the twenty-six-year-old Black woman from Atlanta mentioned earlier, shared a similar sentiment about how PATM made her feel like she was participating in something bigger than herself: "I felt like I was a part of something big, greater than me. Because at that time, especially when it came to the more recent election with voting for Senate and everything, I felt like, the world was watching Atlanta. So, it definitely made me, and I feel like some more people, feel special."

Another story of voting as a celebration of community was shared by Rita, a Black mother of two young children, who participated in one of our Detroit focus group discussions. For Rita, voting is a celebration of community in many ways. She shared her disappointment at having to cast an absentee ballot in November 2020, instead of voting in person, and related this to being together as part of a community, being able to see one's neighbors. She also said that voting in person reminded her of going to the polls with her grandmother when she was younger:

> I actually wanted to vote in person. But again, because of my schedule. And then my kids, of course, they virtual school and things like that. It just didn't allow me to, but, um, you stated about a sense of community, like, I feel that when I go and vote in person, it just reminds me of being with my grandmother. At the voting polls, when I was a young girl, you get to talk to people that you probably would never see, that literally lives in

your neighborhood, because people don't really engage with each other anymore. For real, you know, you just kind of see each other in passing, if you see them at all, and that is an opportunity to see and meet your neighbors.

For Rita, voting is a social event with one's neighbors. Coming together at the physical polling place brings the community together. We heard a similar sentiment from participants in other focus groups. Meghan, a Black woman born and raised in Philadelphia, shared a similar perspective at a Philadelphia focus group: "I usually stand right in line and have a ball cuz everybody's there. And a lot of times we all get together. That's our, that's our event. And when we see each other, even though we're neighbors, you sometimes you'll see your neighbors while you in line voting." Even without a line, there is something about voting in person on Election Day that our participants said is important to them. As one participant in an Atlanta focus group noted, "It's something about voting on Election Day. For me, it's just a thrill, like, I really get pumped up. Not that my vote counts any differently. But it's just something about voting on the actual Election Day."

Voting as a Duty

Other focus group comments hit on the idea of voting as something one does as a community in other ways. Derek, a participant at a Philadelphia focus group, said voting shows compassion for one's community. While other participants did not directly disagree, two Black women in the same focus group, Blanche and Elizabeth, responded to Derek's comments with more traditional conceptions of voting as a duty. Elizabeth specifically referenced the relatively brief period of time in US history during which Black people have been able to vote (since the 1965 Voting Rights Act):

> DEREK: I think it shows compassion for your community, that you're not only voting for you, but you're voting for your community's best effort no matter where you are located in the city or demographically.
> BLANCHE: I feel like it shows appreciation for our forefathers, our predecessors that didn't get a chance to vote, that were never able to

vote, you know? It gives me a better sense of appreciation to know the struggle that went on, so that I could.

ELIZABETH: Yeah, you know, it's interesting. That's an interesting question, because I never, I don't generally think of myself in that way, like, Oh, I'm a voter, right? I vote. That's what I do. I like come of it, you know, any which way? It's, it's, uh, if I was to think about it more, and maybe I would say, you know, I feel an obligation to vote. Not in a negative way. But for sure, in a way that allows my voice to be heard. And I feel a responsibility to vote. And I feel a responsibility to talk to everybody that I know about the fact that they should be voting. You know, I was asked to participate in a short video to get Black women and women, you know, excited about voting, really. The question was, Why do you vote? Why do you vote? And something that I said, which to me, is still like, shocking that, you know, it wasn't until 1965! 1965! I just, I am fifty-four and I will be fifty-five in January. In 1965, which is a year before I was born, is when it became actually legal for African Americans to vote, like across the board, not kind of saying like, yes, you can vote, but then not allowing you to get to the polls and all that other stuff that happened. Like, one year before I was born! That's insane to me. Right, like, so, having that knowledge and knowing that, like, I'm going to vote until I can't do it anymore.

For Elizabeth, voting is about appreciating her ability to do so, without "all that other stuff" that prevented Black Americans from doing so before passage of the Voting Rights Act. Knowing how much effort went into securing the franchise, and how recently, has instilled in her a lifelong commitment to participation. Similar statements were shared by multiple participants across our focus groups. Another great example of this sentiment comes from Dolores, a Black woman who participated in one of our Philadelphia focus group discussions:

I feel like it's a duty to vote in every election. . . . If I can make it there, my goal is to always vote. And, you know, sometimes it really has nothing to do with who's running or not, but just knowing the fight that Black people had to go through to gain the right to vote, and women as well. So as a Black woman, I have double duty, you know, as a Black woman, to exercise my right to vote because people gave people's lives, just so that I can have the right to vote. So, I am definitely going to exercise that right, to honor them. If nothing else, you voted in person. I always vote in person.

Cheyenne, a Black woman who participated in another Philadelphia focus group, shared a similar comment and noted the sacrifices made by Black people such as John Lewis, who led the march across the Edmund Pettus Bridge during the fight for the Voting Rights Act. Cheyenne noted,

> You know, voting is . . . I do take it seriously. It's our right to vote not, you know, often think back to so many people who sacrifice so much wants to have the right to vote. And it's just a very sacred thing that we, that I cherish about in our democracy here. And I think about John Lewis and all them on the bridge. And, you know, there's so many people who are just treated so with violence and all just to get Black people the right to vote. So, it's just the sacred right to me.

Lakiba, a focus group participant in Atlanta, touched on the perspective of Black women like her, given that they were the last major demographic group to win the franchise, in responding to a prompt about whether she considers herself a voter. Noting that her camera was not turned on in the Zoom call, Lakiba identified herself as a Black woman in her response:

> I do consider myself a voter. I've only missed two elections, since I turned eighteen. And I'm significantly older than eighteen. Now, one was because I injured my leg. And the other, somehow, I don't know how I missed that one. But only two. I consider myself a voter. I am a voter I consider um, as it is. It was a right of citizenship. And as that is a responsibility, and I consider because I am an African American female, you can't see me but you can tell by the voice. And we were the last ones to get the right to vote. So, I want to honor all those sisters before me that fought so that I would have this right and this responsibility to vote. So, I take it very serious. And my children, when you could see the names on election roll, before we became automatic, if my children went in there, and they didn't see I had voted, my phone would blow up. That happened one time, that was the time I injured myself and had to go to the hospital—"Where are you? You're the first person to vote, where are you?" 'Cause I am always the first person in line.

Lakiba is such a consistent voter, and always first in line, that the one time she failed to do so (because of an injury), her phone blew up with her children wondering where she was. Voting is important to her as a Black woman, reflecting the suffrage struggles of both Black Americans and women. Vanessa, a Black woman in an Atlanta focus group, shared a similar sentiment about the duty to vote, albeit more succinctly: "I think as an American, it's a choice. I think as a Black woman, it's a duty."

These traditional perspectives on Black turnout—as deeply connected to respecting those who fought, or even died, to win passage of the Voting Rights Act and ensure Black Americans were able to exercise their right to vote—are not unique to the participants in the PATM cities. At a campaign rally at Morehouse College in Atlanta on October 23, 2020, vice-presidential candidate Kamala Harris urged Black voters to vote, noting, "Voting is about honoring those ancestors, honoring what they fought for and what they sacrificed for our right to vote." During that same electoral cycle, the Los Angeles Urban League (2020) issued a call to vote, stating, "We must show up this election. We must vote. We must participate. We must honor those who gave their lives for our right to do so." Years before he became a candidate for the US Senate, Reverend Raphael Warnock of the Ebenezer Baptist Church in Atlanta, the church once led by the Reverend Martin Luther King Jr., told Black parishioners on the Sunday before Election Day in 2010, "Go to the polls Tuesday in the name of our ancestors. Know that your ballot is a blood-stained ballot. This is a sacred obligation" (NewsOne 2010). From Oprah Winfrey to rapper E-40, Black Americans are constantly reminded that their ancestors fought and died for the right to vote and are urged to vote in the next election to honor their sacrifice (Giorgis 2018). These entreaties to vote out of duty to civil rights movement ancestors are common, but they are not the only way in which Black voters think about their duty to participate.

Our focus group participants had other perspectives on voting, including as an instrumental act—as a means of keeping elected officials accountable and of generating changes in public policy. Grace, a forty-six-year-old Black mother from Detroit, likened voting to giving customer feedback when one has complaints or concerns about a product. She said she uses that analogy when talking to her children about the importance of voting: "I always tell my kids, if they don't like something, or they bought something, and it broke; I always say, email the company. I tell them all the time, or call the company or send them email, cuz they always complain to me and I say, the website right there, it says questions or comments." She compared customer feedback on products to voter feedback via elections—as a way to be heard and generate change.

Because of how the PATM program was structured, most of the people we talked to in our interviews and focus groups in Baltimore, Detroit and Philadelphia were older Black women. Another striking theme in these conversations was how often they mentioned their adult children or other youth, and how they encouraged those younger Black individuals to vote. The boxes fostered these conversations by including something for everyone that could be shared with household members. The conversation between our interviewer and Shelley, a Black mother who has lived in Baltimore for her whole life, is illustrative of how the box was used by multiple household members so that everyone felt part of the PATM experience:

> INTERVIEWER: And so, how did you participate with everything that was in the box? Did you put anything in your mailbox? Did you post anything on social media?
>
> SHELLEY: Yeah, I did. Um, because I have a three-year-old daughter. So even though she's obviously far away from getting into anything political, but I was just making sure that she knows that, you know, you need to vote, whether it's political or whether it's you deciding on if you want a green or purple crayon, you need to vote and always have a voice in what you want. So, I was just making, you know, making sure that I posted the Baltimore votes on the refrigerator. She saw me wearing the T-shirt. It came with some cookies in there. So, she, she ate the cookie. And then also, my boyfriend got engaged into it, too. He was like, Oh, I want one. I'm like, I'm sorry, I didn't get you one. But he really enjoyed that. He really enjoyed the Under Armour mask that was put in there. And I think that much because everything that was going on, you know, that's going on. Now, that is definitely an essential part of your attire every day. So, he took the Under Armour mask, because that was too small for me. But yeah, it was, it was a great experience. And I definitely made sure that I posted it all on social media, Twitter, Instagram, Facebook, and

everyone was like, Well, how do I get one? and then they went to the Instagram page and signed up.

Many of our respondents gave similar feedback: The coloring book engaged youth, and the snacks and other items allowed recipients of the box to engage other voting-age members of their households. Every time Shelley's boyfriend wore his Under Armour mask, he likely recalled that it was part of the PATM box and that the election was coming. When she shared the box contents on social media, her friends wanted to sign up and take part in the fun.

Often, the Black women we spoke to reported that their conversations with younger members of their households about voting meant reminding them of the sacrifices that were made to get the franchise, including the march at the Edmund Pettus Bridge in Selma, or the power of the vote to generate positive change. But the PATM boxes opened up a different theme to those conversations, focused more on voting as a celebration of community. We heard this theme in our interview with Kindra, a Black single mother of two from Detroit: "It was actually kind of cool. . . . It seemed like a cool idea especially to get—this makes me sound old—but, the younger generation involved in voting. Once I got my packets in the mailbox, it made . . . my daughter said 'oh' so she became interested, because she's nineteen. . . . She kind of got excited about learning about the politicians and what they were saying. Was so good. So, I enjoyed that part of it. It got them interested." Kindra also commented on how the box made her feel included, as part of something beyond herself, and in something enjoyable:

> INTERVIEWER: So, how did participating in the Party at the Mailbox efforts make you feel?
>
> KINDRA: It made me feel included. Like it mattered. Yeah, basically made me feel included. Like, it was okay to be happy about something politically, I guess. That's the wrong way to say it. But it just made me feel included, because normally, it's just that, oh, who am I vote for, you know, kind of boring type of thing. But it may be engaging in conversation with other people, and to celebrate other people making choices, you know, to make big decisions. So, I just, it was interesting. It made it more interesting and more fun for me.

Another quote from Kindra that stood out concerned the way PATM was different from outreach conducted by political parties or candidates. One consistent finding from get-out-the-vote research is that nonpartisan appeals are more effective than partisan appeals. This is rooted in the intrinsic difference between these get-out-the-vote requests: Nonpartisan appeals tend to focus on the political voice of individual voters, on making sure that they are able to exert their political power and be included; partisan appeals, in contrast, are asking voters to help them win—the voter is being asked to vote in order to generate a certain electoral outcome. They are instrumental to something desired by the candidate or the political party (Green and Gerber 2024). Kindra touched on this in her conversation with our interviewer when asked why she thought PATM was effective.

> I think . . . because you're not looking for money. You just want them to get out and make their voices heard. And I think that that's the important part of getting people interested in voting. Because if you go in with like a specific political party, the Democrats, Green Party, whatever, Republicans, a macho vote, but then they want you to donate a lot of money. . . . You were just asking for people to make their choices heard. So, I think that that, you know, was a big part, that was a big part of it for me. I don't like people begging for money.

We heard a similar story from Shayla, a forty-five-year-old Black mother of two who has lived in Atlanta her entire life. Shayla didn't get a box, but she attended the PATM virtual party on Facebook and was struck by the celebratory tone of the larger project.

> SHAYLA: The box was an extra, like, icing on the cake to let people know, like, you know, we're not, this is not just, you know, like not a gift to you to say, well, we're giving you this because you voted; no, this is just a token because you took the time out, it's a party. You know, because we wanted to thank you for either making your choice, or making this your duty to come out and do what you did, regardless of who you voted for. And why you voted. You did it. And we want to just to celebrate you. Because you did, you know, you did it. Yeah. You know. So, in the, you know, that was exciting, because

it was a lot of young people, old people, people from all walks of life, all different views, and they was excited. And it made it excited. It was the first time in my life, lifetime to see people so excited about just coming together to make a change for whatever that reason was, regardless of what the purpose of what they were voting. That was exciting and Party at the Mailbox made it fun.

INTERVIEWER: That's so good to hear. So, did you say you did receive a box?

SHAYLA: No, I didn't receive my box. But you know, it didn't matter because even just to see how people were excited about it and just seeing everybody . . . when they did the virtual DJ party, it was like, it took me back to when I was young, and the music they played, you know, it was exciting, you know, to be in a virtual world and still have people to just to take time out to think of all kinds of ways just to make you know . . . it may have saved somebody's life, not just because [it was] about voting, necessarily. You know, it's something to be happy about . . . We're here. With what's going on in the world right now, let's have a party. Yes. Yeah. Who doesn't like a party? You know?

In Atlanta, we noticed a very different tone in our interviews and focus groups when asking participants to talk about their city and their communities. While voters in every city were proud to be from that city (e.g., Philadelphians bragging about their city's prominent role in US history), voters from Atlanta shared the unique position Atlanta holds as part of the New Great Migration. The New Great Migration, a reversal of the Great Migration, refers to the pattern of migration back to the South that started in the 1970s and has picked up steam in recent decades. Atlanta has benefited more than any other city from this trend, thanks in part to the concentration of Black wealth in the city, earning it the informal titles of the capital of the New South (Frey 2022) and as the "black mecca" (Robinson 2014, 188) because of a long history of Black political and economic advancement. Participants in Atlanta noted the unique sense of pride they have in living in a city with so many Black professionals and Black-owned businesses—a Black community that is flourishing. They also were proud to be from the same place as Stacey Abrams, the 2018 candidate for Georgia governor—while unsuccessful in her bid in that election, she served as an inspiration for many. Reflecting the timing of our qualitative data collection efforts, immediately after the January 2021 US Senate runoff election, voters knew that in the 2020 presidential election they had turned Georgia blue for the first time in half a century, and they also took pride in that. Leila, a Black woman who has lived in Atlanta for her entire life, summed it up this way: "I love Atlanta. I think it's an area where a lot of Black people have been thriving for years and decades. A lot of people look at Atlanta as a scene full of opportunity. And this is a place where a lot of Black people are just doing very well for themselves."

The Atlanta effort also differed in that it was far more spread out. This meant that the community effect of the project was diluted. Vivian, a Black woman who participated in an Atlanta focus group, noted that this made the large number of posters in the box somewhat unnecessary: "I guess if you're living in the city where it's more connectivity and walkability, you could put it in your window, but it wouldn't matter in my window." Vivian understood that the point of the posters was to help spread the word about voting in her community, but she didn't live in the type of community where that would make a difference because she didn't live downtown. This suggests that PATM and other efforts that cultivate voting as a celebration of community need to be attentive to the density and nature of that community. In downtown Detroit or Baltimore, posters might be more visible, as these are neighborhoods where many folks walk or socialize outdoors. In less dense counties, however, those posters might need to be replaced by other means of bringing the community together—for example, through social media. Maya, a Black woman who participated in a different Atlanta focus group, noted that living in a community with a larger proportion of residents who are Black makes it feel more like a community, and also that she sees more of a community commitment to voting:

> When I got married, I moved, we moved to an area that was more, more Black people, more minority. But before that I lived in heavily whiter areas, you would see a few of us spread out. And there's two things. One, I feel like in the area that I'm in currently, which is a Blacker area, but being gentrified, things are changing and everything, older people are moving out the house, the houses are being flipped, blah, blah, blah. We moved into a

house that was older that then had been flipped. And anyways, basically, I see the people in the area I live in now more involved in voting, more, the Black people, more into, we got to make a change. When I lived in the areas where it was more white, the Black people who live in that area were not as involved as the Black people in the area that I currently live in. I don't know if it's because in the area I live in now people where they see more, they experience more. And maybe I felt like I was kind of blindsided living in the whiter area. I lived in a veil, I just pretty much went to my day to day; they ain't messed with us, we ain't messed with them, we just lived our lives. But it's almost a more sense of a community in a Blacker area than it is in the whiter area.

Maya noted that in her old neighborhood, where there were more white residents, the Black residents seemed less politically involved. They tried to live without drawing attention to themselves as a group or working to make change. In her new neighborhood, where the majority of residents are Black, she sees far more political involvement and a stronger sense of community.

This is the sense of community that is the basis for our VCCM. Uniquely in majority-Black neighborhoods with a strong sense of community, PATM is able to harness that community spirit, and what voting means to Black Americans, to generate increases in voter turnout.

Voting as a Duty, Voting for Joy

Duty has been used in traditional voter behavioral models since the 1960s to explain why people still vote even when the cost may exceed the benefit or their vote is unlikely to affect the outcome of the election (Riker and Ordeshook 1968). It is generally understood as a civic duty to support democracy and to fulfill the social norm of participation or a sense of duty to one's political party (Fieldhouse et al. 2022). Black Americans, however, often see their duty to vote as tied more to a duty to honor ancestors who fought for the franchise and as a duty to protect others within the community. We heard these same distinctive perspectives on the duty of voting in our focus groups.

The PATM project made participants feel like they were part of a larger collective effort, while the local themes of the boxes made the experience feel local to their own city. Together, these perspectives cultivated the message that voting is a celebration of community. Recall Faith, the Black woman in Philadelphia who said that she saw PATM as something good "amongst all this muck." Faith felt that she was part of something bigger than even her own community, because she knew PATM was also going on in other cities, but also felt that it was a local effort. It was a positive experience for her not just because of the fun items in the box but because of the connection and collective spirit it engendered.

While many Black voters spoke of having a duty to vote, the conversations we had about PATM were more about the joy of voting—that PATM generated a unique, celebratory perspective to their participation that was particularly welcome during the dark times of 2020–2021. They were still able to enjoy voting and sharing in the celebration with their housemates and neighbors while staying within the safety of their homes during a global pandemic. Yet these PATM-led household parties extended beyond the four walls of houses or apartments. Posters and signage could be seen throughout neighborhoods, bringing otherwise isolated families together as one community.

Even individuals who were in the control group felt like part of the celebration, and in many of the same ways. While they didn't have their own signs or T-shirts, they were able to join in the fun via social media and as they took walks around town. PATM normalized talking about voting and encouraged people to share their voting intentions and behavior on social media. The boxes were a catalyst for raising the subject, an observation shared by many of our participants. Voters in the PATM project cities commented about the presence of signs in their neighborhoods and mentions of PATM on social media. They saw people in their PATM T-shirts taking photos as they went to drop off their ballots. Even if individuals didn't receive a box, they felt the presence of the PATM program in their communities, and it made them happy. As noted earlier, one focus group respondent called the use of signs and balloons in her neighborhood a form of "communicating through our porches."

To further drive the message that civic engagement was a collective, celebratory activity, PATM boxes included engaging materials for children such as coloring books and stickers. The inclusion of children's items was intentional. As noted by theorists such as Hanes Walton Jr., family in the Black community is an important socializing agent for

Black political thought and Black political consciousness. Contrary to conventional wisdom overstating the limitations of Black political socialization in politics and behavior, Walton contends that oral knowledge of American presidents, party affiliations, and their significance to the Black community is transmitted to Black Americans within family units. This tradition has significant effects on Black political attitudes and behavior by encouraging perceptions of voting as a duty rather than as a right (Walton 1985).

The inclusion of children's items in the PATM boxes reflects Black Girls Vote's understanding of Walton's theory and how Black families can operate as socializing agents for Black political behavior. Not only are these included items a means of continuing to stimulate these family conversations, but they also situate these conversations within a celebratory moment and feeling about the political process that can have a lasting effect on generations of Black voters to come. Another way in which the box materials generated a community-wide celebration was the sharing of posters and balloons in spaces visible to the public—in car and home windows, on sidewalk mailboxes, and in other shared community spaces. The balloons and posters were a visible signal of collective voter celebration that conveyed that voting is a civic activity tied to one's racial and local identity.

Pamela, the Black woman from the Atlanta focus group that we met earlier in this chapter, shared how the balloons and coloring book helped her start a conversation with her three-year-old son: "I thought it was really nice that it included stuff for the kid, as well, because my three-year-old, you know, blew up 'Atlanta votes' balloons and stuff. And he had those, and the coloring book. And so that was a conversation starter for us about why Mommy goes to vote, because when it was safe before COVID, I would take him with me like parents used to do me. So, it was really cool to have that coloring book and stuff to be able to start that conversation with him." This socializing effect of the boxes was not limited to small children. Our conversation with Laverne, a Black mother of two young adults, illustrates how the box was used by recipients to motivate low-propensity voters in their households.

INTERVIEWER: How did participating in the Party at the Mailbox effort make you feel?

LAVERNE: Oh, it made me feel wonderful. I thought that it was so gracious that they gave us those boxes and even such exciting things like Black Girls Vote. You know, little flyers, they gave us stickers, T-shirts. You know, they gave us a bag of chips—things were pertaining to our race. Which was very, it was very exciting. So, my daughter loved it and everything.

INTERVIEWER: And so then, in your opinion, how successful do you think the Party at the Mailbox campaign was in getting people to vote?

LAVERNE: Very successful. Very.

INTERVIEWER: Okay. And do you think that Party at the Mailbox had any other effects?

LAVERNE: I mean, it just gave us a voice. It gave us an initiative like, look—I have two daughters that are of age. One is twenty, and one is eighteen. So, my eighteen-year-old, she's always participated, since she's turned eighteen, she's like, oh I wanna vote, so me and her she's always participated. So, my twenty-year-old when she sees the box, and she's seeing everything in there, then she wanted to participate. It gave her a boost, you know, what I'm saying like, see, this is really what it is, you see, we have a voice.

Laverne is a committed voter who sees voting as a duty; she likely would have voted regardless of whether PATM sent her a box. But she was able to use the box to start a conversation with her adult daughters about participating.

The boxes also contained educational materials, and those were appreciated as well. In one of the November focus groups with Baltimore participants, Phyllis, a Black woman in her late thirties, noted, "I liked the education piece as well. That it wasn't just like, Oh, we doing some rah, rah. You also had information in there as well. . . . And I think that's a good way to get it in because sometimes when you try to give people information, they tend to shy away if they think you're talking to them and not with them. And this was kind of a talking with type of thing and it wasn't so much more [inaudible] choice. People were more adept to get it and listen." Phyllis shared that her son had just turned eighteen and was voting for the first time, and that she used the PATM materials to talk to him about the election. The educational materials were accessible, and recipients were open to receiving them, perhaps because they were accompanied by the other items in the box. To be clear, however, most of our participants, when we asked them to reflect on the items in the boxes, noted the celebratory items—the balloons, noisemakers, coloring books, and snacks—rather than the educational materials. At the same time, the educational materials were available and accessible for recipients to share with their household members.

The spirit of community persisted long after the elections were over. As noted in chapter 3, leaders of partner organizations told us they were still noting folks wearing the PATM T-shirts and displaying PATM signs in the windows of homes and businesses long after the packages had been delivered. This likely is linked to the increased likelihood that PATM resulted in statistically significant increases in turnout in cities where we distributed packages a second time—the initial PATM efforts were memorable, and important, to participants, and so they kept wearing their shirts and displaying their signs. When we came back, we were able to build on those memories and goodwill, and to re-spark the feelings of duty, community, and joy that generate voter participation in Black communities.

Conclusion

Come Join the Party

Elections are serious business. Billions of dollars are spent on campaign marketing plans, materials, and consultants. Voter focus groups test political messages, survey companies collect public opinion data, and local election officials refine their voting materials and processes to ensure a smooth and accurate count. But elections are also a time of celebration. Candidates arrange election-night parties to celebrate their victories (or to commiserate about their losses). Fundraising events bring like-minded people together to raise enthusiasm and dollars for their preferred political parties and elected officials. Houses of worship arrange for Souls to the Polls gatherings after Saturday or Sunday services. The Divine Nine organize their local neighborhoods to stroll to the polls. Drag performers drag out the vote with glitter and high heels. Colleges and universities host campus election festivals.

These election celebrations are also community celebrations—celebrations of geographic communities, of ideological communities, of Greek communities, and of queer communities. They are celebrations of identity and collaboration to achieve a common goal, whether that goal is to promote democracy and the power of the ballot box, to advocate for a specific policy priority or political party, or to celebrate a shared identity. Reminding voters that voting is not just a duty but also a celebration of their identity and community membership can increase their sense of political efficacy and their likelihood of turning out to vote. Some voters, indeed, participate out of a sense of civic duty, and they see these election festivals as a celebration of that sacred trust. We saw this sentiment expressed time and time again through our conversations with voters across the country. Others participate as an instrumental act, to achieve a desirable outcome—they feel passionate about a particular issue or candidate. Regardless of the community with which they identify or the core reason that they participate, they are all celebrating something. Reminding voters that they are part of a community and guiding them to think of voting as a way of celebrating and supporting that community increases their sense of political efficacy and their likelihood of turning themselves, and others, out to vote.

Party at the Mailbox (PATM) did just that. In communities where the project operated, individuals who interacted with it felt part of something larger than themselves and celebrated the collective act of voting as a member of that community. In some iterations of the PATM project, this generated quantifiable increases in voter turnout, either among targeted recipients of the PATM materials or among their household members, and sometimes among both. In other cities, particularly in contexts of very high-salience races, quantitative evidence was negligible, but we see evidence of the power of PATM in the qualitative data from our hundreds of conversations with community members. PATM was born out of necessity during the 2020 COVID-19 lockdown, where more traditional parties at polling places became too risky, but early successes generated momentum and enthusiasm (and donations) that allowed us to continue to explore its ability to motivate voters in subsequent elections as the pandemic eased. In multiple iterations, PATM was able to generate the same sense of joy and community membership as have traditional in-person election festivals. Moving forward, similar efforts can be used to cultivate celebrations and increase turnout. Long-term investments in Black communities can generate future payoffs in the form of increased voter participation.

Carolyn Cohen, one of the first funders to agree to support PATM, saw right away that the celebratory nature of the project would cultivate joy and increase engagement. When asked why she donated, Cohen said it was about Nyki Robinson and her relationships with the community, but also about the specifics of the PATM plan: "Nyki, number one. Just the person that she is, and the enthusiasm that she has, is inspiring. I think it was about the celebratory element of it, that created this immersive engagement that was about joy and hope" (personal communication, May 9, 2022). Anger, threat, and anxiety often motivate political participation (Valentino et al. 2011; Albertson and Gadarian 2015; Phoenix 2019; DeMora et al. 2023). In recent elections, framed by Trump candidacies and presidency and by the pandemic, perceptions of threat and negative affect motivated turnout on both sides of the partisan aisle and by multiple communities (Cruz Nichols and Garibaldo Valdéz 2020; Mason et al. 2021; Parker 2021; Ahn and Mutz 2023; Phillips and Plutzer 2023). Anger's ability to motivate a range of political behaviors makes sense because anger is an action-oriented emotion (Lerner and Tiedens 2006; Groenendyk and Banks 2014; Huddy et al. 2015). However, it is not the only action-oriented emotion. Some individuals are motivated to take political action through positive emotions like joy or enthusiasm (Fredrickson 2001; Groenendyk and Banks 2014; DeMora 2022; DeMora et al. 2023). In the realm of voting, the power of positive emotion is illustrated by research on gratitude-based get-out-the-vote (GOTV) messaging (Panagopoulos 2011), which is now a best practice adopted in most mobilization campaigns. There is also some scholarly evidence that positively framed descriptive norms about voting are just as effective at motivating turnout as are negatively descriptive norms (Gerber et al. 2018). Robinson, Cohen, and other PATM supporters believed emphasizing joy and celebration was what many people needed in the midst of the dual pandemic of 2020; political science scholarship suggested it would be effective.

Robinson's involvement in her community and her belief in the power of celebrating community identity were reflected in the materials provided in the PATM boxes, and this played a key role in promoting a sense of community engagement. The T-shirt images and snacks included in the boxes, and the color schemes of the contents (the shirts, the posters and signs, and even the balloons and confetti), reflected the local history of each city and helped to foster a sense of belonging among voters. The contents of the PATM boxes generated immersive engagement, including materials not just for the primary recipient but clearly meant to be shared with household members, friends, and neighbors. The snacks, coloring books, and crayons helped engage younger children and spark conversations about voting. Posters and balloons encouraged recipients to decorate their homes and cars, and to post about the project on social media, further sparking conversations and a sense of a shared experience. The local theme of the boxes encouraged recipients and their household members to think of PATM and voting as something they were doing together, not just with their families and their children but also with other members of their local community.

Our randomized controlled trials (RCTs) in Baltimore in June and November 2020, which used the original (classic) PATM boxes, generated large increases in voter turnout (see chapter 3). However, to fully understand the impact of the PATM interventions, we also need to examine the negligible results from the initial roadshow cities of Detroit and Philadelphia. In these cities, where the classic boxes were distributed for the November 2020 elections, we do not see the same evidence of increases in turnout in the validated data. Delving into the details of those electoral contexts as well as the specific PATM implementations in those roadshow cities helps refine our Voter Community Celebration Model (VCCM). The lessons we learned in Atlanta, Detroit, and Philadelphia in 2020 and 2021 were crucial in our planning efforts in expanding to a variety of other contexts. Every PATM effort built on the one before it, allowing us to better understand the factors that contribute to successful PATM efforts, as well as to refine VCCM.

What were the differences between the 2020 PATM efforts that created a quantifiable difference in turnout and those that did not? One potential explanation for the very strong results in Baltimore is the stronger community links between the main organizations involved in the project—Black Girls Vote and Baltimore Votes—and Baltimore. Because PATM began in Baltimore and the core team was located within the Baltimore area, they were able to more effectively coordinate the campaign locally than were organizers of the PATM efforts in roadshow cities. Our qualitative data suggest that more voters in Baltimore heard about PATM from one of these local organizations, making it feel more homegrown than it would have if they had heard about it on social media.

At the same time, the PATM efforts in Atlanta, Detroit, and Philadelphia in 2020 and 2021 were conducted in contexts of extreme polarization and unrest, including the pandemic, Black Lives Matter protests, and continued episodes of police violence against Black people. PATM was built on the idea that voting and community are to be celebrated. It seeks to emphasize joy around election time. This may be a more elusive goal in broader contexts that elicit fear or anger. One can imagine that cultivating a sense of celebration in Philadelphia might be more challenging when the governor has deployed the National Guard in your community (see chapter 4). In Atlanta in 2022, there was increased suspicion and anxiety around packages during election time given the efforts against

Black organizers in Georgia who received suspicious items in the mail (see chapter 5). This is not to say that PATM can't be effective under these conditions, but rather that the broader context is an important consideration when evaluating observed outcomes.

Another possible explanation for why some PATM efforts created a quantifiable difference in turnout while others did not is the electoral context of our efforts. In November 2020, Detroit and Philadelphia were battleground cities in battleground states, as was Atlanta in January 2021 and November 2022. Looking at these results as well as those from efforts in Richmond in November 2021, Detroit in November 2022, and Philadelphia in November 2024, our data indicate that PATM had only negligible effects in most of these higher-salience electoral contexts. Thus, we conclude that the measurable successes in Baltimore are due in part to the lower salience of those two elections in 2020. That the project was successful in Detroit in 2022 but not 2020 bolsters this conclusion: The Detroit election in 2022, while still competitive, was far less salient than the 2020 contest.

Our data also indicates that returning to a geographic location for a second time boosts the effectiveness of PATM. For the June 2020 pilot, our RCT and evaluation were limited to the city of Baltimore, but PATM was also actively distributing boxes in the larger (and geographically distinct) area of Baltimore County. When PATM returned to both Baltimore City and Baltimore County in November 2020, the measurable success may also have been due in part to recipients' familiarity with the project from the primary election cycle just a few months earlier. Results in Detroit in 2022 but not 2020, and in Philadelphia in 2024 but not 2020, follow a similar pattern, in that PATM returned to cities where it had been unknown in 2020 (and had negligible results) but was more familiar in 2022 and 2024, generating increases in turnout.

Moving from the classic box to the skinny sleeve, we explored the power of unsolicited PATM materials to motivate voters in Richmond, Detroit, Atlanta, and Philadelphia (chapter 5). As with the roadshow, these extensions of the original project were conducted far from Baltimore. Robinson and her team had to work harder to find community partners (and to properly personalize the boxes to feel local). The election contexts also varied, with lower-salience contests in Richmond in November 2021 and Detroit in November 2022, but higher-salience races in Atlanta in November 2022, where again the balance of power of the US Senate was in play, and in Philadelphia in November 2024. The skinny sleeve still cultivated a homegrown feeling, including similar (but fewer) locally themed items, and PATM was promoted in collaboration with local community organizations. Mirroring findings from the PATM classic box efforts, our RCTs generated statistically significant increases in turnout in Richmond, Detroit, and Philadelphia, but not in Atlanta. In Richmond and Detroit, effects were focused on package recipients, while in Philadelphia we generated notable increases in turnout among both recipients and among their household members. Because the skinny sleeve model did not include advance sign-ups in most cases, and sometimes due to the rush of getting packages delivered, we lack the immensely rich qualitative data for these efforts that we had in iterations of the project that used the classic box. Future replications should find a way to also collect qualitative data from skinny sleeve locations, to better understand the program's full range of effects on attitudes and behaviors.

Overall, PATM generated measurable increases in turnout in six of the nine iterations of the project where we were able to collect robust data (table C.1). Beyond this simple numerical record, however, the variations in the programs across locations, and the supplemental qualitative data, generate an understanding of when and how similar projects in future elections can most effectively increase turnout in Black communities. Combining our qualitative and quantitative data, as well as narrative data from each election, we generate the following best practices for successful PATM celebrations:

1. PATM is more effective in lower- and medium-salience elections, when efforts to get out the vote are less likely to be dismissed as transactional, and when voters feel that they are coming together for their community rather than to help generate a desired outcome.
2. PATM is more effective when it is made to feel local and home-grown, due either to a dense geographic focus that allows for spillover effects and word-of-mouth or to effective partnerships with trusted local community organizations.

Table C.1: PATM Outcomes Summary

		Type of Election	Classic box or skinny sleeve	Return location	Statistically significant effect on box/sleeve addressees (Hosts)	Statistically significant effect on household members (guests)
1	Baltimore City, June 2020	Presidential Primary	Box	n/a	No	Yes
2	Baltimore City, November 2020	Presidential (non-battleground)	Box	Yes	No	Yes
3	Baltimore County, November 2020	Presidential (non-battleground)	Box	Yes[a]	No	Yes
4	Detroit, November 2020	Presidential (battleground)	Box	No	No	No
5	Philadelphia, November 2020	Presidential (battleground)	Box	No	No	No
6	Richmond, November 2021	Gubernatorial	Box vs. Sleeve	No	Yes	No
7	Atlanta, November 2022	US Senate runoff	Sleeve	Yes	No	No
8	Detroit, November 2022	Gubernatorial	Sleeve	Yes	Yes	No
9	Philadelphia, November 2024	Presidential (battleground)	Sleeve	Yes	Yes	Yes

[a] While we did not conduct an RCT or evaluation in Baltimore County in June 2020, the PATM project was active there and distributed boxes to voters.

3. PATM is more effective when the project returns to the same location over time.

Overall, we find strong support for VCCM. Voters in PATM cities felt appreciated and felt like they were participating in a shared community event, and voting meant that they were participating in something bigger than themselves. From the boxes hand-delivered to homes in Baltimore to the mailed sleeves and subsequent polling festival in Detroit, participants felt PATM was fun and celebratory. They were motivated by the project to share PATM materials on social media and in their local communities, and to have conversations with household members and others about their intention to vote. The project generated increased feelings of community-based or city-based identity, increased individuals' identification as voters, and increased feelings of political efficacy. Motivating voters to participate as a celebration of community can generate large increases in turnout among low-propensity voters in majority-Black cities.

Research in Black Communities

As noted in chapter 1, our project was unique in its focus on Black voter participation, as well as the use of RCTs to test the effectiveness of the PATM project. Before the 2020 Baltimore City pilot, there were few published RCTs focused on increasing Black turnout, and many of these failed to generate statistically significant results. The nine RCTs described in this book thus represent a huge leap forward in our understanding of how to effectively increase Black turnout. They also build on and confirm findings from those previous efforts.

One area of such confirmation concerns the clear importance of working with local community organizations. Local partners bring community wisdom and knowledge to the project, and their involvement increases trust and thus the efficacy of outreach to voters. By collaborating with local community organizations, researchers can better understand the unique cultural, social, and political dynamics that shape voter behavior in particular contexts. In the case of the PATM project, this meant having local expertise in certain neighborhoods and communities within PATM cities. The involvement of local organizations in voter outreach efforts is also important to ensure messaging is culturally appropriate and resonates with the community's values and beliefs. In addition to building trust with voters, partnering with local groups can help mitigate potential concerns about outsider intervention and cold outreach efforts that tend to feel more transactional than celebratory. This is not necessarily new—previous RCTs also speak to the value of partnering with local, trusted groups. Research has shown that local organizations can play a critical role in facilitating voter mobilization efforts, particularly among historically marginalized populations. Furthermore, partnering with local organizations can help build long-term relationships and networks that can be called on for future outreach efforts.

One such RCT was the first among Black voters. Conducted in 2000 in collaboration with the National Association for the Advancement of

Colored People (NAACP), the effort used direct mail and commercial phone banks for outreach (Green 2004). The partnership with the NAACP meant voters were hearing from a trusted messenger and brought expertise about the Black community to the project. Unfortunately, the effort encountered multiple operational issues, including contamination of the control group (some members of the control group received phone calls or direct mail encouraging them to vote). In addition, randomization was at the individual level rather than at the household level, making it possible for a household to include both treatment and control individuals. At the same time, it was also a very ambitious project, including hundreds of thousands of registered voters across ten states. Perhaps due to these issues, the estimated effects on turnout were not statistically significant.

Other early RCTs designed to measure efforts to increase Black turnout also did not generate measurable increases in participation. In 2002, Andra Gillespie, then a graduate student at Yale University, coordinated with two Black candidates in Newark, New Jersey (Cory Booker and Ronald Rice Jr.), to conduct experiments in the May 2002 mayoral election and the June 2002 municipal council runoff election. Gillespie combined face-to-face canvassing with reminder postcards. Canvassing was conducted by Yale undergraduate and graduate students recruited by Gillespie, which may have undermined their effectiveness. Gillespie notes,

> Despite the fact that all of the Yale canvassers were students of color, their demeanor, carriage and speech patterns betrayed that they were from out of town. This did not seem to be a problem until the weekend before the election, when voters began to question our origin. Some of us were even accused of being opportunistic and working for Booker so that we could land jobs in his administration. Booker's opposition actually used the fact that he had out-of-town volunteers to their advantage and spread rumors in the city that our intentions in campaigning for Booker were ill-conceived and selfish. (2005, 80)

In addition, as with the NAACP effort in 2000, this RCT's control group was contaminated, due to canvassing conducted by other Booker campaign workers. In her smaller follow-up RCT for the June runoff, Gillespie used only regular Booker campaign workers. Yet, for both rounds, she found no statistically significant effects on turnout.

In 2018, organizers of a door-to-door effort hoped to increase Black turnout in two majority-Black wards of Washington, DC, and even partnered with a local organization (the local branch of the League of Women Voters). However, the effort used mostly white canvassers from other parts of Washington, DC, and had negligible effects (Scott, Michelson, and DeMora 2021). This null result points to the sensitivity and attention to detail needed to carry out successful GOTV campaigns in historically marginalized communities. Effective GOTV campaigns need to be designed and implemented with a deep understanding of the cultural, social, and historical context of the community. As reflected in our PATM efforts, success is more likely if a GOTV project engages community members in both the planning and execution phases of the project, and when it prioritizes appropriate representation and cultural competence in all aspects of the work on the ground.

More consistently positive effects on Black voter turnout have been generated by door-to-door canvassing efforts conducted in coopera- tion with local community organizations. In 2001 and 2003, RCTs in the predominantly Black cities of Detroit (then 94 percent Black) and Kansas City, Missouri (64 percent), were conducted in cooperation with the Association of Community Organizations for Reform Now (ACORN), a well-known national organization with trusted local chap- ters committed to community organizing (Fisher 2009). In Detroit, the door-to-door canvassing effort increased turnout by 7.8 percentage points. In 2003, a similar RCT with another ACORN chapter increased turnout in Kansas City by 8.5 percentage points (Green and Michelson 2009). In 2006 and 2008, door-to-door canvassing efforts by members of the local organization Strategic Concepts in Organizing and Policy Education effectively increased Black voter turnout in South Los Angeles (García Bedolla and Michelson 2012). A smaller effort in 2018 conducted by a community organization in Ohio with majority-Black low-income pub- lic housing residents did not generate statistically significant increases in participation, but the scholars evaluating that RCT attribute this result to their small sample size (Grumbach et al. 2024).

PATM includes a considerable face-to-face component, in that many of the earlier iterations of the project included home deliveries with a wrapped PATM van. Organizers personally went to homes to deliver the PATM boxes in a celebratory way. PATM partner organizations hosted in-person events where the project was boosted and even, sometimes, where local residents could take home a PATM box. But, as the name implies, most of the party (i.e., boxes and sleeves) came in the mail. There is even less of a scholarly record as to how well direct mail works to increase Black participation, compared with previous work using canvassing and live telephone calls. Early efforts with the NAACP and with political campaigns (Green 2004; Gillespie 2005) generated negligible results. These RCTs encouraged turnout but did not include what is now widely considered a best practice for direct mail GOTV: social pressure. In 2006 a group of scholars piloted a social-pressure direct mail GOTV message. When told that their voting behavior was being monitored and might be shared with household members or neighbors, recipients of these pieces of direct mail were far more likely to vote (Gerber et al. 2008). Dozens of RCTs in various electoral contexts have since replicated and refined this approach. In November 2009, a team of scholars used positive social-pressure mailers encouraging recipients to "join your neighborhood's Civic Honor Roll of perfect voters" to successfully increase Black voter turnout in New Jersey's gubernatorial election (Panagopoulos 2013b, 275).

Our PATM efforts also used direct mail, but they involved far more than just thanking voters for their prior civic engagement or applying social pressure. Mailers that thank registered voters for prior turnout or for registering to vote and remind them that voting is a matter of public record are encouraging recipients to vote as a means of fulfilling their civic duty and conforming with social norms, and these are well-documented GOTV best practices. PATM did more. The packages invited recipients to celebrate the election as something they were doing together with their local community, as something they should do out of civic duty, but also as an activity that cultivates Black joy. This is a very different emotional process from one that focuses squarely on social pressure and norms alone.

Black voters are uniquely influenced to participate in elections due to well-understood behavioral norms and social expectations. A handful of RCTs document the effectiveness of local efforts at mobilizing Black voters, as noted earlier. In addition, scholars have documented the pervasive and productive mobilizing efforts conducted by community organizations that serve Black Americans, including churches and social networks (Harris 1999; McDaniel 2008; Philpot et al. 2009; I. White and Laird 2020). PATM combines these threads of scholarship in support of a new theory for how to most effectively motivate members of local Black communities to go to the polls. VCCM builds on historical understandings of Black group consciousness and social norms to better harness expressions of Black joy and feelings of civic duty into local voting celebrations. Especially when conducted in cooperation with local organizations, and in ways that helped residents see their neighbors participating in the program, PATM generated large and meaningful increases in Black turnout. More than that, it generated a stronger sense of community-wide belonging, and in some cases boosted political efficacy—making voters feel like they matter, that their votes matter, and that their community matters.

At the same time, not every iteration of the project was successful in the same ways; these results helped us refine our VCCM and better understand when and where PATM has the best chance of generating statistically significant effects. In addition to the factors already noted (e.g., election salience, local partners), the project also struggled at times due to assumptions about Black voter preferences and concerns about legal challenges. Given the high stakes of some of these elections, and the well-documented preference for Democratic Party candidates by Black voters, concerns were raised by some partnering organizations and donors that the project was not truly nonpartisan. There were additional fears that PATM may have been eliding legal restrictions about nonpartisan voter mobilization with the goal of helping Democratic candidates win elections. This meant time and money were spent on legal advice and responses to these concerns that might otherwise have been devoted to the PATM project, and it also meant that Robinson, Novey, and other organizers were unable to give their full attention to the PATM project. These distractions were particularly notable during the November 2020 and January 2021 PATM projects. Future efforts at mobilizing Black or other communities with historically strong preferences for one political party should keep these challenges in mind.

Another challenge is the labor-intensive and otherwise costly nature of the PATM program's efforts to create celebrations of community. The original Party at the Polls efforts (see chapter 1) increased voter turnout by 2.6 percentage points on average across fourteen voting festival sites. The average cost per vote in these early programs was about $28. In PATM's first pilot program during the Baltimore primary election, our cost per vote was significantly higher—around $87. The total cost of the boxes alone was $27 but, again, there were elements of our pilot program that were very labor intensive. We needed people to pack boxes locally and then to hand-deliver boxes to participants. Had labor and the content of PATM boxes been donated, the cost per vote could have dropped to $23.44. When the program pivoted to using skinny sleeves, our material costs dropped from $27 to $13. While cost is a consideration in implementing programs like PATM in the future, it is not an insurmountable obstacle given the potential for significant cost reduction through the use of volunteers and donations.

Other Considerations for Future GOTV Efforts

Social media played a major role in PATM. In several of our PATM cities, we utilized social media to spread the word about our efforts. Black Girls Vote and partner organizations posted about PATM on multiple social media platforms. On one day in October 2020, Robinson was allowed to take over Lady Gaga's Instagram feed to promote PATM. We also used social media to engage in virtual community celebrations—making them safe in the middle of the pandemic. These virtual events had massive turnout (as discussed in chapter 3). When we returned to Atlanta, one of the in-person party headliners, Omeretta the Great, had recently gone viral online for her song "Sorry Not Sorry," where she lists each local suburb that "is not Atlanta," boosting visibility of her participation in the event. Technology and social media that allowed for the spread of PATM information, for our celebration in Baltimore, and for this local artist's national recognition will continue to play an increasingly important role in shaping how people interact with information and their own communities.

Social media plays a critical role in modern Black politics and in the Black community—evident perhaps by the existence of "Black Twitter" (S. McDonald 2014). Until recently, Black people used X (formerly known as Twitter) at higher rates than any other racial or ethnic group, and they are more likely than any other group to use social media to engage in activism (Auxier 2020). (Many Black users have left X since the November 2024 election and are working to reestablish the community on other social media sites, e.g., Blacksky on Bluesky (Adams and McCorvey 2024, Parham 2024)). PATM efforts were designed to be local, but also included messaging about how similar efforts were being conducted in multiple cities. Social media is helpful for cultivating a broader sense of community that links events across geographic locations. Future efforts might increase their effectiveness by making broader use of virtual spaces including Bluesky, Instagram, and other platforms.

The focus of the PATM efforts was on in-person celebrations, but social media can certainly enhance VCCM, and further research is needed to assess the impact of virtual events (like the ones hosted by Robinson and Black Girls Vote) on the local level. Conversely, investigating how nonlocal voters may be influenced by exposure to these intentionally localized events through online platforms would be a valuable direction for future research. We don't know how these local celebrations might inspire *other* communities or affect them in other ways.

We assume that future virtual celebrations will broaden the effort's overall reach, create cost-effective and convenient ways to participate, amplify community voices, and increase the overall accessibility of the celebrations. However, these are mere assumptions. We don't know for certain what the potential impacts are of future local community-based efforts that engage in outreach virtually, and this is an area where future research will be critical. Again, moving forward, the future of PATM-style celebrations will likely require a combination of continued innovation, creative use of technology and social media (e.g., varying or expanding to use new platforms, live streaming, and incorporating the involvement of online influencers), and continued strategic partnerships to effectively engage with the Black community.

This book exists because of our partnership with Black Girls Vote, and Black Girls Vote succeeded in their efforts to pursue the PATM project because of their partnership with our academic team. Arguments can be made both in favor of and against such partnerships. Partnering with a community organization increases the ability of academics to conduct research ethically and with cultural competency; scholars learn from local experts who have the real-world experience and knowledge that is often absent from scholarly books and journals. In turn, this perspective increases the relevance of the work to the real world. For scholars like us who are interested in work that actively engages with and improves the world we live in, that is an important outcome. For community organizations, partnering with scholars increases their ability to evaluate the effectiveness of their efforts and to conduct work that benefits from previous research. The resulting white papers and academic products can be shared with community members and funders as evidence of their effectiveness. This increases their ability to raise funds and to lobby for change. At the same time, of course, there are challenges. Working with community organizations means giving up some amount of control—randomized studies are still possible, but not everything will be as tightly controlled as in projects in which academics make all the decisions. And community organizations have different goals and timelines, which may not always align with those of their academic partners. Still, we found that the benefits far outweigh the challenges. We encourage other scholars to seek community organizations whose work they support in order to form partnerships, to learn from those community experts, and to engage in work that is grounded in real-world conditions and has real-world relevance. These partnerships allow us to give back to our communities and neighbors, building our academic résumés while also building a better world.

Community Celebrations

While not the focus of this book, other contemporary GOTV efforts also harness the power of community celebrations. In California, the Student Civic and Voter Empowerment Act of 2019 (AB 963) requires colleges to take an active role in celebrating voting, including mandated campuswide emails with reminders about civic holidays such as National Voter Registration Day. National Voter Registration Day was first celebrated in 2012; in 2020, three more civic holidays were added: National Voter Education Day, Vote Early Day, and Election Hero Day. Schools, communities, and workplaces are encouraged to recognize these civic holidays to "strengthen and celebrate" American democracy (Civic Holidays, n.d.). Many college campuses around the country now host election festivals and celebrate these civic holidays, often with the support of national organizations. Each election cycle, the Students Learn

Students Vote Coalition conducts a Campus Takeover in cooperation with hundreds of campuses to help them host celebratory events around the different civic holidays.

To date, no RCTs have been conducted to evaluate the effectiveness of voting festivals held on college campuses, but qualitative data suggest such efforts raise awareness and engagement. In 2022, the nonpartisan Student Public Interest Research Groups held events at 150 campuses, making nearly two hundred thousand GOTV contacts with students through fun events such as Donut Forget to Vote and Instagram stories (Student Public Interest Research Groups, n.d.). Since 2016, Civic Nation has partnered with campuses across the country to host election festivals; in 2022, this included fifteen events with historically Black colleges and universities that reached twenty-five thousand students (Civic Nation 2023). In 2018, former First Lady Michelle Obama created When We All Vote, a national organization aiming to increase voter turnout, as the name implies (When We All Vote is now part of Civic Nation). One component of When We All Vote's work is the Party at the Polls initiative. Their website notes, "Party at the Polls brings our communities together with food, music, and fun activities for the whole family as we make our voices heard at the ballot box" (When We All Vote, n.d.).

These and other festival-based GOTV efforts are inspired by the polling-place parties studied by Donald Green and his collaborators between 2005 and 2018 (see chapter 1), where turnout in treatment neighborhoods increased by an average of 2.5 percentage points in 2006, 3.8 percentage points in 2016, and 3.5 percentage points at early-voting festivals in 2018, although a larger sample of Election Day festivals in 2017 and 2018 generated null results (Addonizio et al. 2007; Green and McClellan 2017, 2020). These mixed results from the later analyses notwithstanding, many community organizations were inspired by the stronger early findings to generate their own community parties at the polls. They weren't using RCTs to estimate impacts on turnout, but their eyes and ears told them that the festivals made a difference, and they have continued to fund and organize them.

In 2018, Baltimore Votes hosted polling-place parties at nearly 20 percent (80 of 297) of all precincts in Baltimore City. In 2020, Black Girls Vote and Baltimore Votes hoped to expand that effort to all 297 precincts. That plan was interrupted by the COVID-19 pandemic, but

Robinson and Novey instead launched the PATM project. Whether via live celebrations at polling places or via the mail and social media, the core insight of the eighteenth-century Election Day festivals among enslaved Black people, the parties at the polls piloted by Green in 2005, and the PATM iterations of 2020, 2021, 2022, and 2024 remains the same: Encouraging voters to celebrate voting brings communities together and increases turnout.

The LGBTQ community has also used the power of celebration to motivate voter participation. In recent years, this has involved channeling the power and popularity of drag to mobilize voters. Drag—the art form of challenging and breaking gender norms, most often with male-identified gay men wearing makeup and glamorous clothing traditionally worn by women—has always been a celebration of LGBTQ identity and expression, and it has always been political. In 2016, drag performers on the popular television show *RuPaul's Drag Race* used their national platform to encourage viewers to register and to vote (Kornhaber 2017; Middlemost 2020), as did local drag performers (Greenhalgh 2018) and panelists at DragCon, an annual *Drag Race* fan convention (Villarreal 2018). *Drag Race* has continued to promote voter turnout in subsequent elections, including a (pre-taped) appearance by Vice President Harris in 2024 (Weissert 2024). Drag Out the Vote, a national effort launched in 2020 to use the celebrity of drag performers to motivate people to register and to vote, channels the joyful, community spirit engendered by the art form to attract attention to their GOTV message. As Edward Kammerer Jr. and Melissa Michelson note in their study of the Drag Out the Vote project, "Everyone loves a party, and drag is a party" (2022, 657).

In part due to evidence generated by RCTs, the use of celebrations to motivate voter turnout has experienced a renaissance in the twenty-first century, harking back to the joyful events of the first half century of the new United States, when elections were "an opportunity to let loose and party" (Blakemore 2019). This is increasingly relevant in the modern era, when many potential voters, especially young voters, view electoral politics with cynicism and distaste. Encouragements to view elections as something to celebrate, as something that brings people together with hope and joy, make it less likely that voters will opt out of participating. Election festivals are an antidote to the apprehension generated by today's polarized politics.

A multicampus study of college student attitudes and participation in the 2020 presidential election revealed that many of them experienced anxiety when discussing politics, particularly when conversing with family and friends on the subject (Osorio et al. 2023). One participant expressed feeling anxious due to the differing political views within their household, which often resulted in arguments rather than constructive dialogue. Another student recounted a poignant experience of being judged and alienated by their peers after receiving a text from the Joe Biden campaign. Programs like PATM may help to mitigate the tension present in political conversations by introducing a lighthearted and enjoyable approach to celebrating voting and civic engagement. These programs enable families and friends to come together and participate in the democratic process—and celebrate being part of a democracy—without having to delve into discussions about specific campaigns or candidates. In doing so, they can effectively circumvent the apprehension commonly associated with political discourse.

It's Not Just a Box

Across all nine RCTs and throughout the PATM project, Robinson repeatedly reminded the academic team and community partners, "It's not just a box, it's an experience." The community engagement and joy cultivated with the boxes spilled over to household members, neighbors, and social media networks that shared in the PATM experience. Black residents in the communities we worked in felt appreciated, felt excited, and felt joy as they came together to celebrate their electoral power and to come out to vote. They were motivated by civic duty to their ancestors and to their families and neighbors, but also by their group consciousness as members of cohesive Black communities and as members of a project bigger than themselves. The VCCM GOTV engagement method (1) acknowledges and intentionally celebrates individual voters as active participants in American democracy, (2) messages that voting is a fun and educational family activity, and (3) celebrates voting as an act of public service in a voter's residential community. From our pilot effort in Baltimore for the June 2020 primary through our skinny sleeve iteration in Philadelphia for the November 2024 general election, we cued these three messages with PATM packages and online and in-person events, often (and most successfully) in partnership with deeply embedded local community organizations. The successes documented in this book support VCCM and provide a strong road map for future PATM iterations, as well as for other celebrations of community, including election festivals and Souls to the Polls. Despite the sometimes hostile and often polarizing nature of recent election cycles, celebrations can still bring people together to encourage the prosocial behavior of voting as an expression of community power and joy.

ACKNOWLEDGMENTS

When the COVID-19 pandemic shut down the country in early 2020, it disrupted everything. Get-out-the-vote campaigns struggled with whether it was safe to engage in door-to-door canvassing. Schools shifted to remote instruction. We wore masks to the store and wiped down our groceries before bringing them indoors. People were scared and dying. But the race for the White House continued. While some states moved to delay their spring elections, there was little wiggle room for the presidential election cycle. COVID-19 fears notwithstanding, the election show had to go on. Three states (Arizona, Florida, and Illinois) held their primaries on March 17, 2020, as scheduled, but in many other states the primary elections were delayed, sometimes with extended rules allowing for expanded use of absentee ballots or adopting vote-by-mail procedures for almost all voters (Corasaniti and Saul 2020).

In Wisconsin, Democratic Governor Tony Evers issued an executive order to postpone in-person voting and extend the deadline for absentee ballots to June, but the order was successfully blocked by Republican legal challenges. Other states moved to vote-by-mail elections (or almost completely vote-by-mail elections), including Alaska (also delaying the election from March 24 to April 10), Wyoming (delaying from April 4 to April 17), Ohio (delaying from March 17 to April 28), Kansas (May 2), Hawaii (May 22), and Indiana (delayed from May 5 to June 2). The governors of Maryland, Pennsylvania, and Rhode Island moved those state primaries from April 28 to June 2 and shifted to vote-by-mail elections. In Georgia, Secretary of State Brad Raffensperger first moved the primary from March 24 to May 19, responding to Governor Brian Kemp's declaration of a state public health emergency; when that state of emergency was extended, the primary was again moved, to June 9, but the election retained its in-person format. In-person primaries were delayed in West Virginia (from May 12 to June 9), Kentucky (from May 19 to June 23),

New York (from April 28 to June 23), Virginia (from June 9 to June 23), and New Jersey (from June 2 to July 7). New York tried to cancel the election altogether but was ordered by a federal judge to follow through with the June 23 contest. Delaware postponed its primary election from April 28 to July 7 and also sent all registered voters a vote-by-mail ballot. Louisiana delayed its primary twice, from April 4 to June 20, and then to July 11. Similarly, Puerto Rico postponed its Democratic primary from March 29 to April 26, and then to July 12. Connecticut postponed its primary from April 28 to June 2 and then to August 11. The Alabama Republican primary race for a US Senate seat was postponed from March 31 to July 14. Even the Democratic National Convention was delayed, from July 13–16 to the week of August 17.

State and local election officials implemented these procedural changes to allow voters to cast their ballots safely, citing the health risks posed by crowded polling places. The broader use of vote-by-mail ballots, in particular, aimed to minimize in-person interactions and reduce the risk of virus transmission at polling stations. Many jurisdictions extended early-voting periods and set up secure drop boxes for mail-in ballots in order to reduce the number of people showing up at polling places on Election Day.

Community organizations had to adapt to the new reality imposed by the pandemic as well. In West Baltimore, Maryland, Black Girls Vote founder Nyki Robinson was determined to ensure that her community voted, and in a moment of inspiration created the Party at the Mailbox (PATM) project. Understanding the importance of community-based collaboration, she first pitched her idea to Sam Novey, cofounder of Baltimore Votes and a longtime community partner. Together, Robinson and Novey then reached out to political scientists who might help them design PATM in a way that would ensure a robust evaluation of its effectiveness. Their goal was to create a data-driven, evidence-based approach that could be replicated in other communities facing similar challenges.

The multiracial, intergenerational team of scholars that conducted this research reflects the uniqueness of the project. Melissa Michelson, a senior scholar with decades of experience in the subfield of get-out-the-vote research and the analytical method of randomized controlled trials, was the initial point of contact with Black Girls Vote. Michelson recognized the project's need for expertise in Black politics and immediately reached out to colleagues to recruit an appropriate team. Reflecting her longtime commitment to mentorship and to increasing the diversity of the discipline, she also recruited to the project team multiple women of color in earlier stages of their academic careers. The final group of graduate students and faculty who contributed to the project thus included early-career women and Black women. Both coauthors of this book are early career women: Sarah Hayes is a Black graduate student and Stephanie DeMora was a graduate student when the project began and is now an assistant professor. Both were essential members of that team and are experts in political behavior.

The rest, as they say, is history. For the next few years, our academic team worked hand in hand with Robinson and Novey and their practitioner and community colleagues to determine just how powerful the PATM project was and could be for motivating voter participation in majority-Black communities. Together, we crafted a strategy that incorporated targeted outreach, voter education, and community mobilization through community celebration and expressions of Black joy. Through these collaborative efforts, the PATM project not only aimed to increase voter turnout but also sought to empower Black communities by instilling a sense of membership and pride in the electoral process.

Eventually, the moment came where we realized, "This is a book," and we turned our attention from writing brief white papers and funder presentations to drafting chapters. The book delves into the development, implementation, and impact of the PATM project, shedding light on the potential of grassroots efforts to drive civic participation. It offers valuable insights into the role of community organizations in promoting voter engagement, as well as into the power of innovation and collaboration in addressing complex societal challenges. By sharing the PATM story, we hope to inspire other communities to adopt similar strategies and foster a stronger sense of civic responsibility across the nation.

A book is always a major project with many, many people involved. We are enormously grateful first to Robinson and Novey, who believed in us and trusted us to not only crunch their data but write about their work. We are grateful to the many other members of the PATM project at their organizations, Black Girls Vote and Baltimore Votes. This project would not be possible without the input of scholars like Ashley C. J. Daniels and folks on the ground in each of our cities. We give special thanks to our qualitative data coordinators who worked on organizing focus groups and in-depth interviews with community members and local organizers: Kimberly R. Moffitt (Baltimore 2020), Camille Burge and Nyron Crawford (Philadelphia 2020), Christine Slaughter (Detroit 2020), Kamri Hudgins (Detroit 2022), Lakeyta M. Bonnette-Bailey and Teri Platt (Atlanta 2021), and Kevin Sparrow (Atlanta 2022). We are also extremely grateful to team members who conducted focus groups and held interviews either locally or over Zoom. It is largely due to their local expertise and cultural competency that we were able to collect such rich data from across the country: Annabella Cockerell, Abigail Cohen, David Denton, Joshua Griffin, Caitlyn Grunert, Shannon Hicks, Jason James, Anthony Nichols, Kyle Patel, Eugenia Quintanilla, Ignanelli Salinas-Muniz, Jonathan Santos, Kendall Turro, Tyra Walker, Zoe Walker, Niiaja Wright, and Rosalind Wynne. Our data team was invaluable in ensuring that our quantitative data were of the highest possible quality. For this, we must thank Josh Allen, Jazz Applewhite, Joel Beauchamp, Jade Carr, Kate Cohee, Maria V. DeMora, Taj Farmer, Rebecca Frost-Brewer, Adriana Ninci, Busra Nur Ozguler, Maricruz Ariana Osorio, Sofia Sciascia, Morgan Smith, Undariya Tegshbayar, and Ozlem Tuncel.

All of the people working with Robinson and Black Girls Vote played a critical role in ensuring that the party actually happened. People like Ashley Daniels, Savannah Frazier, Natasha Murphey, Sam Novey, Rebecca Phillips, Cortney Robertson, Tasmin Swanson, Dea Thomas, Tenne Thrower, Akil Trice, Patricia Watson, and many more made sure that the program worked, and that PATM boxes were designed, put together, addressed, and delivered.

We also owe enormous debts to our colleagues who helped us think through the project, including the Voter Community Celebration Model that pulls it all together, and who gave feedback at various political science association meetings. Thank you to Tova Wang for reaching out to Melissa and introducing her, way back in April 2020, to Novey and Robinson. In addition, we received instrumental assistance and support from Vin Arceneaux, Don Green, Michael Hanmer, Tyson King-Meadows, Chris Mann, and Lester Spence.

The PATM project itself exists and succeeded because of the financial support of various entities and institutions, including crucial initial donors Carolyn and Joe Cohen. We also received valuable financial support from Melissa's home institution, Menlo College. Our thanks also go to PATM's external partners and funders, including the Alliance for Youth Organizing; Baltimore Votes; Chambers Fund; City Fund; Civic Georgia; Corinthian International Foundation; the David Rockefeller Foundation; Detroit vs. Everybody; Globe at MICA; the Movement Team; Movement Voter Project; the National Conference on Citizenship; the National Domestic Workers Alliance; the National Philanthropic Trust; the New Birth Baptist Missionary Church; the Open Society Institute; OSI Baltimore; the Partnership for Safe Voting/New Venture Fund; Public Wise; She Can Win; the Students Learn, Students Vote Coalition; and Under Armour.

We benefited from feedback presented at various conferences, including annual meetings of the National Conference of Black Political Scientists, the American Political Science Association, the Midwest Political Science Association, and the Western Political Science Association, as well as from the University of California, Riverside, graduate colloquium, Stony Brook University, and the University of Virginia. The feedback we received at those presentations helped refine and improve the work.

We are also very grateful to our editors at New York University Press, Sonia Tsuruoka for her early enthusiasm and support of the project, and Ilene Kalish for taking us across the finish line, including helping secure an amazing cover that recognizes the project's partnership with the Globe Press at the Maryland Institute College of Art. Our two editors were a delight to work with at every step along the way.

Finally, thank you to our families. Melissa thanks her husband Christopher Gardner, and her sons Colin, Jackson, Joshua, and Zachary, for their love and support, and for understanding why she sometimes sits at her computer on nights and weekends, or even while "on vacation." Stephanie owes a debt of gratitude to her husband and best friend, Gary Rettberg; daughter, Anna Elise; parents, Priscilla and Daniel; sisters, Meghan and Maria; grandparents, Carole, Elaine, Daniel, and Paul; and dear friends Brittany and Brighton for their unending love and encouragement during these efforts and beyond. Sarah thanks her mother, Linda; sister, Candice; nephew, Nathanial; friends Alexandra and Rosalinda; and mentors, Nadia and Jamil, for their unwavering support and continued encouragement throughout this journey.

Finally, we must thank the communities in which we implemented PATM. To the community members in Baltimore, Philadelphia, Detroit, Atlanta, and Richmond: Thank you for welcoming us into your neighborhoods and inviting us to the party. At times the work of pushing back against voter disenfranchisement and disinformation can seem daunting, and the negativity and polarization of modern politics can make it tempting to turn away and leave politics to others. Your dedication to democracy and to your neighbors is testament to the power of Black joy and community organizing, and we are better people for having learned from you.

Baltimore Pilot June 2020

Respondent age ranged from 18 to 77 (mean = 42.5). Most respondents (87.9 percent) identified as female, 11.5 percent as male, and 0.6 percent as nonbinary. Most (63.6 percent) identified as Black or as multiple races including Black, another 29 percent identified as white (non-Hispanic), and the remaining respondents identified as Asian only, Hispanic only, Middle Eastern or Arab, mixed race not including Black, or other. Of those providing a partisan identification, most (91 percent) identified as Democrats (including leaners).

Table A.1: Political Efficacy, Party at the Mailbox, Baltimore Pilot Survey

Control group average	Treatment group average	Difference
Full sample		
Agree that the government in Baltimore cares what people like me think		
1.47	1.39	−0.08
Agree that people like me have a say in what the federal government does		
1.54	1.41	−0.13
Agree that the government in Washington cares what people like me think		
1.11	1.04	−0.07
Black sample		
Agree that the government in Baltimore cares what people like me think		
1.55	1.30	−0.25
Agree that people like me have a say in what the federal government does		
1.46	1.34	−0.12
Agree that the government in Washington cares what people like me think		
1.03	0.93	−0.10

Notes: Efficacy scores here range on a scale from 0 to 3 with higher scores indicating higher levels of political efficacy. We included encouragement scores in our other surveys (see later in the appendix), but they are not included here due to a programming error.

Table A.2: Identity Strength, Party at the Mailbox, Baltimore Pilot Survey

Identity as a . . .	Control group average	Treatment group average	Difference
Full sample			
Baltimorean	2.11	2.30	0.19*
American	2.12	2.16	0.04
Voter	2.63	2.70	0.07
Black sample			
Baltimorean	2.00	2.40	0.40*
American	2.03	2.15	0.12
Voter	2.56	2.69	0.13*

Notes: Identity survey items are coded 0 (not at all) to 3 (very well). Differences noted with an asterisk are statistically significant.

Baltimore November 2020

Respondent age ranged from 19 to 77 (mean = 40.51). Most respondents (93.1 percent) identified as female, 5.5 percent as male, 1 percent identified as nonbinary, and 0.4 percent identified as a transgender male. Most (86 percent) identified as Black or as multiple races including Black, another 9 percent identified as white, 9 percent non-Hispanic, and the remaining 5 percent of respondents identified as Asian only, Hispanic only, Middle Eastern or Arab, mixed race not including Black, or other. Of those providing a partisan identification, most (92 percent) identified as Democrats (including leaners).

Detroit November 2020

Respondent age ranged from 18 to 77 (mean = 41.03). Most respondents (87.8 percent) identified as female, 11.8 percent as male, and 0.4 percent identified as transgender male. Most (92.5 percent) identified as Black or as multiple races including Black, another 3.1 percent identified as white, non-Hispanic (3 percent), and the remaining respondents (5 percent) identified as Asian only, Hispanic only, Middle Eastern or Arab, mixed race not including Black, or other. Of those providing a partisan identification, most (90 percent) identified as Democrats (including leaners).

Table A.3: Efficacy and Encouragement, Party at the Mailbox, Baltimore General Survey

Control group average	Treatment group average	Difference
Full sample		
Agree that the government in Baltimore cares what people like me think		
0.457	0.431	−0.026
Agree that people like me have a say in what the federal government does		
0.307	0.332	0.025
Agree that the government in Washington cares what people like me think		
0.568	0.579	0.011
Encourage others to vote		
3.144	3.349	0.205
Black sample		
Agree that the government in Baltimore cares what people like me think		
0.450	0.435	−0.015
Agree that people like me have a say in what the federal government does		
0.292	0.317	0.025
Agree that the government in Washington cares what people like me think		
0.567	0.580	0.013
Encourage others to vote		
3.214	3.393	0.179

Notes: Efficacy scores here range on a scale from 0 to 1, with higher scores indicating higher levels of political efficacy. Encouragement scores here are additive, indicating the number of other types (e.g., friends, family, co-workers, etc.) of individuals that the respondent reported encouraging to vote.

Table A.4: Identity Strength, Party at the Mailbox, Baltimore General Survey

Identity as a . . .	Control group average	Treatment group average	Difference
Full sample			
Baltimorean	2.226	2.210	−0.016
American	2.433	2.325	−0.108
Voter	2.659	2.655	−0.004
Black sample			
Baltimorean	2.229	2.214	−0.015
American	2.469	2.323	−0.146
Voter	2.646	2.649	0.003

Note: Identity survey items are coded 0 (not at all) to 3 (very well).

Table A.5: Efficacy and Encouragement, Party at the Mailbox, Detroit General Survey

Control group average	Treatment group average	Difference
Full sample		
Agree that the government in Detroit cares what people like me think		
0.404	0.413	0.009
Agree that people like me have a say in what the federal government does		
0.320	0.293	−0.027
Agree that the government in Washington cares what people like me think		
0.603	0.567	−0.036
Encourage others to vote		
3.277	3.432	0.155
Black sample		
Agree that the government in Detroit cares what people like me think		
0.394	0.404	0.010
Agree that people like me have a say in what the federal government does		
0.317	0.289	−0.028
Agree that the government in Washington cares what people like me think		
0.593	0.577	−0.016
Encourage others to vote		
3.273	3.452	0.179

Notes: Efficacy scores here range on a scale from 0 to 1, with higher scores indicating higher levels of political efficacy. Encouragement scores here are additive, indicating the number of other types of individuals that the respondent reported encouraging to vote.

Table A.6: Identity Strength, Party at the Mailbox, Detroit General Survey

Identity as a . . .	Control group average	Treatment group average	Difference
Full sample			
Detroiter	2.698	2.744	0.046
American	2.500	2.467	−0.033
Voter	2.693	2.707	0.014
Black sample			
Detroiter	2.686	2.765	0.079
American	2.483	2.482	−0.001
Voter	2.672	2.728	0.056

Note: Identity survey items are coded 0 (not at all) to 3 (very well).

Philadelphia November 2020

Respondent age ranged from 18 to 79 (mean = 43.97). Most respondents (90 percent) identified as female, 9 percent as male, 0.2 percent identified as nonbinary, and 0.2 percent as something else. Most (83.5 percent) identified as Black or as multiple races including Black, another 9.1 percent identified as white, non-Hispanic (9 percent), and the remaining respondents (8 percent) identified as Asian only, Hispanic only, Middle Eastern or Arab, mixed race not including Black, or other. Of those providing a partisan identification, most (94 percent) identified as Democrats (including leaners).

Table A.7. Efficacy and Encouragement, Party at the Mailbox, Philadelphia General Survey

Control group average	Treatment group average	Difference
Full sample		
Agree that the government in Philadelphia cares what people like me think		
0.455	0.453	0.002
Agree that people like me have a say in what the federal government does		
0.343	0.352	0.009
Agree that the government in Washington cares what people like me think		
0.576	0.585	0.009
Encourage others to vote		
3.209	3.184	−0.025
Black sample		
Agree that the government in Philadelphia cares what people like me think		
0.446	0.460	0.014
Agree that people like me have a say in what the federal government does		
0.335	0.354	0.019
Agree that the government in Washington cares what people like me think		
0.574	0.588	0.014
Encourage others to vote		
3.282	3.280	−0.002

Notes: Efficacy scores here range on a scale from 0 to 1, with higher scores indicating higher levels of political efficacy. Encouragement scores here are additive, indicating the number of other types of individuals that the respondent reported encouraging to vote.

Table A.8. Identity Strength, Party at the Mailbox, Philadelphia General Survey

Identity as a . . .	Control group average	Treatment group average	Difference
Full sample			
Philadelphian	2.537	2.513	−0.024
American	2.412	2.412	0.000
Voter	2.699	2.647	−0.052
Black Sample			
Philadelphian	2.563	2.524	−0.039
American	2.367	2.395	0.028
Voter	2.711	2.683	−0.028

Note: Identity survey items are coded 0 (not at all) to 3 (very well).

Atlanta Runoff January 2021

Respondent age ranged from 18 to 79 (mean = 37.6). Most respondents (84.8 percent) identified as female, 14.6 percent as male, 0.2 percent identified as nonbinary, 0.2 percent identified as a transgender female, and 0.2 percent identified as something else. Most (86.5 percent) identified as Black or as multiple races including Black, another 9 percent identified as white, non-Hispanic, and the remaining respondents identified as Asian only, Hispanic only, Middle Eastern or Arab, mixed race not including Black, or other. Of those providing a partisan identification, most (86 percent) identified as Democrats (including leaners).

Baltimore June 2020 Survey

Consent
You are invited to participate in a research study about voting and public opinion around the 2020 presidential primary, being conducted by Baltimore Votes, Black Girls Vote, and researchers at Menlo College. Your participation in this study will help us understand why residents of Baltimore, MD participate in politics. If you decide to take part in this study, you will be asked to complete a survey that will take between 8–10 minutes of your time. We will also ask basic demographic questions and others related to political attitudes and behavior. At the end of this

Table A.9: Identity Strength, Party at the Mailbox, 2021 Atlanta Survey: Full Sample

	Control group average	Treatment group average	Difference
Identity as an Atlantan			
Everyone	2.02	2.20	0.18*
Hosts	2.16	2.20	0.04
Guests	1.36	2.23	0.87*
Identity as an American			
Everyone	2.08	2.39	0.31*
Hosts	2.12	2.38	0.26*
Guests	1.92	2.53	0.61*
Identity as a voter			
Everyone	2.53	2.76	0.23*
Hosts	2.63	2.77	0.14*
Guests	2.02	2.66	0.64*
Agree that the government in Atlanta cares what people like me think			
Everyone	0.60	0.63	0.03
Hosts	0.62	0.63	0.01
Guests	0.49	0.66	0.17*
Agree that people like me have a say in what the federal government does			
Everyone	0.65	0.72	0.07*
Hosts	0.67	0.73	0.06*
Guests	0.58	0.64	0.06
Agree that the government in Washington cares what people like me think			
Everyone	0.42	0.46	0.04*
Hosts	0.42	0.47	0.05*
Guests	0.41	0.43	0.02

Notes: Identity survey items are coded 0 (not at all) to 3 (very well). Efficacy items are coded on a scale from 0 to 1, with higher scores indicating higher levels of political efficacy. Differences noted with an asterisk are statistically significant. Data collected January 19–February 8, 2021.

survey, you will be asked for an email address at which you will receive compensation upon successful completion of the survey. Participation in this study is entirely voluntary. You must be 18 years or older, a U.S. citizen, and fluent in English to participate. You may decline to answer particular survey questions or choose to end your participation at any time without penalty. Confidentiality will be maintained at all times. Each survey will contain a random identification number. The data collected from this study will be stored on secure computers. This study should not include any risks or discomforts for you that you would not encounter in everyday life. You may feel uncomfortable answering some of the survey questions, but you are free to skip any that you do not want to answer. There will be no direct benefit to you for participating in this study; however, we hope to learn more about your views on politics. Additionally, you will be given an option to list your email at the end of this survey to receive a $10 Amazon gift card.

If you have any questions for the researchers or would like information about the study results, please contact Dr. Melissa Michelson, Department of Political Science, melissa.michelson@menlo.edu or by phone at (650) 543-3844. By clicking yes below, I agree to participate in the study.

☐ Yes
☐ No

Thank you for taking part in our survey of opinions among residents of Baltimore, MD. By agreeing to take this survey, you certify that you are 18 years of age or older.

☐ Yes, I am 18 or older.
☐ No, I am not 18 or older.

1. Did you have a chance to vote in the presidential **primary** election in **April of 2016?** That was the election when voters weighed in on who should be the nominees for president, a race eventually won by Hillary Clinton on the Democratic side and Donald Trump on the Republican side. There was also a crowded Democratic field to replace Mayor Stephanie Rawlings-Blake, which was won by Catherine Pugh. [Response options: Yes; No; Not sure/Don't know]

2. Did you have a chance to vote in the presidential **general** election in **November of 2016?** That was the race between Hillary Clinton and Donald Trump, and when Catherine Pugh was elected mayor, edging out Sheila Dixon, Alan Walden, and Joshua Harris. [Yes; No; Not sure/Don't know]

3. Did you have a chance to vote in the presidential **primary** election (**June 2020** election)? That was the election held just a few weeks ago to choose the Democratic nominee for the presidency and the nominees for mayor, which was won by Democrat Brandon Scott and Republican Shannon Wright. [Yes; No; Not sure/Don't know]
4. Different people feel differently about voting.
   [Below statements are presented in random order.]
   > For some, voting is a DUTY. They feel that they should vote in every election however they feel about the candidates and parties.
   > For others, voting is a CHOICE. They feel free to vote or not to vote in an election depending on how they feel about the candidates and parties.
   > For you personally, voting is FIRST AND FOREMOST a: [Duty; Choice; Not sure]
   4A. How strongly do you feel personally that voting is a [DUTY/ CHOICE]? [Very strongly; Somewhat strongly; Not very strongly]
5. Did you encourage anyone to vote in the **June 2020 primary** election? [Yes; No]
   5A. [If Yes] Please select all that apply:
      ◦ I encouraged a friend to vote in the 2020 primary election
      ◦ I encouraged a co-worker to vote in the 2020 primary election
      ◦ I encouraged my children to vote in the 2020 primary election
      ◦ I encouraged my spouse or partner to vote in the 2020 primary election
      ◦ I encouraged another household member to vote in the 2020 primary election
      ◦ I encouraged my followers to vote via social media posts
      ◦ Other (Please specify)
6. How likely are you to vote in the next presidential **general** election in **November 2020**? [Very likely; Likely; Somewhat likely; Not at all likely; Don't know]
7. Generally speaking, do you usually think of yourself as a: [Democrat; Republican; Independent; Other party (please specify)]

7A. [If Democrat] Would you call yourself a strong Democrat or a not very strong Democrat? [Strong Democrat; Not very strong Democrat]

7B. [If Republican] Would you call yourself a strong Republican or a not very strong Republican? [Strong Republican; Not very strong Republican]

7C. [If Independent] Do you think of yourself as closer to the Republican Party or to the Democratic Party, or equally close to the Republican Party and Democratic Party? [The Republican Party; The Democratic Party; Neither]

8. How well does the term "Baltimorean" describe you? [Extremely well; Very well; Not very well; Not at all]

9. How well does the term "voter" describe you? [Extremely well; Very well; Not very well; Not at all]

10. How well does the term "American" describe you? [Extremely well; Very well; Not very well; Not at all]

11. How well do the following terms describe you? [Extremely well; Very well; Not very well; Not at all]
    A. Woman
    B. Man
    C. Black or African American
    D. White (Non-Hispanic)
    E. Asian American, Pacific Islander
    F. American Indian, Alaska Native

    Please indicate the extent to which you agree or disagree with the following statements:

12. "Sometimes politics and government seem so complicated that a person like me can't really understand what's going on." [Strongly disagree; Somewhat disagree; Somewhat agree; Strongly agree]

13. "People like me don't have any say about what the government in **Washington** does." [Strongly disagree; Somewhat disagree; Somewhat agree; Strongly agree]

14. "People like me don't have any say about what the government in **Baltimore** does." [Strongly disagree; Somewhat disagree; Somewhat agree; Strongly agree]

15. "Public officials in **Washington** don't care much what people like me think." [Strongly disagree; Somewhat disagree; Somewhat agree; Strongly agree]

16. "Public officials in **Baltimore** don't care much what people like me think." [Strongly disagree; Somewhat disagree; Somewhat agree; Strongly agree]

17. When it comes to election policy, how much confidence, if any, do you have in each of the following parts of government to act in the best interests of the public? [A great deal; A fair amount; Not too much; No confidence at all]
    A.   State elections officials
    B.   The Maryland State Board of Elections
    C.   City of Baltimore election officials
    D.   The governor of Maryland
    E.   The Maryland state legislature
    F.   The Federal government

18. Generally speaking, to what extent do you think the following parts of government use elections to find out what citizens want? [To a very large extent; To a large extent; To a moderate extent; To a small extent; To a very small extent]
    A.   State elections officials
    B.   The Maryland State Board of Elections
    C.   City of Baltimore election officials
    D.   The governor of Maryland
    E.   The Maryland state legislature
    F.   The Federal government

19. Generally speaking, to what extent do you think the following parts of government explain their policies to citizens? [To a very large extent; To a large extent; To a moderate extent; To a small extent; To a very small extent]
    A.   State elections officials
    B.   The Maryland State Board of Elections
    C.   City of Baltimore election officials
    D.   The governor of Maryland
    E.   The Maryland state legislature
    F.   The Federal government

20. Generally speaking, when it comes to elections to what extent do you think the following parts of government try to accommodate citizen wishes? [To a very large extent; To a large extent; To a moderate extent; To a small extent; To a very small extent]
    A. State elections officials
    B. The Maryland State Board of Elections
    C. City of Baltimore election officials
    D. The governor of Maryland
    E. The Maryland state legislature
    F. The Federal government

21. **During the past 12 months**, have you done any of the following? [Yes; No; Don't know]
    A. Attended a meeting of a town or city government or school board?
    B. Donated money to a candidate or political issue?
    C. Donated to a religious organization?
    D. Donated to some other charitable cause?
    E. Signed a petition about a political or social issue?
    F. Joined a protest, march, rally, or demonstration?
    G. Contacted a government official to express your views?
    H. Attended a virtual political webinar or information session?
    I. Volunteered with a civic engagement focused organization?

22. **Looking ahead to the next 12 months**, what is the likelihood that you will engage in the following activities? [Not at all likely; Somewhat likely; Likely; Very likely]
    A. Attend a meeting of a town or city government or school board?
    B. Donate money to a candidate or political issue?
    C. Donate to a religious organization?
    D. Donate to some other charitable cause?
    E. Sign a petition about a political or social issue?
    F. Join a protest, march, rally, or demonstration?
    G. Contact a government official to express your views?
    H. Attend a virtual political webinar or information session?
    I. Volunteer with a civic engagement focused organization?

23. What do you think is the most important problem facing the **United States** today?

24. What do you think is the most important problem facing **Maryland** today?

25. What do you think is the most important problem facing **Baltimore** today?

26. In the past 12 months, have you been contacted by any of the following? [Yes; No; Not sure; Don't know]
    A. The Republican Party
    B. The Democratic Party
    C. A political candidate
    D. A political campaign
    E. A community group involved in politics

27. Given the COVID-19 pandemic, getting enough food can be a problem for some people. In the **last 7 days**, which of these statements best describes the food eaten in your household? Select only one answer. [Enough of the kinds of food (I/we) wanted to eat; Enough, but not always the kinds of food (I/we) wanted to eat; Sometimes not enough to eat; Often not enough to eat]

    27A. [If NOT Enough of the kinds of food (I/we) wanted to eat]: Why did you not have enough to eat (or not what you wanted to eat)? Choose all that apply. [Couldn't afford to buy more food; Couldn't get out to buy food; Afraid to go or didn't want to go out to buy food; Couldn't get groceries or meals delivered to me; The stores didn't have the food I wanted]

28. How confident are you that your household will be able to afford the kinds of food you need for the **next four weeks**? [Not at all confident; Somewhat confident; Moderately confident; Very confident]

Thank you for answering those questions. Now I just have a few questions to help classify your answers. Please note that these are only for statistical purposes and your answers will be kept confidential.

29. What year were you born?

30. Did you receive a "Party at the Mailbox" box? [Yes; No]

31. Did someone in your household receive a "Party at the Mailbox" box? [Yes; No]

32. Are you currently registered to vote? [Yes; No; Not sure/Don't know]

33. What is your gender? [Male; Female; Transgender female; Transgender male; Non-binary; Something else (please specify)]

34. What is your race? Choose as many as apply. [White (Non-Hispanic); Black or African American; American Indian or Alaska Native; Asian; Native Hawaiian or Pacific Islander; Hispanic or Latino; Middle-Eastern or Arab; Other (please specify)

     34A. [If more than one Race selected]: With which of the following racial or ethnic groups do you identify most strongly? [White (Non-Hispanic); Black or African American; American Indian or Alaska Native; Asian; Native Hawaiian or Pacific Islander; Hispanic or Latino; Middle-Eastern or Arab; Other (please specify)]

35. What is the highest level of school you have completed or the highest degree you have received? [Less than high school; High school graduate or GED; Some college, but no degree; Associate's Degree (2-year degree); Bachelor's Degree (4-year degree); Master's Degree (including MA, MS, MEng, MEd, MSW, MBA); Advanced/Professional degree (including MD, DDS, DVM, LLB, JD, PhD, EdD); Other (please specify)]

36. Thinking back over the last year, what was your family's annual income? [Under $15,000; Less than $19,999; $20,000–$39,999; $40,000–$59,999; $60,000–$79,999; $80,000–$99,999; $100,000–$149,999; $150,000–$199,999; $200,000 or more; Prefer not to say]

37. Do you have any children under age 18 currently living in your household? [Yes; No]

38. In years, how long have you lived in Baltimore?

Thank you for your participation!

Please indicate which e-mail address would you like us to contact you about the Amazon gift card:

November 2020 Survey

Consent
You are invited to participate in an evaluation effort about voting and public opinion around the 2020 presidential election, being conducted by the Party at the Mailbox project and analysts at Menlo College. Your

participation in this evaluation will help us understand why residents of [CITY] participate in politics. If you decide to take part in this evaluation, you will be asked to complete a survey that will take about 10 minutes of your time. We will also ask basic demographic questions and others related to political attitudes and behavior. At the end of this survey, you will be asked for an email address at which you will receive compensation upon successful completion of the survey. Participation in this survey is entirely voluntary. You must be 18 years or older and a U.S. citizen to participate. You may decline to answer particular survey questions or choose to end your participation at any time without penalty. Confidentiality will be maintained at all times. Each survey will contain a random identification number. The data collected from this survey will be stored on secure computers. This survey should not include any risks or discomforts for you that you would not encounter in everyday life. If you feel uncomfortable answering any of the survey questions, you are free to skip any that you do not want to answer. There will be no direct benefit to you for participating in this survey; however, we hope to learn more about your views on politics. Additionally, you will be given an option to list your email at the end of this survey to receive a $10 Amazon gift card.

If you have any questions for the researchers or would like information about the study results, please contact Dr. Melissa Michelson, Department of Political Science, melissa.michelson@menlo.edu or by phone at (650) 543-3844. By clicking yes below, I agree to participate in the study.

☐ Yes
☐ No

Thank you for taking part in our survey of opinions among residents of [CITY]. By agreeing to take this survey, you certify that you are 18 years of age or older.

☐ Yes, I am 18 or older.
☐ No, I am not 18 or older.

1. Did you have a chance to vote in the **presidential** election on **November 3, 2020,** including early voting and vote by mail? That was the election when voters weighed in on who should be president, choosing between Donald Trump and Joe Biden. [Response

options: Yes; No; Not sure/Don't know; Was not old enough/Was not eligible to vote]

2. Thinking about the November 2020 presidential election, would you say that when you voted you personally cared a good deal who would win the presidential election, or that you didn't care very much who would win? [Cared a good deal; Didn't care very much who would win]

3. Different people feel differently about voting.
   [Below statements are presented in random order.]
   For some, voting is a DUTY. They feel that they should vote in every election however they feel about the candidates and parties.
   For others, voting is a CHOICE. They feel free to vote or not to vote in an election depending on how they feel about the candidates and parties.

4. For you personally, voting is FIRST AND FOREMOST a: [Duty; Choice; Not sure]

5. How strongly do you feel personally that voting is a [duty; choice]? [Very strongly; Somewhat strongly; Not very strongly]

6. Did you encourage anyone to vote in the **November 2020** election? [Yes; No]

   6A. [If Yes] Please select all that apply: [I encouraged a friend to vote in the November 2020 election; I encouraged a co-worker to vote in the November 2020 election; I encouraged my children to vote in the November 2020 election; I encouraged my spouse or partner to vote in the November 2020 election; I encouraged another household member to vote in the November 2020 election; I encouraged my followers to vote via social media posts; Other (Please specify)]

7. Which of these issues mattered most when you were deciding whether to vote this year? [Racial inequality; The coronavirus pandemic; Crime and safety; Health care policy; Jobs and the economy; Other (please specify)]

8. What is your gender? [Male; Female; Transgender female; Transgender male; Non-binary; Something else (please specify)]

9. What is your race? Choose as many as apply. [White (Non-Hispanic); Black or African American; American Indian or Alaska

Native; Asian; Native Hawaiian or Pacific Islander; Hispanic or
Latino; Middle-Eastern or Arab; Other (please specify)]

9A. [If more than one RACE selected]: With which of the follow-
ing racial or ethnic groups do you identify most strongly?
[White (Non-Hispanic); Black or African American;
American Indian or Alaska Native; Asian; Native Hawaiian or
Pacific Islander; Hispanic or Latino; Middle-Eastern or Arab;
Other (please specify)]

10. Generally speaking, do you usually think of yourself as a:
[Democrat; Republican; Independent; Other party (please
specify)]

10A. [If Democrat] Would you call yourself a strong Democrat
or a not very strong Democrat? [Strong Democrat; Not very
strong Democrat]

10B. [If Republican] Would you call yourself a strong Republican
or a not very strong Republican? [Strong Republican; Not
very strong Republican]

10C. [If Independent] Do you think of yourself as closer to the
Republican Party or to the Democratic Party, or equally
close to the Republican Party and Democratic Party? [The
Republican Party; The Democratic Party; Neither]

11. How well does the term "[CITY]an" describe you? [Extremely well;
Very well; Not very well; Not at all]

12. How well does the term "voter" describe you? [Extremely well;
Very well; Not very well; Not at all]

13. How well does the term "American" describe you? [Extremely well;
Very well; Not very well; Not at all]

*Please indicate the extent to which you agree or disagree with the
following statements:*

14. "Sometimes politics and government seem so complicated that
a person like me can't really understand what's going on."
[Strongly disagree; Somewhat disagree; Somewhat agree; Strongly
agree]

15. "People like me don't have any say about what the government
in **Washington** does." [Strongly disagree; Somewhat disagree;
Somewhat agree; Strongly agree]

16. "People like me don't have any say about what the government in [STATE] does." [Strongly disagree; Somewhat disagree; Somewhat agree; Strongly agree]

17. "People like me don't have any say about what the government in [CITY] does." [Strongly disagree; Somewhat disagree; Somewhat agree; Strongly agree]

18. "Public officials in **Washington** don't care much what people like me think." [Strongly disagree; Somewhat disagree; Somewhat agree; Strongly agree]

19. "Public officials in [STATE] don't care much what people like me think." [Strongly disagree; Somewhat disagree; Somewhat agree; Strongly agree]

20. "Public officials in [CITY] don't care much what people like me think." [Strongly disagree; Somewhat disagree; Somewhat agree; Strongly agree]

21. How important is being a [GENDER] to your identity? [Very important; Somewhat important; Not very important]

22. How important is being [RACE] to your identity? [Very important; Somewhat important; Not very important]

23. How important is being a [RACE+GENDER] to your identity? [Very important; Somewhat important; Not very important]

24. Where do you mostly get your news about politics and current affairs? [Social media: Facebook, Twitter, Instagram; Television news; Newspapers; Radio; Conversations at place of worship; Family and friends]

25. Have you or has anyone in your household been diagnosed with the coronavirus? [Yes, me personally; Yes, someone in my immediate family; No]

26. Do you think the reasons why Black people in our country have been hospitalized with and died due to the coronavirus at higher rates than other racial or ethnic groups have more to do with people's choices and lifestyles, or circumstances beyond people's control? [People's choices and lifestyles; Circumstances beyond people's control]

27. At any point since the start of the coronavirus outbreak, have you or has anyone in your household had serious problems paying the bills, including the rent or the mortgage? [Yes; No; Not sure/Don't know]

28. From what you've read and heard, how do you feel about the Black Lives Matter movement? [Strongly support; Somewhat support; Somewhat oppose; Strongly oppose]

29. Thinking about your own experience, have you ever experienced discrimination or been treated unfairly because of your race, ethnicity, or gender? [Yes, regularly; Yes, from time to time; No]

   29A. [If YES] Which of the following have personally happened to you because of your gender or race? (click all that apply) [Been unfairly stopped by police; Been unfairly denied a job or promotion; People acted as if they were suspicious of you; Been subjected to slurs or jokes; Feared for your personal safety; Been treated unfairly when seeking medical treatment; None of these have happened to me]

30. How strongly do you identify as a feminist (if at all)? [A great deal; A lot; A moderate amount; A little; Not at all]

31. What year were you born?

32. Did you receive a "Party at the Mailbox" box? [Yes; No]

   32A. [If NO]: Did someone in your household receive a "Party at the Mailbox" box? [Yes; No]

33. Did you attend the online (virtual) Party at the Mailbox celebration on November 3? [Yes; No]

   33A. [If YES]: How did that celebration make you feel? [Happy; Excited; Connected; Anxious; Other (Please specify)]

Thank you for answering those questions. Now I just have a few questions to help classify your answers. Please note that these are only for statistical purposes and your answers will be kept confidential.

34. Generally speaking, do you consider yourself to be [Very Liberal; Liberal; Moderate; Conservative; Very Conservative]

35. What is the highest level of school you have completed or the highest degree you have received? [Less than high school; High school graduate or GED; Some college, but no degree; Associate's Degree (2-year degree); Bachelor's Degree (4-year degree); Master's Degree (including MA, MS, MEng, MEd, MSW, MBA); Advanced/Professional degree (including MD, DDS, DVM, LLB, JD, PhD, EdD); Other (please specify)]

36. Thinking back over the last year, what was your family's annual income? [Under $15,000; Less than $19,999; $20,000–$39,999; $40,000–$59,999; $60,000–$79,999; $80,000–$99,999; $100,000–$149,999; $150,000–$199,999; $200,000 or more; Prefer not to say]
37. Do you have any children under age 18 currently living in your household? [Yes; No]
38. In years, how long have you lived in [CITY]?

Thank you for your participation!

Please indicate which e-mail address would you like us to contact you about the Amazon gift card:

Atlanta January 2021 Survey

Consent

You are invited to participate in an evaluation effort about voting and public opinion around the 2021 U.S. Senate runoff elections, being conducted by the Party at the Mailbox project and analysts at Menlo College. Your participation in this evaluation will help us understand why residents of the Atlanta metropolitan area participate in politics. If you decide to take part in this evaluation, you will be asked to complete a survey that will take about 10 minutes of your time. We will also ask basic demographic questions and others related to political attitudes and behavior. At the end of this survey, you will be asked for an email address at which you will receive compensation upon successful completion of the survey. Participation in this survey is entirely voluntary. You must be 18 years or older and a U.S. citizen to participate. You may decline to answer particular survey questions or choose to end your participation at any time without penalty. Confidentiality will be maintained at all times. Each survey will contain a random identification number. The data collected from this survey will be stored on secure computers. This survey should not include any risks or discomforts for you that you would not encounter in everyday life. If you feel uncomfortable answering any of the survey questions, you are free to skip any that you do not want to answer. There will be no direct benefit to you for participating in this survey; however, we hope to learn more about your views on politics.

Additionally, you will be given an option to list your email at the end of this survey to receive a $10 Amazon gift card.

If you have any questions for the analysts or would like information about the evaluation results, please contact Dr. Melissa Michelson, Department of Political Science, melissa.michelson@menlo.edu or by phone at (650) 543-3844. By clicking yes below, I agree to participate in the evaluation effort.

☐ Yes
☐ No

Thank you for taking part in our survey of opinions among residents of the Atlanta metropolitan area. By agreeing to take this survey, you certify that you are 18 years of age or older.

☐ Yes, I am 18 or older
☐ No, I am not 18 or older

1. Did you have a chance to vote in the **U.S. Senate runoff elections on January 5, 2021**, including early voting and vote by mail? That was the election when voters weighed in on who should represent the state of Georgia in the U.S. Senate, choosing between David Perdue and Jon Ossoff for one seat and between Kelly Loeffler and Rev. Raphael Warnock for another seat. [Response options: Yes; No; Not sure/Don't know]

   1A. [If YES]: Thinking about the January 2021 U.S. Senate runoff elections, would you say that when you voted you personally cared a good deal who would win the two elections, or that you didn't care very much who would win? [Care a good deal; Didn't care very much who would win]

2. Different people feel differently about voting.
   [Below statements are presented in random order.]
   For some, voting is a DUTY. They feel that they should vote in every election however they feel about the candidates and parties.
   For others, voting is a CHOICE. They feel free to vote or not to vote in an election depending on how they feel about the candidates and parties.

3. For you personally, voting is FIRST AND FOREMOST a: [Duty; Choice; Not sure]

4. How strongly do you feel personally that voting is a [duty; choice]? [Very strongly; Somewhat strongly; Not very strongly]

5. Did you encourage anyone to vote in the **January 2021 runoff** elections? [Yes; No]

   5A. [If YES]: Select all that apply: [I encouraged a friend to vote in the January 2021 elections; I encouraged a co-worker to vote in the January 2021 elections; I encouraged my children to vote in the January 2021 elections; I encouraged my spouse or partner to vote in the January 2021 elections; I encouraged another household member to vote in the January 2021 elections; I encouraged my followers to vote via social media posts; Other (Please specify)]

6. Which of these issues mattered most when you were deciding whether to vote this year? [Racial inequality; The coronavirus pandemic; Crime and safety; Health care policy; Jobs and the economy; Whether Democrats or Republicans control the U.S. Senate; Other (please specify)]

7. What is your gender? [Male; Female; Transgender female; Transgender male; Non-binary; Something else (please specify)]

8. What is your race? Choose as many as apply. [White (Non-Hispanic); Black or African American; American Indian or Alaska Native; Asian; Native Hawaiian or Pacific Islander; Hispanic or Latino; Middle-Eastern or Arab; Other (please specify)]

   8A. [If more than one RACE selected]: With which of the following racial or ethnic groups do you identify most strongly? [White (Non-Hispanic); Black or African American; American Indian or Alaska Native; Asian; Native Hawaiian or Pacific Islander; Hispanic or Latino; Middle-Eastern or Arab; Other (please specify)]

9. Generally speaking, do you usually think of yourself as a: [Democrat; Republican; Independent; Other party (please specify)]

   9A. [If Democrat] Would you call yourself a strong Democrat or a not very strong Democrat? [Strong Democrat; Not very strong Democrat]

9B. [If Republican] Would you call yourself a strong Republican or a not very strong Republican? [Strong Republican; Not very strong Republican]

9C. [If Independent] Do you think of yourself as closer to the Republican Party or to the Democratic Party, or equally close to the Republican Party and Democratic Party? [The Republican Party; The Democratic Party; Neither]

10. How well does the term "Atlantan" describe you? [Extremely well; Very well; Not very well; Not at all]

11. How well does the term "voter" describe you? [Extremely well; Very well; Not very well; Not at all]

12. How well does the term "American" describe you? [Extremely well; Very well; Not very well; Not at all]

Please indicate the extent to which you agree or disagree with the following statements:

13. "Sometimes politics and government seem so complicated that a person like me can't really understand what's going on." [Strongly disagree; Somewhat disagree; Somewhat agree; Strongly agree]

14. "People like me don't have any say about what the government in **Washington** does." [Strongly disagree; Somewhat disagree; Somewhat agree; Strongly agree]

15. "People like me don't have any say about what the **Georgia state government** does." [Strongly disagree; Somewhat disagree; Somewhat agree; Strongly agree]

16. "People like me don't have any say about what my **local city government** does." [Strongly disagree; Somewhat disagree; Somewhat agree; Strongly agree]

17. "Public officials in **Washington** don't care much what people like me think." [Strongly disagree; Somewhat disagree; Somewhat agree; Strongly agree]

18. "**State government** public officials in **Georgia** don't care much what people like me think." [Strongly disagree; Somewhat disagree; Somewhat agree; Strongly agree]

19. How important is being a **[GENDER]** to your identity? [Very important; Somewhat important; Not very important]

20. How important is being **[RACE]** to your identity? [Very important; Somewhat important; Not very important]

21. How important is being a **[RACE+GENDER]** to your identity? [Very important; Somewhat important; Not very important]

22. Where do you mostly get your news about politics and current affairs? [Social media: Facebook, Twitter, Instagram; Television news; Newspapers; Radio; Conversations at place of worship; Family or friends; Other]

23. Are your political beliefs influenced by celebrities? [Yes; No; Don't know/Not Sure]

    23A. [If YES]: Do celebrities influence your political beliefs a great deal, a lot, a moderate amount, a little, or not at all? [A great deal; A lot; A moderate amount; A little; Not at all]

24. Have you or has anyone in your household been diagnosed with the coronavirus? [Yes, me personally; Yes, someone in my immediate family; No]

25. Do you think the reasons why Black people in our country have been hospitalized with and died due to the coronavirus at higher rates than other racial or ethnic groups have more to do with people's choices and lifestyles, or circumstances beyond people's control? [People's choices and lifestyles; Circumstances beyond people's control]

26. At any point since the start of the coronavirus outbreak, have you or has anyone in your household had serious problems paying the bills, including the rent or the mortgage? [Yes; No; Not Sure/Don't know]

27. From what you've read and heard, how do you feel about the Black Lives Matter movement? [Strongly support; Somewhat support; Somewhat oppose; Strongly oppose]

28. Thinking about your own experience, have you ever experienced discrimination or been treated unfairly because of your race, ethnicity, or gender? [Yes, regularly; Yes, from time to time; No]

    28A. [If YES]: Which of the following have personally happened to you because of your gender or race? (click all that apply) [Been unfairly stopped by police; Been unfairly denied a job or promotion; People acted as if they were suspicious of you;

Been subjected to slurs or jokes; Feared for your personal safety; Been treated unfairly when seeking medical treatment; None of these have happened to me]

29. How strongly do you identify as a feminist (if at all)? [A great deal; A lot; A moderate amount; A little; Not at all]

30. What year were you born?

31. Did you receive a "Party at the Mailbox" box? [Yes; No]

    31A. [If NO]: Did someone in your household receive a "Party at the Mailbox" box? [Yes; No]

32. Would you likely participate in a future Party at the Mailbox program if we return to Georgia? [Yes; No]

33. Did you attend the online (virtual) Party at the Mailbox celebration on January 5? [Yes; No]

    33A. [If YES]: How did that celebration make you feel? [Happy; Excited; Connected; Anxious; Other (Please specify)]

Thank you for answering those questions. Now I just have a few questions to help classify your answers. Please note that these are only for statistical purposes and your answers will be kept confidential.

34. Generally speaking, do you consider yourself to be [Very Liberal; Liberal; Moderate; Conservative; Very Conservative]

35. What is the highest level of school you have completed or the highest degree you have received? [Less than high school; High school graduate or GED; Some college, but no degree; Associate's Degree (2-year degree); Bachelor's Degree (4-year degree); Master's Degree (including MA, MS, MEng, MEd, MSW, MBA); Advanced/Professional degree (including MD, DDS, DVM, LLB, JD, PhD, EdD); Other (please specify)]

36. Thinking back over the last year, what was your family's annual income? [Under $15,000; Less than $19,999; $20,000–$39,999; $40,000–$59,999; $60,000–$79,999; $80,000–$99,999; $100,000–$149,999; $150,000–$199,999; $200,000 or more; Prefer not to say]

37. Do you have any children under age 18 currently living in your household? [Yes; No]

38. In years, how long have you lived in the Atlanta metropolitan area?

Thank you for your participation!

Please indicate which e-mail address would you like us to contact you about the Amazon gift card:

39. Do you have a household member who may want to complete this survey? [Yes; No]
    39A. [If YES] Please do not refer someone to us or share their contact information with us unless you have their permission to do so.
    What is their full name?
    What is their email address?

Please share this survey link with the household member you listed previously: [LINK]

If your household member chooses to complete the survey, please make sure they use the same email address you are providing to us. Otherwise, we will not be able to allow them to complete the survey and receive their Amazon gift card.

Atlanta and Detroit 2022 Survey (Shared via QR Code)

Do you live in Georgia or Michigan? [Georgia; Michigan; Someplace else]

Before you proceed to the survey, please complete the captcha below.

You are invited to participate in an evaluation effort about voting and public opinion around the [STATE] 2022 election, being conducted by the Party at the Mailbox project and analysts at [redacted]. Your participation in this evaluation will help us understand why residents of [CITY] participate in politics. If you decide to take part in this evaluation, you will be asked to complete a survey that will take about 10 minutes of your time. We will also ask basic demographic questions and others related to political attitudes and behavior. At the end of this survey, you will be asked for an email address so that we can enter you into a raffle upon successful completion of the survey. Participation in this survey is entirely voluntary. You must be 18 years or older and a U.S. citizen to participate. You may decline to answer particular survey questions or choose to end your participation at any time without penalty. Confidentiality will be maintained at all times. Each survey will contain a random identification number. The data collected from this survey will be stored on secure computers. This survey should not include any risks or discomforts for you that you would not encounter in everyday life. If you feel uncomfortable answering any of the survey questions, you are free to skip any that you do not want to answer. There will be no direct benefit to you for participating in this survey; however, we hope to learn more about your views on politics. Additionally, you will be entered into a raffle where 5 winners will receive a $100 Amazon gift card.

If you have any questions for the analysts or would like information about the evaluation results, please contact Dr. Melissa Michelson, Department of Political Science, melissa.michelson@menlo.edu or by phone at (650) 543-3844. By clicking yes below, I agree to participate in the evaluation effort.

☐ Yes

☐ No

Thank you for taking part in our survey of opinions among residents of [CITY], [STATE]. By agreeing to take this survey, you certify that you are 18 years of age or older.

☐ Yes, I am 18 or older.

☐ No, I am not 18 or older.

1. Did you have a chance to vote in the **[STATE] election on November 8, 2022**, including early voting and vote by mail? That was the election when voters weighed in on who should represent the state of [STATE] as Governor, choosing between [Stacey Abrams, Brian Kemp, Elbert Bartell and President Boddie; Gretchen Whitmer, Tudor Dixon, and Mary Buzuma]. Voters also weighed in on who should represent them as Lieutenant Governor, Attorney General, Secretary of State, and in the U.S. Senate. [Response options: Yes; No; Not sure/Don't know; Was not old enough/Was not eligible to vote]

    1A. [If YES]: Thinking about the [STATE] 2022 election, how much would you say you cared about who won? [Cared a good deal; Didn't care very much who would win]

2. Were you excited about voting during this election? [Yes; No; Don't know]

3. Different people feel differently about voting.
   [Below statements are presented in random order.]
   For some, voting is a DUTY. They feel that they should vote in every election however they feel about the candidates and parties.
   For others, voting is a CHOICE. They feel free to vote or not to vote in an election depending on how they feel about the candidates and parties.

4. For you personally, voting is FIRST AND FOREMOST a: [Duty; Choice; Not sure]

5. How strongly do you feel personally that voting is a [duty; choice]? [Very strongly; Somewhat strongly; Not very strongly]

6. Did you encourage anyone to vote in the **[STATE] November 2022** election? [Yes; No]

   6A. [If YES]: Select all that apply: [I encouraged a friend to vote in the [STATE] November 2022 election; I encouraged a co-worker to vote in the [STATE] November 2022 election; I encouraged my children to vote in the [STATE] November 2022 election; I encouraged my spouse or partner to vote in the [STATE] November 2022 election; I encouraged another household member to vote in the [STATE] November 2022 election; I encouraged my followers to vote via social media posts; Other (Please specify)]

7. Which of these issues mattered most when you were deciding whether to vote this year? [Racial inequality; The coronavirus pandemic; Crime and safety; Health care policy; Jobs and the economy; Whether [STATE]'s Governor is a Democrat or Republican; Education; Misinformation; Abortion; Inflation; Other (please specify)]

8. Did you or someone in your household get a Party at the Mailbox package? [Yes, an envelope addressed to me; Yes, an envelope addressed to someone else in my household; No]

   8A. [If YES]: How did the package make you feel? Select the top 3 emotions that you felt. [Happy; Hopeful; Connected; Proud; Like part of my larger community; Surprised; Appreciated; Excited; Enthusiastic; Afraid; Anxious; Suspicious; Angry; Disappointed]

8B. In your own words, why did you feel this way? [Fill in response]

9. Did you attend the voting celebration on October 28th? [Yes; No]

9A. [If YES]: How did the celebration make you feel? Select the top 3 emotions that you felt. [Happy; Hopeful; Connected; Proud; Like part of my larger community; Surprised; Appreciated; Excited; Enthusiastic; Afraid; Anxious; Suspicious; Angry; Disappointed]

9B. In your own words, why did you feel this way? [Fill in response]

10. Overall, how much impact do you think people like you can have in making your community a better place? [A big impact; A moderate impact; A small impact; No impact at all]

11. What is your gender? [Man; Woman; Non-binary; Something else (please specify)]

12. Would you describe yourself as transgender? [Yes; No]

13. What is your race? Choose as many as apply. [White (Non-Hispanic); Black or African American; American Indian or Alaska Native; Asian; Native Hawaiian or Pacific Islander; Hispanic or Latino; Middle-Eastern or Arab; Other (please specify)]

13A. [If more than one RACE selected] With which of the following racial or ethnic groups do you identify most strongly? [White (Non-Hispanic); Black or African American; American Indian or Alaska Native; Asian; Native Hawaiian or Pacific Islander; Hispanic or Latino; Middle-Eastern or Arab; Other (please specify)]

14. How well does the term "[CITY]n/er" describe you? you? [Extremely well; Very well; Not very well; Not at all]

15. How well does the term "voter" describe you? [Extremely well; Very well; Not very well; Not at all]

16. How well does the term "American" describe you? [Extremely well; Very well; Not very well; Not at all]

17. What color is grass?
Sometimes, people think about their answers carefully when they are answering a survey, and sometimes they get a bit distracted. So we're just checking in here. Please select purple so that we know you are paying attention. [Green; Red; Purple]

18. Are you a member of a community organization or group (i.e., neighborhood association, social club, community group, fraternal group, parent-teacher association)? [Yes; No]
19. What religion, if any, do you best identify with? [Buddhist; Muslim; Hindu; Christian (Non-Denominational); Baptist; Methodist; Catholic; Other (please specify)]
20. How often do you attend religious services? [At least once a week; Once or twice a month; Once or twice a year; Never]
21. Has your local religious group/organization participated in any bipartisan voter outreach initiatives within the last two election cycles (i.e., voter registration drives)? [Yes; No]
22. Would you likely participate in a future Party at the Mailbox program if we return to [STATE]? [Yes; No]

Thank you for answering those questions. Now I just have a few questions to help classify your answers. Please note that these are only for statistical purposes and your answers will be kept confidential.

23. What year were you born?
24. Generally speaking, do you consider yourself to be [Very Liberal; Liberal; Moderate; Conservative; Very Conservative]
25. Generally speaking, do you usually think of yourself as a: [Democrat; Republican; Independent; Other party (please specify); Don't know]
    25A. [If Democrat] Would you call yourself a strong Democrat or a not very strong Democrat? [Strong Democrat; Not very strong Democrat]
    25B. [If Republican] Would you call yourself a strong Republican or a not very strong Republican? [Strong Republican; Not very strong Republican]
    25C. [If Independent] Do you think of yourself as closer to the Republican Party or to the Democratic Party, or equally close to the Republican Party and Democratic Party? [The Republican Party; The Democratic Party; Neither]
26. What is the highest level of school you have completed or the highest degree you have received? [Less than high school; High school graduate or GED; Some college, but no degree; Associate's

Degree (2-year degree); Bachelor's Degree (4-year degree); Master's Degree (including MA, MS, MEng, MEd, MSW, MBA); Advanced/ Professional degree (including MD, DDS, DVM, LLB, JD, PhD, EdD); Other (please specify)]

27. Thinking back over the last year, what was your family's annual income? [Under $15,000; Less than $19,999; $20,000–$39,999; $40,000–$59,999; $60,000–$79,999; $80,000–$99,999; $100,000–$149,999; $150,000–$199,999; $200,000 or more; Prefer not to say]

28. In years, how long have you lived in [CITY], [STATE]?

Thank you for your participation!

Please indicate which e-mail address would you like us to contact you about the Amazon gift card raffle:

29. Would you like to volunteer to participate in a focus group? Please note that not everyone who volunteers will be contacted. If you are selected, we will be able to thank you with a $50 Amazon gift card. [Yes; No]

Votelanta Music Festival Survey

[Note: This survey was primarily used for focus group invites and open-ended questions.]

Before you proceed to the survey, please complete the captcha below.

You are invited to participate in an evaluation effort about voting and public opinion around the Georgia 2022 election, being conducted by the Party at the Mailbox project and analysts at Menlo College. Your participation in this evaluation will help us understand why residents of Atlanta, Georgia participate in politics. If you decide to take part in this evaluation, you will be asked to complete a survey that will take about 10 minutes of your time. We will also ask basic demographic questions and others related to political attitudes and behavior. At the end of this survey, you will be asked for an email address so that we can enter you into a raffle upon successful completion of the survey. Participation in this survey is entirely voluntary. You must be 18 years or older and a U.S.

citizen to participate. You may decline to answer particular survey questions or choose to end your participation at any time without penalty. Confidentiality will be maintained at all times. Each survey will contain a random identification number. The data collected from this survey will be stored on secure computers. This survey should not include any risks or discomforts for you that you would not encounter in everyday life. If you feel uncomfortable answering any of the survey questions, you are free to skip any that you do not want to answer. There will be no direct benefit to you for participating in this survey; however, we hope to learn more about your views on politics. Additionally, you will be entered into a raffle where 5 winners will receive a $100 Amazon gift card.

If you have any questions for the analysts or would like information about the evaluation results, please contact Dr. Melissa Michelson, Department of Political Science, melissa.michelson@menlo.edu or by phone at (650) 543-3844. By clicking yes below, I agree to participate in the evaluation effort.

☐ Yes
☐ No

Thank you for taking part in our survey of opinions among residents of Atlanta, Georgia. By agreeing to take this survey, you certify that you are 18 years of age or older.

☐ Yes, I am 18 or older.
☐ No, I am not 18 or older.

1. Did you have a chance to vote in the **Georgia election on November 8, 2022**, including early voting and vote by mail? That was the election when voters weighed in on who should represent the state of Georgia as Governor, choosing between Stacey Abrams, Brian Kemp, Elbert Bartell and President Boddie. Voters also weighed in on who should represent them as Lieutenant Governor, Attorney General, Secretary of State, and in the U.S. Senate. [Response options: Yes; No; Not sure/Don't know; Was not old enough/Was not eligible to vote]

    1A. [If YES]: Thinking about the Georgia 2022 election, how much would you say you cared about who won? [Cared a good deal; Didn't care very much who would]

2. Were you excited about voting during this election? [Yes; No; Don't know]

3. Different people feel differently about voting.
   [Below statements are presented in random order.]
   For some, voting is a DUTY. They feel that they should vote in every election however they feel about the candidates and parties.
   For others, voting is a CHOICE. They feel free to vote or not to vote in an election depending on how they feel about the candidates and parties.

4. For you personally, voting is FIRST AND FOREMOST a: [Duty; Choice; Not sure]

5. How strongly do you feel personally that voting is a [duty; choice]? [Very strongly; Somewhat strongly; Not very strongly]

6. Did you encourage anyone to vote in the **Georgia November 2022** election? [Yes; No]

   6A. [If YES]: Please select all that apply: [I encouraged a friend to vote in the Georgia November 2022 election; I encouraged a co-worker to vote in the Georgia November 2022 election; I encouraged my children to vote in the Georgia November 2022 election; I encouraged my spouse or partner to vote in the Georgia November 2022 election; I encouraged another household member to vote in the Georgia November 2022 election; I encouraged my followers to vote via social media posts; Other (Please specify)]

7. Which of these issues mattered most when you were deciding whether to vote this year? [Racial inequality; The coronavirus pandemic; Crime and safety; Health care policy; Jobs and the economy; Whether Georgia's Governor is a Democrat or Republican; Education; Misinformation; Abortion; Inflation; Other (please specify)]

8. Did you or someone in your household get a Party at the Mailbox package? [Yes, an envelope addressed to me; Yes, an envelope addressed to someone else in my household; No]

   8A. [If YES]: How did the package make you feel? Select the top 3 emotions that you felt. [Happy; Hopeful; Connected; Proud; Like part of my larger community; Surprised; Appreciated;

Excited; Enthusiastic; Afraid; Anxious; Suspicious; Angry; Disappointed]

8B. In your own words, why did you feel this way? [Fill in response]

9. Did you attend the voting celebration on October 28th? [Yes; No]

9A. [If YES]: How did the celebration make you feel? Select the top 3 emotions that you felt. [Happy; Hopeful; Connected; Proud; Like part of my larger community; Surprised; Appreciated; Excited; Enthusiastic; Afraid; Anxious; Suspicious; Angry; Disappointed]

9B. In your own words, why did you feel this way? [Fill in response]

10. Overall, how much impact do you think people like you can have in making your community a better place? [A big impact; A moderate impact; A small impact; No impact at all]

11. What is your gender? [Man; Woman; Non-binary; Something else (please specify)]

12. Would you describe yourself as transgender? [Yes; No]

13. What is your race? Choose as many as apply. [White (Non-Hispanic); Black or African American; American Indian or Alaska Native; Asian; Native Hawaiian or Pacific Islander; Hispanic or Latino; Middle-Eastern or Arab; Other (please specify)]

13A. [If more than one RACE selected]: With which of the following racial or ethnic groups do you identify most strongly? [White (Non-Hispanic); Black or African American; American Indian or Alaska Native; Asian; Native Hawaiian or Pacific Islander; Hispanic or Latino; Middle-Eastern or Arab; Other (please specify)]

14. How well does the term "Atlantan" describe you? [Extremely well; Very well; Not very well; Not at all]

15. How well does the term "voter" describe you? [Extremely well; Very well; Not very well; Not at all]

16. How well does the term "American" describe you? [Extremely well; Very well; Not very well; Not at all]

17. What color is grass?
Sometimes, people think about their answers carefully when they are answering a survey, and sometimes they get a bit distracted. So, we're just checking in here. Please select purple so that we know you are paying attention. [Green; Red; Purple]

18. Are you a member of a community organization or group (i.e., neighborhood association, social club, community group, fraternal group, parent-teacher association)? [Yes; No]
19. What religion, if any, do you best identify with? [Buddhist; Muslim; Hindu; Christian (Non-Denominational); Baptist; Methodist; Catholic; Other (please specify)]
20. How often do you attend religious services? [At least once a week; Once or twice a month; Once or twice a year; Never]
21. Has your local religious group/organization participated in any bipartisan voter outreach initiatives within the last two election cycles (i.e., voter registration drives)? [Yes; No]
22. Would you likely participate in a future Party at the Mailbox program if we return to Georgia? [Yes; No]

Thank you for answering those questions. Now I just have a few questions to help classify your answers. Please note that these are only for statistical purposes and your answers will be kept confidential.

23. What year were you born?
24. Generally speaking, do you consider yourself to be [Very Liberal; Liberal; Moderate; Conservative; Very Conservative]
25. Generally speaking, do you usually think of yourself as a: [Democrat; Republican; Independent; Other party (please specify); Don't know]
    25A. [If Democrat] Would you call yourself a strong Democrat or a not very strong Democrat? [Strong Democrat; Not very strong Democrat]
    25B. [If Republican] Would you call yourself a strong Republican or a not very strong Republican? [Strong Republican; Not very strong Republican]
    25C. [If Independent] Do you think of yourself as closer to the Republican Party or to the Democratic Party, or equally close to the Republican Party and Democratic Party? [The Republican Party; The Democratic Party; Neither]
26. What is the highest level of school you have completed or the highest degree you have received? [Less than high school; High school graduate or GED; Some college, but no degree; Associate's Degree (2-year degree); Bachelor's Degree (4-year degree); Master's

Degree (including MA, MS, MEng, MEd, MSW, MBA); Advanced/
Professional degree (including MD, DDS, DVM, LLB, JD, PhD,
EdD); Other (please specify)]

27. Thinking back over the last year, what was your family's annual
income? [Under $15,000; Less than $19,999; $20,000–$39,999;
$40,000–$59,999; $60,000–$79,999; $80,000–$99,999; $100,000–
$149,999; $150,000–$199,999; $200,000 or more; Prefer not to say]

28. In years, how long have you lived in Atlanta, Georgia?

Thank you for your participation!
Please indicate which e-mail address would you like us to contact you
about the Amazon gift card raffle:
(Please allow up to two weeks processing time)

29. Please confirm your e-mail address. [Fill in response]

30. Would you like to volunteer to participate in a focus group? Please
note that not everyone who volunteers will be contacted. If you are
selected, we will be able to thank you with a $50 Amazon gift card.
[Yes; No]

Additional Qualitative Information

- Interview Script
- Interview Recruitment Processes
- Focus Group Recruitment Processes

Individual Party at the Mailbox Interviews, November 2020

[Note: These interviews were conducted via phone or Zoom, not
face-to-face.]

INTRODUCTION

My name is _____ and I'm working on the PATM interview team.
Thank you for helping us out with this project and helping us learn
more about voters in [Baltimore/Detroit/Philadelphia]. I'd like to record
our conversation to make sure I accurately represent your thoughts, and
so that I can concentrate on our conversation instead of taking notes.

Only I and the professors heading this project will have access to the recording. If at any time you want me to turn off the recorder, just let me know.

We may use your input in our research or consider it while framing further outreach activities. We will not directly identify you by your name for any part of the interview.

BACKGROUND

Let's start with some background about yourself.

1. How long have you lived in [Baltimore/Detroit/Philadelphia]? [probe for details including when/where they came from if not "always"]
2. Tell me a little about yourself. [see if they mention anything political, but don't prime it]
3. Tell me a little about your community. What are its strengths and challenges?
4. Tell me a little about how you think about [Baltimore/Detroit/Philadelphia]. What are its strengths and challenges? [Probe for details including city vs. county issues]

POLITICAL ACTIVITY

Next, I have a few questions for you about politics and government.

1. Would you say that you are interested in politics—do you pay attention to political news? [probe for details including local vs. national]
   ◦ Where do you get most of your political news?
2. Would you say that you are involved in politics—do you belong to any groups that are active in politics? Do you personally engage in politics, maybe on social media, or going to meetings?
   ◦ [Probe here for voting, protesting, marching, contacting gov't officials, signing petitions, volunteerism, etc.]
   ◦ [If NO, probe for belonging and/or participation in non-politically centered groups (communities of faith, sororities, fraternities, sport teams, art groups, etc.)]
   ◦ [Also, probe for belonging and/or participation in non-politically centered groups (communities of faith, sororities, fraternities, sport teams, art groups etc.)]

3. Different people feel different about voting. How do you feel about voting? [probe: Do you see voting as more of a duty or a choice? (Duty = They feel that they *should* vote in every election however they may feel about the candidates or parties. Choice = They feel that they are free to vote or not depending on how they feel about the candidates and parties.)]

4. Can you tell me a little more about how you feel about your personal understanding of politics?
   - Do you feel that you have a say in what the **federal government in Washington** does? Why do/don't you think so?
   - Do you feel that you have a say in what the **state government** in [Maryland/Michigan/Pennsylvania] does? Why do/don't you think so?
   - Do you feel that you have a say in what the **local government** in [Baltimore/Detroit/Philadelphia] does? Why do/don't you think so?
   - Where do you think you have a bigger say?
   - Do you feel that the **local government** in [Baltimore/Detroit/Philadelphia] really cares about what you think? Why do/don't you think so?
   - Do you feel that the **state government** in [Maryland/Michigan/Pennsylvania] really cares about what you think? Why do/don't you think so?
   - Do you feel that the **federal government in Washington** really cares about what you think? Why do/don't you think so?

ORGANIZATIONAL CHARACTERISTICS

Now I want to ask you some questions about local organizations you may have had interactions with recently.

1. Can you share any organizations working in [Baltimore/Detroit/Philadelphia] that come to mind, if any?
   1A. If any were shared: In your opinion, which groups would you say are most influential in local issues?
   1B. If none were shared: Have you heard of Black Girls Vote (others)? How about Baltimore Votes?

2. Do you have any kind of relationship with _____ [influential organization(s) mentioned above]?

3. If multiple: How influential would you say this group is, in comparison to the others you mentioned?

4. In what ways do you think **community leaders** engage in civic activities? (PROBE W/THE FOLLOWING)

   4A. Attend meetings on local issues

   4B. How about writing to elected officials?

   4C. Circulating petitions or letter-writing campaigns

   4D. Organizing or participating in rallies or demonstrations

   4E. Registering people to vote? Voting in local elections?

   4F. Talking to reporters or writing letters to the editor

   4G. Arranging meetings with elected officials to discuss concerns

   4H. Hosting virtual events or informational sessions

   [** follow-up as needed re: ways this has changed due to pandemic]

5. And what about local organizations? Are there any that are politically active locally? (PROBE:)

   5A. Attend meetings on local issues

   5B. How about writing to elected officials?

   5C. Circulating petitions or letter-writing campaigns

   5D. Organizing or participating in rallies or demonstrations

   5E. Registering people to vote? Voting in local elections?

   5F. Talking to reporters or writing letters to the editor

   5G. Arranging meetings with elected officials to discuss concerns

   5H. Hosting virtual events or informational sessions

   [** follow-up as needed re: ways this has changed due to pandemic]

PARTY AT THE MAILBOX

Next, I would like to ask you some questions specifically about Get Out the Vote efforts and the Party at the Mailbox program.

6. How would you describe your experience, if you have one, with the Party at the Mailbox efforts overall?

   6A. [**if they received a box**]: What did you do with your Party at the Mailbox box?

   [probe for household member involvement, social media]

6B. How did participating in the Party at the Mailbox efforts make you feel?

6C. In your opinion, how successful do you think the Party at the Mailbox campaign was at getting people to vote?

6D. In your opinion, did the Party at the Mailbox have any other effects? [Probe: Community-building effects]?

6E. How comfortable would you be inviting people you know to partner with or volunteer for this Party at the Mailbox efforts?

6F. Would you be interested in being put in contact with other participating organizations like Black Girls Vote or Baltimore Votes?

6G. How do you think others involved felt about the Party at the Mailbox effort? [probe: did you tell friends/neighbors/relatives/others about it? What did you tell them? How did they respond?]

6H. How do you think other community members feel about Party at the Mailbox? [probe: was that people in your neighborhood, or your network on social media?]

6I. Speaking from your personal experience, how might the program be improved?

VOTER CHALLENGES

Finally, I just have a few questions about challenges and opportunities that you see in your community.

7. What sort of challenges do you see your community facing in the coming months and years? [*DEPENDING on answer, PROBE for following:*]

7A. Does your community face any challenges in terms of being politically active?

7B. [IF YES:] Can you tell me a bit about these challenges?

8. Has non-profit or organizational involvement in your community changed in the past few years?

8A. [IF YES] How so?

9. What about **voting**? What are the challenges you see for your community?

10. And what about opportunities? Have opportunities to participate in politics improved in the last 5 years?
    10A. If so, what do you think explains that shift?
11. Do you feel that the leadership of your city mirrors the diversity of its population? [probe for specifics re: race, gender, etc.]
12. What do you hope will change as a product of the work organizations like Black Girls Vote and Baltimore Votes are doing in Baltimore?

THANK YOU SO MUCH FOR YOUR TIME; THIS HAS BEEN REALLY HELPFUL!

Interview Recruitment Processes

2020 PRIMARY (PILOT) INTERVIEW INVITATION
Dear [NAME],
I reached out to you earlier this week to let you know that I might be following up to request an interview—this is that follow up!

I was wondering whether you would be available to participate in an interview with one of our team members by phone or by zoom sometime in the next week? If so, please let me know which days work best for you, and you will hear from one of our team members shortly to coordinate an interview time.

As a reminder, completed interviews will mean that we can thank you with **a $50 gift card**. Thank you for your support of Party at the Mailbox and hope to hear from you soon.

2020 GENERAL INTERVIEW INVITATION
Dear Community Member,
I reached out to you earlier this week to let you know that I might be following up to request an interview—this is that follow up!

I was wondering whether you would be available to participate in an interview with one of our team members by phone or by zoom sometime in the next week? If so, please let me know which days work best for you, and you will hear from one of our team members shortly to coordinate an interview time.

As a reminder, completed interviews will mean that we can thank you with **a $25 gift card**.

Thank you for your support of Party at the Mailbox and hope to hear from you soon.

2021 ATLANTA INTERVIEW AND FOCUS GROUP INVITATION

Dear [NAME],

Thank you for completing the Party at the Mailbox survey. I am following up with your interest in participating in a focus group or interview about your experience in the 2021 Senate election. If you are still interested, please fill out this form here. As noted in the survey, after completion of an interview we will be able to thank you for your participation with a $50 Amazon gift card.

If you have any questions or concerns, please feel free to reach out to me at [redacted].

Focus Group Recruitment Processes

2020 PRIMARY (PILOT) FOCUS GROUP INVITATION

Dear Voter,

You are invited to join our focus group discussion for a research study about how Baltimore voters think about politics. This project is being conducted by Baltimore Votes, Black Girls Vote, and researchers at Menlo College. You are invited because you are a resident of the city and expressed some interest in politics by signing up for a Party at the Mailbox box of goodies for the June 2020 primary election. We are having discussions like this with several groups of similar people.

We are asking participants to select **ONE focus group date** to attend virtually, utilizing Zoom. The session will take **between 60–90 minutes** of your time. We will ask basic demographic questions and open-ended questions related to political attitudes and behavior. Within two weeks of completing the discussion, you will receive compensation in the form of a **$50 Amazon gift card**.

Please complete this google form to register or decline participation: [LINK]

Thank you in advance for your willingness to share your thoughts as a Baltimore voter!

2020 GENERAL FOCUS GROUP INVITATION

Dear Voter,

You are invited to join our focus group discussion for a research study about how voters think about politics. This project is being conducted by Black Girls Vote, the National Conference on Citizenship, and analysts at Menlo College. You are invited because you are a resident of the city and expressed some interest in politics by signing up for a Party at the Mailbox box of goodies for the November 2020 general election. We are having discussions like this with several groups of similar people.

We are asking participants to select **ONE focus group date** to attend virtually, utilizing Zoom. The session will take **between 60–90 minutes** of your time. We will ask basic demographic questions and open-ended questions related to political attitudes and behavior. Within two weeks of completing the discussion, you will receive compensation in the form of a **$50 Amazon gift card**.

Please complete this google form to register or decline participation: [LINK]

Thank you in advance for your willingness to share your thoughts as a voter!

PARTY AT THE MAILBOX FOCUS GROUP REGISTRATION: GOOGLE FORM

I am interested in participating in ONE of the focus group sessions:
- ☐ Yes
- ☐ No

I would like to register for the following session:
- ☐ Sunday, July 19th 3–5 p.m.
- ☐ Monday, July 20th 12 noon–2 p.m.
- ☐ Wednesday, July 22nd 6–8 p.m.

Email Address (to receive gift card for participation):

Mobile/Cell Phone:

Please indicate which means you would like to receive updates:
- ☐ Email
- ☐ Mobile/cell phone

ATLANTA 2022 FOCUS GROUP EMAIL INVITATION
Hello Everyone,

Thank you for agreeing to participate in our focus group. We are very excited to learn about your experience voting.

My name is [NAME] and I will be monitoring our discussion. The focus group will occur this Thursday, November 10th, 2022 at 6 pm. Please try to arrive 30 minutes prior to the start of the event. The location is [ADDRESS] and parking is free. The discussion will last roughly an hour, and all participants will be paid $50 cash at the end of the focus group.

Please respond to this email directly if you can attend. I look forward to seeing everyone on Thursday.

Best,
[NAME]

ATLANTA 2022 FOCUS GROUP GUIDE
Instructions to Focus Group Facilitators
Introduce yourself first and then introduce the study using the following script:

> *"Good afternoon and welcome. Thanks for taking the time to join our discussion about our community here in Atlanta. My name is [redacted] and I am working with Menlo College on this project. We are collecting information about how people who live in Atlanta think about politics. You were invited because you attended a local party at the polls or voting festival. We are having discussions like this with groups of similar people around the country. Before we begin, I would like to formally ask for your consent to participate in the study."*

Hand out CONSENT FORMS to participants. Read the consent form. Offer an opportunity for participants to ask questions.

As participants sign their consent forms, record information about the focus group on the PARTICIPANT ROSTER.

Collect consent forms and confirm that all present have assented to participate and have assented to an audio recording of the discussion. If permitted, start the audio recorder. Continue with the script:

"There are no wrong answers but rather differing points of view. Please feel free to share your point of view even if it differs from what others have said. Keep in mind that we're just as interested in negative comments as positive comments, and at times the negative comments are the most helpful.

"You've probably noticed the electronic device(s) that are recording us. I am recording the session because I don't want to miss any of your comments. People often say very helpful things in these discussions and I can't write fast enough to get them all down. I will be on a first name basis tonight, and I won't use any names in my reports.

"Well, let's begin. Let's find out some more about each other by going around the table and introducing ourselves with your name and the neighborhood you live in."

Then, ask questions using the QUESTION GUIDELINE and take notes as needed. When completed, thank the participants for their time and record the end time.

Question Guideline
- What words would you use to describe yourself?
  - How about as a voter, do you all identify yourselves as voters? **What does that mean to you, to be a voter?**
  - How about as an Atlantan? What does that mean to you, to be a Atlantan?
- How does voting make you feel? Which emotions come to mind when you think about voting?
  - PROBE what is it about voting that evokes those emotions?
  - Have you always felt this way about voting, or was this year different?
- Different people feel differently about why they vote. For some, voting is a DUTY. They feel that they should vote in every election however they feel about the candidates and parties. For others, voting is a CHOICE. They feel free to vote or not to vote in an election depending on how they feel about the candidates and parties. How do you think about voting?
- How about voting to support the community? Do you think that voting is about community?
- Is voting something you enjoy? [PROBE here for why or why not]

- How did you hear about the election party last Friday?
- What did you think of it? What was good about it? What would you do differently? How did it make you feel?
- When you think about voting, is there something about voting that you find difficult? [PROBE why does [ANSWER] make it harder to vote?]
- What would make voting easier?
- Did you talk about voting with your family or friends? When you talk about voting with other people, what do you talk about? [PROBE do you talk about issues you care about? Do you talk about candidates you like? How do those conversations make you feel?]
- Of all the things that we discussed today, what to you is the most important? Is there anything that you would like to add?
- Have we missed anything? What other question or questions should we be asking?

NOTES

CHAPTER 1. A HISTORY OF PARTYING TO THE POLLS

1 Following the lead of our partner organization, Black Girls Vote, we use the term *Black* in this book to refer to members of the African American diaspora living in the United States. *Black* is a coconstructed term that recognizes the social importance of race but also the degree to which race is not based in genetics or science. It is based to some degree on skin tone and other physical characteristics but is also continually being reconstructed.

2 Names of individual voters in this book are pseudonyms.

3 In New Haven, Connecticut, the festival was held in a neighborhood that is 37 percent African American, 36 percent non-Latino white, and 21 percent Latino. Other neighborhoods were less racially diverse.

4 These same social pressures make Black Americans more likely to overreport their voting behavior compared with other Americans (Cassel 2019); this emphasizes the importance of basing conclusions about how to best get out the vote among Black Americans on studies using validated voter turnout data, as we do in this book.

CHAPTER 2. BLACK IDENTITIES AND BLACK TURNOUT

1 The Divine Nine are Alpha Phi Alpha Fraternity, Kappa Alpha Psi Fraternity, Omega Psi Phi Fraternity, Alpha Kappa Alpha Sorority, Delta Sigma Theta Sorority, Zeta Phi Beta Sorority, Sigma Gamma Rho Sorority, Phi Beta Sigma Fraternity, and Iota Phi Theta Fraternity (Ross 2019).

CHAPTER 3. BALTIMORE VOTES

1 The larger treatment group is a factor of having a finite number of sign-ups where we pulled those assigned to both treatment and control groups. The organizations on the ground had the resources to put together and deliver 680 boxes, so 680 individuals who signed up were randomly assigned to the treatment condition and the remaining 418 individuals who signed up were randomly assigned to the control condition.

2 Voter propensity scores were provided by Catalist for the Baltimore pilot but were calculated with voter histories and demographic variables provided in local voter files for the follow-up RCTs (for methodology, see Barber et al. 2014). We categorize participants into two groups based on these scores—low-propensity (<50 percent likely) and high-propensity (≥50 percent likely) voters.

3 All *p* values are one-tailed.

4 The control for race here captures additional races that individuals selected where one of their racial identities is "Black or African American."

CHAPTER 4. THE PATM ROADSHOW

1 Dave Wasserman (@Redistrict), Twitter, January 5, 2021, https://twitter.com /Redistrict/status/1346700089352474625?s=20&t=xC1DuUUXSkPBiTYkTOKqkQ.

2 Other partners in Atlanta included Year Up, National Council of Urban League Guilds, Future Coalition, The Georgia Youth Poll Worker Project, Refuge Coffee Co., Nora Lee Walker Foundation, Workforce Strong, Alliance for Black Lives, King of Pops, Black Girls Read, Campus Vote Project, The People's Uprising, Branded Hearts Church, Justice for GA, Synergy Services Group, Jada Helps, Daddy's Girl BBQ, Underground Comics of Atlanta Show, Emerging 100 Atlanta, PROOF Incorporated, Refugee Women's Network, Our Women in Politics, Take the Torch, Crystal in the City, Muslimahs Endure, 18by Vote, Perreo404, Holloway's Gift of Life Foundation, Middle Georgia State University Student Government Association, Lift Our Vote 2020, Caribbean American Chamber of Commerce of Georgia, Twinmommy 101, Social Change, Westview Community Organization, US Uplift Strategies, TILA Studios, Restore More, Teens4Justice, Social Justice Café for Girls, Georgia National Organization for Women, Clayton County Federation of Democratic Women, Maryland Peer Advisory Council, Amber Worthy, Promote Positivity Movement, On Point Communications, Albany State University, Boots on the Ground, Cobb County NAACP, ExtraOrdinary Educational Enterprises, Incorporated, Frontline Impact Inc., New Georgia Project, Special Needs Siblings, Stewart Foundation, True Community Foundation, and UVOTE.

REFERENCES

Adams, Char, and J.J. McCorvey. 2024. "Black Twitter Helped Define the Internet—So Where Will the Exodus From X Lead?" NBC News, November 17. www.nbcnews.com.

Addonizio, Elizabeth M., Donald P. Green, and James M. Glaser. 2007. "Putting the Party Back into Politics: An Experiment Testing Whether Election Day Festivals Increase Voter Turnout." *PS: Political Science & Politics* 40 (4): 721–727.

Ahn, Chloe, and Diana C. Mutz. 2023. "The Effects of Polarized Evaluations on Political Participation: Does Hating the Other Side Motivate Voters?" *Public Opinion Quarterly* 87 (2): 243–266.

Albertson, Bethany, and Shana Kushner Gadarian. 2015. *Anxious Politics: Democratic Citizenship in a Threatening World.* New York: Cambridge University Press.

Alex-Assensoh, Yvette, and Karin Stanford. 1997. "Gender, Participation, and the Black Urban Underclass." In *Women Transforming Politics: An Alternative Reader*, edited by Cathy J. Cohen, Kathleen B. Jones, and Joan C. Tronto, 398–411. New York: New York University Press.

Allen, Richard L., Michael C. Dawson, and Ronald E. Brown. 1989. "A Schema-Based Approach to Modeling an African-American Racial Belief System." *American Political Science Review* 83 (2): 421–441.

Arceneaux, Kevin, and David W. Nickerson. 2009. "Who Is Mobilized to Vote? A Re-Analysis of 11 Field Experiments." *American Journal of Political Science* 53 (1): 1–16.

Asmelash, Leah. 2020. "Why This Bus Tours the South to Get Disenfranchised Voters to the Polls." CNN, November 2. www.cnn.com.

Austin, Sharon D. Wright. 2018. *The Caribbeanization of Black Politics: Race, Group Consciousness, and Political Participation in America.* Albany: State University of New York Press.

Auxier, Brooke. 2020. "Social Media Continue to Be Important Political Outlets for Black Americans." Pew Research Center, December 11. www.pewresearch.org.

Azari, Julia, and Ebonya Washington. 2006. "Results from a 2004 Leafleting Field Experiment in Miami-Dade and Duval Counties, Florida." Unpublished Manuscript. Institution for Social and Policy Studies, Yale University.

Baltimore Heritage. n.d. "Baltimore's Civil Rights Heritage." Accessed January 28, 2025. https://baltimoreheritage.github.io.

Barber, Michael J., Christopher B. Mann, J. Quin Monson, and Kelly D. Patterson. 2014. "Online Polls and Registration-Based Sampling: A New Method for Pre-Election Polling." *Political Analysis* 22 (3): 321–335.

Barnes, Sandra L. 2006. "Whosoever Will Let *Her* Come: Social Activism and Gender Inclusivity in the Black Church." *Journal for the Scientific Study of Religion* 45 (3): 371–387.

Bascom, Marion. 2006. Interview transcript, November 4. Baltimore '68: Riots and Rebirth Collection, Box 8, R0142-BSR, University of Baltimore Special Collections and Archives.

Bates, Beth Tompkins. 2012. *The Making of Black Detroit in the Age of Henry Ford.* Chapel Hill: University of North Carolina Press.

Bates, Karen Grigsby. 2020. "In Harris, Black Sororities and Fraternities Celebrate One of Their Own." *Code Switch*, NPR, November 9. www.npr.org.

Bergh, Johannes, and Dag Arne Christensen. 2022. "Getting Out the Vote in Different Electoral Contexts: The Effect of Impersonal Voter Mobilization Techniques in Middle and High Salience Norwegian Elections." *Journal of Elections, Public Opinion and Parties* 34 (1): 79–95.

Berlin, Ira. 1980. "Time, Space, and the Evolution of Afro-American Society on British Mainland North America." *American Historical Review* 85 (1): 44–78.

Blais, André, and Christopher H. Achen. 2019. "Civic Duty and Voter Turnout." *Political Behavior* 41 (2): 473–497.

Blakemore, Erin. 2019. "Elections in Colonial America Were Huge, Booze-Fueled Parties." History.com, November 25. www.history.com.

Bobo, Lawrence, and Franklin D. Gilliam Jr. 1990. "Race, Sociopolitical Participation, and Black Empowerment." *American Political Science Review* 84 (2): 377–393.

Booker, Brakkton. 2018. "50 Years Ago Baltimore Burned. The Same Issues Set It Aflame in 2015." NPR, April 7. www.npr.org.

Boyd, Herb. 2017. *Black Detroit: A People's History of Self-Determination.* New York: Amistad.

Brown, Elsa Barkley. 1994. "Negotiating and Transforming the Public Sphere: African American Political Life in the Transition from Slavery to Freedom." *Public Culture* 7 (1): 107–146.

Brown, Lawrence T. 2021. *The Black Butterfly: The Harmful Politics of Race and Space in America.* Baltimore, Maryland: Johns Hopkins University Press.

Brown, Nadia E. 2014. "Political Participation of Women of Color: An Intersectional Analysis." *Journal of Women, Politics & Policy* 35 (4): 315–348.

Brown, Nadia E., and Danielle Casarez Lemi. 2021. *Sister Style: The Politics of Appearance for Black Women Political Elites.* New York: Oxford University Press.

Brown, R. Khari, and Ronald E. Brown. 2003. "Faith and Works: Church-Based Social Capital Resources and African American Political Activism." *Social Forces* 82 (2): 617–641.

Brown, W. O. 1931. "The Nature of Race Consciousness." *Social Forces* 10 (1): 90–97.

BUILD (Baltimoreans United in Leadership Development) Baltimore. n.d. Homepage. Accessed January 31, 2025. www.buildiaf.org.

Burch, Audra D. S. 2021. "Turning Out the Vote in Georgia." *New York Times*, December 29. www.nytimes.com.

Burns, Nancy, Kay Lehman Schlozman, and Sidney Verba. 2001. *The Private Roots of Public Action: Gender, Equality, and Political Participation*. Cambridge, MA: Harvard University Press.

Camp, Stephanie M. H. 2002. "The Pleasures of Resistance: Enslaved Women and Body Politics in the Plantation South, 1830–1861." *Journal of Southern History* 68 (3): 533–572.

Caruso, Stephen. 2020. "Campaign Committees Raise Record $35.4 Million to Spend on Pa. Legislature in 2020 Election." *Pennsylvania Capital-Star*, October 20. https://penncapital-star.com.

Cassel, Carol A. 2019. "Vote Misreporting and Black Turnout Studies in the U.S." *Politics, Groups, and Identities* 7 (3): 574–589.

Center for American Women and Politics. n.d. "Gender Differences in Voter Turnout." Center for American Women and Politics, Eagleton Institute of Politics, Rutgers University–New Brunswick. Accessed January 28, 2025. https://cawp.rutgers.edu.

Centers for Disease Control and Prevention. 2023. "The U.S. Public Health Service Untreated Syphilis Study at Tuskegee." January 9. www.cdc.gov.

Chen, M. Keith, Kareem Haggag, Devin G. Pope, and Ryne Rohla. 2022. "Racial Disparities in Voting Wait Times: Evidence from Smartphone Data." *Review of Economics and Statistics* 104 (6): 1341–1350.

Chisholm, Shirley. 1970. *Unbought and Unbossed*. New York: Avon.

Chong, Dennis, and Reuel Rogers. 2005. "Racial Solidarity and Political Participation." *Political Behavior* 27 (4): 347–374.

Cialdini, Robert B. 2021. *Influence: The Psychology of Persuasion*. New York: HarperCollins.

Civic Holidays. n.d. Homepage. Accessed January 28, 2025. https://civicholidays.org.

Civic Nation. 2023. *Civic Nation 2022 Impact Report*. Washington, DC: Civic Nation. https://civicnation.org.

Clinton, Bill. 1997. "Apology for Study Done in Tuskegee." Clinton White House, May 16. https://clintonwhitehouse4.archives.gov.

Cobb, James C. 1994. *The Most Southern Place on Earth: The Mississippi Delta and the Roots of Regional Identity*. New York: Oxford University Press.

Cohen, Cathy J. 1999. *The Boundaries of Blackness: AIDS and the Breakdown of Black Politics*. Chicago: University of Chicago Press.

Cohn, Nate. 2021. "Why Warnock and Ossoff Won in Georgia." *New York Times*, January 8. www.nytimes.com.

Collins, Patricia Hill. 2000. *Black Feminist Thought: Knowledge, Consciousness, and the Politics of Empowerment*. New York: Routledge.

Corasaniti, Nick, and Stephanie Saul. 2020. "16 States Have Postponed Primaries During the Pandemic. Here's a List." *New York Times*, August 10. www.nytimes.com.

Cotti, Chad D., Bryan Engelhardt, Joshua Foster, Erik Nesson, and Paul Niekamp. 2020. "The Relationship Between In-Person Voting, Consolidated Polling Locations, and Absentee Voting on COVID-19: Evidence from the Wisconsin Primary." SSRN, May 10. https://dx.doi.org.

Cox, Kiana, and Christine Tamir. 2022. "Race Is Central to Identity for Black Americans and Affects How They Connect With Each Other." Pew Research Center, April 14. www.pewresearch.org.

Crenshaw, Kimberlé. 1991. "Mapping the Margins: Intersectionality, Identity Politics, and Violence Against Women of Color." *Stanford Law Review* 43 (6): 1241–1299.

Cruz Nichols, Vanessa, and Ramón Garibaldo Valdéz. 2020. "How to Sound the Alarms: Untangling Racialized Threat in Latinx Mobilization." *PS: Political Science & Politics* 53 (4): 690–696.

Csicsek, Alex. 2011. "Spiro T. Agnew and the Burning of Baltimore." In *Baltimore '68: Riots and Rebirth in an American City*, edited by Jessica I. Elfenbein, Thomas L. Hollowak, and Elizabeth M. Nix, 70–85. Philadelphia: Temple University Press.

Daniels, Ashley C. J. 2021. "Unlocking the Power of the Sister(hood) Vote: Exploring the Opinions and Motivations of NPHC Sorority Black Women Supporting Black Women Candidates." PhD thesis, Howard University.

Daniels, Ashley C. J. 2023. "Thinking Outside the (Ballot) Box: Analyzing the Political Creativity of Black Women-Led Organizations Mobilizing Voters in Baltimore." In *Distinct Identities*, 2nd ed., edited by Nadia E. Brown and Sarah Allen Gershon, 62–77. New York: Routledge.

Daniels, David D., III. 2020. "The Black Church Has Been Getting 'Souls to the Polls' for More Than 60 Years." *The Conversation*, October 30. https://theconversation.com.

Danigelis, Nicholas L. 1977. "A Theory of Black Political Participation in the United States." *Social Forces* 56 (1): 31–47.

Danigelis, Nicholas L. 1978. "Black Political Participation in the United States: Some Recent Evidence." *American Sociological Review* 43 (5) 756–771.

Darmofal, David. 2010. "Reexamining the Calculus of Voting." *Political Psychology* 31 (2): 149–174.

Davis, Angela Y. 1981. *Women, Race and Class*. New York: Random House.

Davis, Angela Y. 1989. *Women, Culture, & Politics*. New York: Vintage Books.

Dawson, Michael C. 1994. *Behind the Mule: Race and Class in African-American Politics*. Princeton: Princeton University Press.

DeMora, Stephanie L. 2022. "Who Supports Her? The Conditions of Gender Specific Voting." PhD diss., University of California, Riverside.

DeMora, Stephanie L., Christian Lindke, Sean Long, Jennifer L. Merolla, and Maricruz A. Osorio. 2023. "The Effect of the Political Environment on White Women's Political Ambition." *Political Research Quarterly* 76 (4): 1987–2003.

DeSilver, Drew. 2020. "Mail-In Voting Became Much More Common in 2020 Primaries as COVID-19 Spread." Pew Research Center, October 13. www .pewresearch.org.

Diaz, Johnny. 2021. "Philadelphia Settles Lawsuit in Fatal Police Shooting of Walter Wallace Jr." *New York Times*, November 8. www.nytimes.com.

Diversity and Disparities. n.d. Homepage. Accessed January 28, 2025. https://s4.ad .brown.edu.

Doubek, James, and Steve Inskeep. 2021. "Black Church Leaders in Georgia on the Importance of 'Souls to the Polls.'" *Morning Edition*, NPR, March 22. www.npr.org.

Douglass, Frederick. 1852. "What to the Slave Is the Fourth of July?" Teaching American History. https://teachingamericanhistory.org.

Dowe, Pearl K. Ford. 2016. "African American Women: Leading Ladies of Liberal Politics." In *Distinct Identities: Minority Women in U.S. Politics*, edited by Nadia E. Brown and Sarah Allen Gershon, 65–78. New York: Routledge.

Downs, Anthony. 1957. *An Economic Theory of Democracy*. New York: Harper.

Driskell, Jay Winston Jr. 2017. *Schooling Jim Crow: The Fight for Atlanta's Booker T. Washington High School and the Roots of Black Protest Politics*. Charlottesville: University of Virginia Press.

Earls, Anita S., Kara Millonzi, Oni Seliski, and Torrey Dixon. 2008. "Voting Rights in Virginia: 1982–2006." *Southern California Review of Law and Social Justice* 17: 761–799.

11Alive. 2020. "Historically Black Sororities in Atlanta Unite for 'Stroll to the Polls' Video, Images, Now Viral." *11Alive*, October 19. www.11alive.com.

Ellison, Christopher G., and Bruce London. 1992. "The Social and Political Participation of Black Americans: Compensatory and Ethnic Community Perspectives Revisited." *Social Forces* 70 (3): 681–701.

Ellison, Christopher G., and David A. Gay. 1989. "Black Political Participation Revisited: A Test of Compensatory, Ethnic Community, and Public Arena Models." *Social Science Quarterly* 70 (1): 101–119.

Elwood, Karina. 2021. "Trump Urges Support for Youngkin the Day Before Virginia's Gubernatorial Election." *Washington Post*, November 1. www.washingtonpost.com.

Epstein, Rachel. 2020. "LaTosha Brown Says a New South Is Rising." *Marie Claire*, November 10. www.marieclaire.com.

Ezratty, Harry A. 2013. *Baltimore in the Civil War: The Pratt Street Riot and a City Occupied*. Charleston, SC: History Press.

Fairdosi, Amir Shawn, and Jon C. Rogowski. 2015. "Candidate Race, Partisanship, and Political Participation: When Do Black Candidates Increase Black Turnout?" *Political Research Quarterly* 68 (2): 337–349.

Farris, Emily M., and Mirya R. Holman. 2014. "Social Capital and Solving the Puzzle of Black Women's Political Participation." *Politics, Groups and Identities* 2 (3): 331–349.

FBI (Federal Bureau of Investigation). 2022. "Foreign Actors Likely to Use Information Manipulation Tactics for 2022 Midterm Elections." Public service announcement, Alert Number I-100622-PSA, October 6. www.cisa.gov.

Feagin, Joe R., and Harlan Hahn. 1970. "The Second Reconstruction: Black Political Strength in the South." *Social Science Quarterly* 51 (1): 42–56.

Feliciano, Ivette, and Connie Kargbo. 2021. "JXN Project Examines the History of One of the First Black Urban Neighborhoods." PBS, May 9. www.pbs.org.

Ferejohn, John A., and Morris P. Fiorina. 1974. "The Paradox of Not Voting: A Decision Theoretic Analysis." *American Political Science Review* 68 (2): 525–536.

Fieldhouse, Edward, David Cutts, and Jack Bailey. 2022. "Who Cares If You Vote? Partisan Pressure and Social Norms of Voting." *Political Behavior* 44 (3): 1297–1316.

Fields, Barbara Jeanne. 1987. *Slavery and Freedom on the Middle Ground: Maryland During the Nineteenth Century.* New Haven: Yale University Press.

Fisher, Robert, ed. 2009. *The People Shall Rule: ACORN, Community Organizing, and the Struggle for Economic Justice.* Nashville: Vanderbilt University Press.

Fraga, Bernard L. 2018. *The Turnout Gap: Race, Ethnicity, and Political Inequality in a Diversifying America.* New York: Cambridge University Press.

Fredrickson, Barbara L. 2001. "The Role of Positive Emotions in Positive Psychology: The Broaden-and-Build Theory of Positive Emotions." *American Psychologist* 56 (3): 218–226.

Frey, William H. 2022. "A New Great Migration is Bringing Black Americans Back to the South." Brookings, September 12. www.brookings.edu.

Frymer, Paul. 1999. *Uneasy Alliances: Race and Party Competition in America.* Princeton, NJ: Princeton University Press.

Fullmer, Elliott B. 2015. "Early Voting: Do More Sites Lead to Higher Turnout?" *Election Law Journal: Rules, Politics, and Policy* 14 (2): 81–96.

García Bedolla, Lisa, and Melissa R. Michelson. 2012. *Mobilizing Inclusion: Transforming the Electorate Through Get-Out-the-Vote Campaigns.* New Haven, CT: Yale University Press.

Gay, Claudine, Jennifer Hochschild, and Ariel White. 2016. "Americans' Belief in Linked Fate: Does the Measure Capture the Concept?" *Journal of Race, Ethnicity and Politics* 1 (1): 117–144.

Gay, Claudine, and Katherine Tate. 1998. "Doubly Bound: The Impact of Gender and Race on the Politics of Black Women." *Political Psychology* 19 (1): 169–184.

Gerber, Alan S., and Donald P. Green. 2000. "The Effects of Canvassing, Telephone Calls, and Direct Mail on Voter Turnout: A Field Experiment." *American Political Science Review* 94 (3): 653–663.

Gerber, Alan S., Donald P. Green, and Christopher W. Larimer. 2008. "Social Pressure and Voter Turnout: Evidence from a Large-Scale Field Experiment." *American Political Science Review* 102 (1): 33–48.

Gerber, Alan S., Gregory A. Huber, Albert H. Fang, and Andrew Gooch. 2017. "The Generalizability of Social Pressure Effects on Turnout Across High-Salience Electoral Contexts: Field Experimental Evidence from 1.96 Million Citizens in 17 States." *American Politics Research* 45 (4): 533–559.

Gerber, Alan S., Gregory A. Huber, Albert H. Fang, and Catlan E. Reardon. 2018. "The Comparative Effectiveness of Turnout of Positively Versus Negatively Framed Descriptive Norms in Mobilization Campaigns." *American Politics Research* 46 (6): 943–1122.

Giddings, Paula. 1984. *When and Where I Enter: The Impact of Black Women on Race and Sex in America.* New York: Amistad.

Giddings, Paula. 1988. *In Search of Sisterhood: Delta Sigma Theta and the Black Sorority Movement.* New York: HarperCollins.

Gilberstadt, Hannah, and Andrew Daniller. 2020. "Liberals Make Up the Largest Share of Democratic Voters, but Their Growth Has Slowed in Recent Years." Pew Research Center, January 17. www.pewresearch.org.

Gillespie, Andra Nicole. 2005. "Community, Coordination, and Context: A Black Politics Perspective on Voter Mobilization." PhD diss., Yale University.

Giorgis, Hannah. 2018. "Oprah, Cousin Pookie, and the Long Tradition of Shaming Black Voters." *Atlantic*, November 8. www.theatlantic.com.

Giovanni, Nikki. 1988. *Sacred Cows . . . and Other Edibles*. New York: Quill/William Morrow.

Goldfarb, Robert S., and Lee Sigelman. 2010. "Does 'Civic Duty' 'Solve' the Rational Choice Voter Turnout Puzzle?" *Journal of Theoretical Politics* 22 (3): 275–300.

Grant, Keneshia N. 2020. *The Great Migration and the Democratic Party: Black Voters and the Realignment of American Politics in the 20th Century*. Philadelphia: Temple University Press.

Gray, Kathleen. 2020. "Democrats Mount an All-Out Effort to Get Detroit to Vote." *New York Times*, October 2. www.nytimes.com.

Green, Donald P. 2004. "Mobilizing African-American Voters Using Direct Mail and Commercial Phone Banks: A Field Experiment." *Political Research Quarterly* 57 (2): 245–255.

Green, Donald P., and Alan S. Gerber. 2024. *Get Out the Vote: How to Increase Voter Turnout*. 5th ed. Washington, DC: Brookings Institution Press.

Green, Donald P., and Melissa R. Michelson. 2009. "ACORN Experiments in Minority Voter Mobilization." In *The People Shall Rule: ACORN, Community Organizing, and the Struggle for Economic Justice*, edited by Robert Fisher, 235–248. Nashville: Vanderbilt University Press.

Green, Donald P., and Oliver A. McClellan. 2017. "The Effects of Election Festivals on Voter Turnout: A Field Experiment Conducted During a Presidential Election." SSRN, July 9. http://dx.doi.org/10.2139/ssrn.2999305.

Green, Donald P., and Oliver A. McClellan. 2020. "Election Festivals and Voter Turnout: An Overview of Recent Research." SSRN, March 4. http://dx.doi.org/10.2139/ssrn.3548959.

Greenhalgh, Ella. 2018. "'Darkness Turned into Power': Drag as Resistance in the Era of Trumpian Reversal." *Queer Studies in Media & Popular Culture* 3 (3): 299–319.

Grimmer, Justin, and Jesse Yoder. 2022. "The Durable Differential Deterrent Effects of Strict Photo Identification Laws." *Political Science Research and Methods* 10 (3): 453–469.

Groenendyk, Eric W., and Antoine J. Banks. 2014. "Emotional Rescue: How Affect Helps Partisans Overcome Collective Action Problems." *Political Psychology* 35 (3): 359–378.

Grumbach, Jacob, Hahrie Han, and Dorian T. Warren. 2024. "Getting Out the Vote in the Projects: Lessons from a Community Organizing Experiment." *Politics, Groups and Identities* 12 (1): 245–256.

Guterbock, Thomas M., and Bruce London. 1983. "Race, Political Orientation, and Participation: An Empirical Test of Four Competing Theories." *American Sociological Review* 48 (4): 439–453.

Harris, Fredrick C. 1999. *Something Within: Religion in African-American Political Activism*. New York: Oxford University Press.

Harris-Lacewell, Melissa. 2004. *Barbershops, Bibles, and BET: Everyday Talk and Black Political Thought*. Princeton: Princeton University Press.

Hayter, Julian Maxwell. 2017. *The Dream Is Lost: Voting Rights and the Politics of Race in Richmond, Virginia*. Lexington: University Press of Kentucky.

Hazelton, Lynette. 2022. "Getting Souls Out to the Polls." *Philadelphia Inquirer*, November 7. www.inquirer.com.

Herron, Michael C., and Daniel A. Smith. 2012. "Souls to the Polls: Early Voting in Florida in the Shadow of House Bill 1355." *Election Law Journal* 11 (3): 331–347.

Higginbotham, Evelyn Brooks. 1993. *Righteous Discontent: The Women's Movement in the Black Baptist Church, 1880–1920*. Cambridge, MA: Harvard University Press.

Hobson, M. J. 2017. *The Legend of the Black Mecca: Politics and Class in the Making of Modern Atlanta*. Chapel Hill: University of North Carolina Press.

Huddy, Leonie, Lilliana Mason, and Lene Aarøe. 2015. "Expressive Partisanship: Campaign Involvement, Political Emotion, and Partisan Identity." *American Political Science Review* 109 (1): 1–17.

Janes, Chelsea. 2020. "Kamala Harris, Supported by a Sea of Sisters." *Washington Post*, October 1. www.washingtonpost.com.

Jardina, Ashley, and Spencer Piston. 2023. "Trickle-Down Racism: Trump's Effect on Whites' Racist Dehumanizing Attitudes." *Current Research in Ecological and Social Psychology* 5:100158. https://doi.org.

Johnson, Ashley. 2020. "'Party at the Mailbox' Campaign Encourages Black Voters in Pennsylvania." *ABC6 Action News*, October 20. https://6abc.com.

Johnson, Jason. 2021. "Battling Georgia's Backlash Against Black Voters." *Slate*, April 2. https://slate.com.

Johnson, Theodore R. 2015. "The Political Power of the Black Sorority." *Atlantic*, April 26. www.theatlantic.com.

Jones, Martha S. 2020. *Vanguard: How Black Women Broke Barriers, Won the Vote, and Insisted on Equality for All*. New York: Basic Books.

Kammerer, Edward F., Jr., and Melissa R. Michelson. 2022. "You Better Vote: Drag Performers and Voter Mobilization in the 2020 Election." *PS: Political Science & Politics* 55 (4): 655–660.

Kenworthy, E. W. 1963. "200,000 March for Civil Rights in Orderly Washington Rally; President Sees Gain for Negro." *New York Times*, August 29. https://archive.nytimes.com.

Kornacki, Steve. 2019. "Journey to Power: The History of Black Voters, 1976 to 2020." *NBC News*, July 29. www.nbcnews.com.

Kornhaber, Spencer. 2017. "Why Drag Is the Ultimate Retort to Trump." *Atlantic*, June. www.theatlantic.com.

Kornweibel, Theodore, Jr. 1976. "An Economic Profile of Black Life in the Twenties." *Journal of Black Studies* 6 (4): 307–320.

Kousser, J. Morgan. 1999. *Colorblind Injustice: Minority Voting Rights and the Undoing of the Second Reconstruction.* Chapel Hill: University of North Carolina Press.

Kyles, Yohance. 2022. "Gucci Mane to Headline Free Votelanta Concert in ATL." AllHipHop.com, October 27. https://allhiphop.com.

Lane, Robert E. 1959. *Political Life: Why and How People Get Involved in Politics.* New York: Free Press.

Lee, Michelle Ye Hee, Reis Thebault, Haisten Willis, and Lenny Bronner. 2021. "Black Voters Powered Democrats to Victory in the Georgia Senate Runoff." *Washington Post*, January 6. www.washingtonpost.com.

Lee, Taeku. 2002. *Mobilizing Public Opinion: Black Insurgency and Racial Attitudes in the Civil Rights Era.* Chicago: University of Chicago Press.

Lerner, Jennifer S., and Larissa Z. Tiedens. 2006. "Portrait of the Angry Decision Maker: How Appraisal Tendencies Shape Anger's Influence on Cognition." *Journal of Behavioral Decision Making* 19 (2): 115–137.

Leroux, Kelly. 2007. "Nonprofits as Civic Intermediaries: The Role of Community-Based Organizations in Promoting Political Participation." *Urban Affairs Review* 42 (3): 410–422.

Levy, Peter B. 2011. "The Dream Deferred: The Assassination of Martin Luther King, Jr., and the Holy Week Uprisings of 1968." In *Baltimore '68: Riots and Rebirth in an American City*, edited by Jessica I. Elfenbein, Thomas L. Hollowak, and Elizabeth M. Nix, 3–25. Philadelphia: Temple University Press.

Lewis, Glenda. 2022. "Human Fliers Is a Grassroots Company Grown Through Mentorship and Teaching Business Skills to Youth." WXYZ Detroit, February 28. www.wxyz.com.

Lewis-Giggetts, Tracey Michae'l. 2020. *Black Joy: Stories of Resistance, Resilience, and Restoration.* New York: Simon and Schuster.

London, Bruce, and Micheal W. Giles. 1987. "Black Participation: Compensation or Ethnic Identification?" *Journal of Black Studies* 18 (1): 20–44.

Long, Sean. 2022. "White Identity, Donald Trump, and the Mobilization of Extremism." *Politics, Groups, and Identities* 11 (3): 638–666.

Lopez, German. 2016. "The Baltimore Protests over Freddie Gray's Death, Explained." *Vox*, August 18. www.vox.com.

Lopez Bunyasi, Tehama, and Candis Watts Smith. 2019. "Do All Black Lives Matter Equally to Black People? Respectability Politics and the Limitations of Linked Fate." *Journal of Race, Ethnicity and Politics* 4 (1): 180–215.

Los Angeles Urban League. 2020. "By Voting We Honor Our Ancestors." October 23. https://laul.org.

Lu, Jessica H., and Catherine Knight Steele. 2019. "'Joy Is Resistance': Cross-Platform Resilience and (Re)invention of Black Oral Culture Online." *Information, Communication and Society* 22 (6): 823–837.

Malhotra, Neil, Melissa R. Michelson, Todd Rogers, and Ali Adam Valenzuela. 2011. "Text Messages as Mobilization Tools: The Conditional Effect of Habitual Voting and Election Salience." *American Politics Research* 39 (4): 664–681.

Mann, Christopher B., and Katherine Haenschen. 2024. "A Meta-Analysis of Voter Mobilization Tactics by Electoral Salience." *Electoral Studies* 87:102729.

Martin, Lerone A. 2016. "Developments in Twenty-First-Century African-American Religion and Politics." In *The Wiley Blackwell Companion to Religion and Politics in the U.S.*, edited by Barbara A. McGraw, 416–427. Hoboken, NJ: John Wiley & Sons.

Mason, Lilliana, Julie Wronski, and John V. Kane. 2021. "Activating Animus: The Uniquely Social Roots of Trump Support." *American Political Science Review* 115 (4): 1508–1516.

Massey, Douglass, and Jonathan Tannen. 2015. "A Research Note on Trends in Black Hypersegregation." *Demography* 52 (3): 1025–1034.

McClain, Paula, Jessica Johnson Carew, Eugene Walton Jr., and Candis Watts. 2009. "Group Membership, Group Identity, and Group Consciousness: Measures of Racial Identity in American Politics?" *Annual Review of Political Science* 12: 471–485.

McClellan, Jennifer L. 2023. "The Voting Rights Act of Virginia: Overcoming a History of Voter Discrimination." *Richmond Public Interest Law Review* 26: 111–153.

McClerking, Harwood K., and Eric L. McDaniel. 2005. "Belonging and Doing: Political Churches and Black Political Participation." *Political Psychology* 26 (5): 721–734.

McDaniel, Eric. 2008. *Politics in the Pews: The Political Mobilization of Black Churches.* Ann Arbor: University of Michigan Press.

McDonald, Michael. n.d. "Voter Turnout Demographics." US Elections Project. Accessed January 29, 2025. www.electproject.org.

McDonald, Soraya Nadia. 2014. "Black Twitter: A Virtual Community Ready to Hashtag Out a Response to Cultural Issues." *Washington Post*, January 20. www.washingtonpost.com.

McDougall, Harold A. 1993. *Black Baltimore*. Temple University Press.

McGrady, Clyde. 2022. "Why a Black Democratic City Won't Have a Black Democrat in the House." *New York Times*, October 24. www.nytimes.com.

McGraw, Bill. 2017. "Bringing Detroit's Black Bottom Back to (Virtual) Life." *Detroit Free Press*, February 27. www.freep.com.

Michelson, Melissa R., and Lisa García Bedolla. 2014. "Mobilization by Different Means: Nativity and GOTV in the United States." *International Migration Review* 48 (3): 710–727.

Middlemost, Renee. 2020. "'Serving Activist Realness': The New Drag Superstars and Activism Under Trump." In *Intercultural Communication, Identity, and Social Movements in the Digital Age*, edited by Margaret U. D'Silva and Ahmet Atay, 48–65. New York: Routledge.

Miller, Arthur H., Patricia Gurin, Gerald Gurin, and Oksana Malanchuk. 1981. "Group Consciousness and Political Participation." *American Journal of Political Science* 25 (3): 494–511.

Mohamed, Besheer, Kiana Cox, Jeff Diamant, and Claire Gecewicz. 2021. "10 New Findings About Faith Among Black Americans." Pew Research Center, February 16. www.pewresearch.org.

Moody-Ramirez, Mia, Dorothy Bland, and Gheni Platenburg. 2023. "The 2020 Presidential Election: An Examination of the Social Media Messaging of Divine-9 Sororities & Fraternities." *Southwestern Mass Communication Journal* 38 (2). https:// swecjmc-ojs-txstate.tdl.org

Morris, Kevin, and Coryn Grange. 2024. "Growing Racial Disparities in Voter Turnout, 2008–2022." Brennan Center for Justice, March 2. www.brennancenter.org.

Moscow, Jason. 2020. "How 'Black Girls Vote' Empowered Baltimore Residents to Get to the Polls." *Forbes*, August 7. www.forbes.com.

Murugesan, Anand. 2020. "Electoral Clientelism and Vote Buying." In *Oxford Research Encyclopedia of Politics*. Oxford University Press, September 28. https://oxfordre.com.

Myrdal, Gunner, Richard Sterner, and Arnold Rose. 1944. *An American Dilemma: The Negro Problem and Modern Democracy*. New York: Harper and Bros.

Myrick-Harris, Clarissa. 2006. "The Origins of the Civil Rights Movement in Atlanta, 1880–1910." *Perspectives on History*, November 1. www.historians.org.

NewsOne. 2010. "Pastors Urge Blacks to Vote 'in the Name of Our Ancestors.'" November 1. https://newsone.com.

Ngunjiri, Faith Wambura, Sharon Gramby-Sobukwe, and Kimberly Williams-Gegner. 2012. "Tempered Radicals: Black Women's Leadership in the Church and Community." *Journal of Pan African Studies* 5 (2): 84–109.

Nichols, Elaine. 2023. "Black Joy: Resistance, Resilience, and Reclamation." *National Museum of African American History and Culture*, January 23. https://nmaahc.si .edu.

Nichter, Simeon. 2008. "Vote Buying or Turnout Buying? Machine Politics and the Secret Ballot." *American Political Science Review* 102 (1): 19–31.

NPR. 2020. "Former Georgia Gubernatorial Candidate on a Push for Voter Turnout." *All Things Considered*, NPR, November 2. www.npr.org.

Olsen, Marvin E. 1970. "Social and Political Participation of Blacks." *American Sociological Review* 35: 682–697.

One Detroit. 2023a. "Detroit's Black Political Representation, Michigan State University Mass Shooting." *American Black Journal*, February 21. www.onedetroitpbs.org.

One Detroit. 2023b. "A Shift in Representation: Detroit's Black Political Past and Present with Adolph Mongo." *American Black Journal*, February 21. www.onedetroitpbs .org.

Orum, Anthony M. 1966. "A Reappraisal of the Social and Political Participation of Negroes." *American Journal of Sociology* 72 (1): 32–46.

Osorio, Maricruz A., Melissa R. Michelson, Stephanie L. DeMora, Kesicia Dickinson, Jasmine Jackson, Jazmine Jimenez, and India Lenear. 2023. "Students as Knowledge Brokers: Voter Information Sharing and the Political Consequences of Informing Students of Color and First-Generation Students on Electoral Politics." Paper presented at the 2023 Student Vote Research Network Workshop, Chicago.

Palast, Greg. 2022. *Vigilante: Georgia's Vote Suppression Hitman.* https://www.imdb.com/title/tt22439720/.

Panagopoulos, Costas. 2011. "Thank You for Voting: Gratitude Expression and Voter Mobilization." *Journal of Politics* 73 (3): 707–717.

Panagopoulos, Costas. 2013a. "Extrinsic Rewards, Intrinsic Motivation and Voting." *Journal of Politics* 75 (1): 266–280.

Panagopoulos, Costas. 2013b. "Positive Social Pressure and Prosocial Motivation: Evidence from a Large-Scale Field Experiment on Voter Mobilization." *Political Psychology* 34 (2): 265–275.

Parham, Jason. 2024. "Blacksky Is Nothing Like Black Twitter—and It Doesn't Need to Be." *Wired*, December 13. www.wired.com.

Parker, Christopher Sebastian. 2021. "Status Threat: Moving the Right Further to the Right." *Daedalus* 150 (2): 56–75.

Parks, Gregory S., and Matthew W. Hughey. 2020. "Kamala Harris and the Political Power of Black Sororities (and Fraternities)." *NYU Press Blog*, August 24. https://nyupress.org.

Parks, Miles. 2022. "2020 Changed How America Votes. The Question Now Is Whether Those Changes Stick." NPR, October 28. www.npr.org.

Phillips, Joseph B., and Eric Plutzer. 2023. "Reassessing the Effects of Emotions on Turnout." *Journal of Politics* 85 (3): 1094–1106.

Philpot, Tasha S., Daron R. Shaw, and Ernest B. McGowen. 2009. "Winning the Race: Black Voter Turnout in the 2008 Presidential Election." *Public Opinion Quarterly* 73 (5): 995–1022.

Phoenix, Davin L. 2019. *The Anger Gap: How Race Shapes Emotion in Politics.* New York: Cambridge University Press.

Raffensperger, Brad. 2022. "Georgia Voters Set All-Time Midterm Early Turnout Record." Georgia Secretary of State, November 5. https://sos.ga.gov.

Ramírez, Ricardo, Romelia Solano, and Bryan Wilcox-Archuleta. 2018. "Selective Recruitment or Voter Neglect? Race, Place, and Voter Mobilization in 2016." *Journal of Race, Ethnicity and Politics* 3 (1): 156–184.

Ray, Rashawn, and Mark Whitlock. 2019. "Setting the Record Straight on Black Voter Turnout." Brookings, September 12. www.brookings.edu.

Reyes, Nino. 2022. "Omeretta the Great: A Rising Atlanta MC." *Bleu*, June 17. https://bleumag.com.

Riker, William H., and Peter C. Ordeshook. 1968. "A Theory of the Calculus of Voting." *American Political Science Review* 62 (1): 25–42.

Robinson, Zandria F. 2014. *This Ain't Chicago: Race, Class, and Regional Identity in the Post-Soul South.* Chapel Hill: University of North Carolina Press.

Ross, Lawrence C., Jr. 2019. *The Divine Nine: The History of African American Fraternities and Sororities.* 2nd ed. New York: Kensington.

Sanchez, Gabriel R., and Edward D. Vargas. 2016. "Taking a Closer Look at Group Identity: The Link Between Theory and Measurement of Group Consciousness and Linked Fate." *Political Research Quarterly* 69 (1): 160–174.

Sanneh, Kelefa. 2016. "Out of the Trap." *New Yorker*, August 8 and 15.

Scott, Jamil. 2022. "It's All About The Money: Understanding How Black Women Fund Their Campaigns." *PS: Political Science & Politics*, 55 (2): 297–300.

Scott, Jamil S., Melissa R. Michelson, and Stephanie L. DeMora. 2021. "Getting Out the Black Vote in Washington DC: A Field Experiment." *Journal of Political Marketing* 20 (3–4): 289–301.

Scott, Jamil, Nadia Brown, Lorrie Frasure, and Dianne Pinderhughes. 2021. "Destined to Run? The Role of Political Participation on Black Women's Decision to Run for Elected Office." *National Review of Black Politics* 2 (1): 22–52.

Searle, David M., and Marisa Abrajano. 2020. "Appealing to Diverse Electorates in the United States." In *Oxford Handbook of Electoral Persuasion*, edited by Elizabeth Suhay, Bernard Grofman, and Alexander H. Trechsel, 258–281. New York: Oxford University Press.

Serwer, Adam. 2015. "The Biggest Mystery of Baltimore's Riots." *Buzzfeed*, April 28. www.buzzfeednews.com.

Shineman, Victoria. 2018. "If You Mobilize Them, They Will Become Informed: Experimental Evidence That Information Acquisition Is Endogenous to Costs and Incentives to Participate." *British Journal of Political Science* 48 (1): 189–211.

Shukla, Aseem, and Michaelle Bond. 2021. "Philly Remains One of the Most Racially Segregated Cities in America." *Philadelphia Inquirer*, October 19. www.inquirer.com.

Silver, Nate. "2020 Election Forecast." FiveThirtyEight. Last modified November 3, 2020. https://projects.fivethirtyeight.com.

Simien, Evelyn. 2005. "Race, Gender, and Linked Fate." *Journal of Black Studies* 35 (5): 529–550.

Simien, Evelyn M., and Rosalie A. Clawson. 2004. "The Intersection of Race and Gender: An Examination of Black Feminist Consciousness, Race Consciousness, and Policy Attitudes." *Social Science Quarterly* 85 (3): 793–810.

Sinclair, Betsy, Margaret McConnell, and Melissa R. Michelson. 2013. "Local Canvassing: The Efficacy of Grassroots Voter Mobilization." *Political Communication* 30 (1): 42–57.

Skene, Lea, and Sarah Brumfield. 2023. "Family of Henrietta Lacks, Whose Cells Were Taken for Research, Settles with Company That Profited." *PBS Newshour*, August 1. www.pbs.org.

Smith, Candis Watts, Tehama Lopez Bunyasi, and Jasmine Smith. 2019. "Linked Fate over Time and Across Generations." *Politics, Groups, and Identities* 7 (3): 684–694.

Smooth, Wendy G. 2018. "African American Women and Electoral Politics: The Core of the New American Electorate." In *Gender and Elections: Shaping the Future of American Politics*, edited by Susan J. Carroll and Richard L. Fox, 171–197. New York: Cambridge University Press.

Spangler, Todd, and Clara Hendrickson. 2022. "Shri Thanedar Wins Democratic Race for Congressional Seat in Detroit." *Detroit Free Press*, August 3. www.freep.com.

Spence, Lester. 2011. *Stare in the Darkness: The Limits of Hip-Hop and Black Politics*. Minneapolis: University of Minnesota Press.

Steady, Filomina Chioma. 1981. "The Black Woman Cross-Culturally: An Overview." In *The Black Woman Cross-Culturally*, edited by Filomina Chioma Steady, 7–42. Cambridge, MA: Schenkman.

Steady, Filomina Chioma. 1987. "African Feminism: A Worldwide Perspective." In *Women in Africa and the African Diaspora*, edited by Rosalyn Terborg-Penn, Sharon Harley, and Andrea Benton Rushing, 3–24. Washington, DC: Howard University Press.

Stephens-Dougan, LaFleur. 2021. "The Persistence of Racial Cues and Appeals in American Elections." *Annual Reviews* 24: 301–320.

Strolovitch, Dara. 2007. *Affirmative Advocacy: Race, Class, and Gender in Interest Group Politics*. Chicago: University of Chicago Press.

Student Public Interest Research Groups. n.d. Homepage. Accessed January 29, 2025. https://studentpirgs.org/.

Tate, Katherine. 1991. "Black Political Participation in the 1984 and 1988 Presidential Elections." *American Political Science Review* 85 (4): 1159–1176.

Taylor, Jessica. 2018. "Georgia's Stacey Abrams Admits Defeat, Says Kemp Used 'Deliberate' Suppression to Win." NPR, November 16. www.npr.org.

Terborg-Penn, Rosalyn. 1985. "Survival Strategies Among African-American Women Workers: Continuing Process." In *Women, Work and Protest: A Century of U.S. Women's Labor History*, edited by Ruth Milkman, 139–155. Boston: Routledge and Kegan Paul.

Thomas, Terrell. 2020. "Voter Education Campaign 'Party at the Mailbox' Launches in Atlanta for Historic Push to Increase Turnout for GA Runoffs." *These Urban Times*, December 30. https://theseurbantimes.com.

Thompson, Ashley B., and Melissa M. Sloan. 2012. "Race as Region, Region as Race: How Black and White Southerners Understand Their Regional Identities." *Southern Cultures* 18 (4): 72–95.

Trépanier, Cécyle. 1991. "The Cajunization of French Louisiana: Forging a Regional Identity." *Geographical Journal* 157 (2): 161–171.

Tullock, Gordon. 1968. *Toward a Mathematics of Politics*. Ann Arbor: University of Michigan Press.

Valentino, Nicholas A., Ted Brader, Eric W. Groenendyk, Krysha Gregorowicz, and Vincent T. Hutchings. 2011. "Election Night's Alright for Fighting: The Role of Emotions in Political Participation." *Journal of Politics* 73 (1): 156–170.

Veasey, Kendall. 2023. "Vote Early." Vimeo video, 4 min, 39 sec., posted February 9. https://vimeo.com/797556908/3c9b0be5d5.

Verba, Sidney, Kay Lehman Schlozman, and Henry E. Brady. 1995. *Voice and Equality: Civic Voluntarism in American Politics*. Cambridge, MA: Harvard University Press.

Verba, Sidney, and Norman H. Nie. 1972. *Participation in America: Political Democracy and Social Equality*. New York: Harper and Row.

Vicente, Pedro C. 2014. "Is Vote Buying Effective? Evidence from a Field Experiment in West Africa." *Economic Journal* 124 (574): F356–F387.

Villarreal, Daniel. 2018. "Drag Queens Are More Political Than Ever. Can They Lead a Movement?" *Vox*, November 5. www.vox.com.

Vroman, Mary Elizabeth. 1965. *Shaped to Its Purpose: Delta Sigma Theta, the First Fifty Years*. New York: Random House.

Walker, Alice. 1983. *In Search of Our Mother's Gardens*. New York: Harcourt Brace Jovanovich.

Walton, Hanes, Jr. 1985. *Invisible Politics: Black Political Behavior*. Albany: State University of New York Press.

Walton, Hanes, Jr., and Robert C. Smith. 2012. *American Politics and the African American Quest for Universal Freedom*. 6th ed. New York: Longman.

Wang, Ching-Hsing. 2016. "Political Trust, Civic Duty and Voter Turnout: The Mediation Argument." *Social Science Journal* 53 (3): 291–300.

Weissert, Will. 2024. "Harris Makes a Pre-Taped Appearance on 'RuPaul's Drag Race All Stars' to Urge Americans to Vote." AP News, July 26. www.apnews.com.

When We All Vote. n.d. "Party at the Polls." Accessed January 29, 2025. https://whenweallvote.org.

Whitby, Kenny J. 2015. "Impact of Organizational Vitality on Black Voter Turnout in the South." *Party Politics* 21 (2): 234–245.

White, Ismail K., and Chryl N. Laird. 2020. *Steadfast Democrats: How Social Forces Shape Black Political Behavior*. Princeton: Princeton University Press.

White, Shane. 1994. "'It Was a Proud Day': African Americans, Festivals, and Parades in the North, 1741–1834." *Journal of American History* 81 (1): 13–50.

Wilcox, Clyde. 1990. "Black Women and Feminism." *Women and Politics* 10 (3): 65–84.

Williams, J. Allen Jr., Nicholas Babchuk, and David R. Johnson. 1975. "Compensatory and Ethnic Community Theories: Are They Generalizable? *American Sociological Review* 40 (1): 117–121.

Williams, Joseph P. 2020. "A Tale of Two Motor Cities." *U.S. News & World Report*, January 22. www.usnews.com.

Winch, Julie, ed. 2000. *The Elite of Our People: Joseph Wilson's Sketches of Black Upper-Class Life in Antebellum Philadelphia*. University Park: Pennsylvania State University Press.

Wolfinger, James. 2013. "African American Migration." *Encyclopedia of Greater Philadelphia*. https://philadelphiaencyclopedia.org.

Wootson, Cleve R., Jr. 2022. "Does Stacey Abrams's Model For Engaging Voters Die With Her Election Loss?" *Washington Post*, December 10. www.washingtonpost.com.

WXYZ Detroit. 2020. "Detroit Pistons Host Get in the Vote Event in Detroit on Saturday, October 24th." October 24. www.wxyz.com.

Yockel, Michael. 2007. "100 Years: The Riots of 1968." *Baltimore Magazine*, May 2007. www.baltimoremagazine.com.

Zinn, Maxine Baca. 1979. "Field Research in Minority Communities: Ethical, Methodological and Political Observations by an Insider." *Social Problems* 27 (2): 209–219.

INDEX

Page references followed by an f or t represent figures or tables.

ABOUT THE AUTHORS

Melissa R. Michelson is Dean of Arts and Sciences and a professor of political science at Menlo College.

Stephanie L. DeMora is an assistant professor of political science at Stony Brook University.

Sarah V. Hayes is a doctoral candidate in the Government PhD program at Georgetown University.